St. Louis Community College

Forest Park
Florissant Valley
Meramec

Instructional Resources
St. Louis, Missouri

a map of
Hope

a map of

Hope

women's writings
on human rights
—an international
literary anthology

edited by marjorie agosín

Rutgers University Press
New Brunswick, New Jersey, and London

Library of Congress Cataloging-in-Publication Data

A map of hope : women's writing on human rights : an international literary
    anthology / edited by Marjorie Agosín.
        p.   cm.
    ISBN 0-8135-2625-6 (cloth : alk. paper). — ISBN 0-8135-2626-4
(pbk. : alk. paper)
    1. Human rights—Literary collections. 2. Women's rights—Literary
collections. 3. Literature—Women authors. I. Agosin, Marjorie.
PN6071.H784M37   1998
808.8'0353—dc21   98-44985
                                                                                        CIP

British Cataloguing-in-Publication data for this book is available from the British Library

This collection copyright © 1999 by Rutgers, The State University. For copyrights to
individual pieces please see Copyrights and Permissions in the back of book.
Introduction copyright © 1999 by Marjorie Agosín

Manufactured in the United States of America

contents

THREE: CHILDHOOD

FOUR: EXILES AND REFUGEES

Five: Domestic and Political Violence

Six: Resistance and Refusal

foreword

"... And only when the danger
was plain in the music could you know
their true measure of rejoicing in

finding a voice where they found a vision."

These lines from Eavan Boland's poem "The Singers" help us to understand the true value of this international literary anthology of women's writings on human rights. It holds the voices and visions of seventy-seven women
expressing with passion, courage and creativity their sense of human rights,
justice, and freedom. From the works of Nadine Gordimer, Marguerite Duras,
Barbara Kingsolver, Wislawa Szymborska, Aun San Su Kye and others, this
human geography of witness is a true map of hope for the twenty-first
century.

We need it!

The World Conference on Human Rights in 1993 set as a priority for governments and the United Nations the achievement of the full and equal en-
joyment by women of all human rights, the integration of human rights into
the United Nations system-wide action and the full participation of women as
both agents and beneficiaries of development. The Beijing Declaration and
Platform for Action reaffirmed that the human rights of women and girl children are an inalienable, integral, and indivisible part of universal human rights
and established a number of specific strategic objectives to ensure that women

enjoy their full human rights. It is clear that the practical realization of those objectives will present a very great challenge to all of us in the years ahead.

Women throughout the world have found that declarations and conventions are not enough to guarantee their human rights. Of the 1.3 billion people living in poverty 70 percent are women; the majority of the world's refugees are women; female illiteracy is invariably higher than male illiteracy; women and girl children are becoming commodities in cross-border prostitution rackets and the pornography industry. Women in every country are regular victims of domestic violence and every day women are targeted in armed conflicts. One of the starkest reflections of the low status accorded to women is the discrimination against them in the law. In many countries, women are not treated as equal to men—whether in property rights, rights of inheritance, laws related to marriage and divorce, or the rights to acquire nationality, manage property, or seek employment.

Fighting for women's human rights is a positive struggle which recognizes the quality of a woman's contribution to every aspect of the community. I am convinced that the best hope for realizing the human rights of women lies in the efforts of women themselves. On many occasions, I had the opportunity and the privilege to meet women living under difficult circumstances, committed to demonstrating that human rights principles belong to all and are compatible with diverse cultures and traditions. The solidarity of women with their sisters in other countries is a powerful force. It is the essence of this map of hope which I, for one, will bring with me on my travels and draw upon in my work. May it serve as an inspiration and source of strength to all human rights defenders.

Mary Robinson
United Nations High Commissioner for Human Rights

acknowledgments

I do not know how this book emerged, became a reality, and took shape in my hands and more so in my soul. Perhaps it happened in some distant past when my family and I prepared to leave Chile in a long and dark night of exile. I read the poems of Pablo Neruda, Gabriela Mistral, and Anna Akhmatova. I then understood that literature had the power to heal and to save. Perhaps at that particular moment I realized that literature was going to be my guide, my path as I left home. And it has come to be so. My years in the United States have allowed me to know more about the world because I live in this first world country and have access to, as well as knowledge of, all the abuses that take place in this land and others. *A Map of Hope* was born because of a passionate desire to bring to witness the atrocities faced by women since the beginning of the century—indeed, since the beginning of time. I also wanted to show through the voices of women throughout the world the power to heal through words as well as the power of resistance.

I am grateful to so many people who have supported me as I completed this anthology: my parents, who taught me about justice and consciousness; my children, who taught me about unconditional love; my colleagues at the Spanish department, who have allowed me to work and to nourish my creativity; and my students, who bring me into day-to-day contact with the tenacity of hope.

I want to especially thank Emi Kamura, my project assistant, who from the very beginning believed in this book and believed that we would be able to navigate through the convoluted world of permissions and inquiries about who owned what. Emi also gave me the calmness and the perspective to be able to finish this work.

I also want to thank all of the authors included in this anthology who so generously donated their work, who waived their fees, and to the publishing houses who also waived their fees. Special thanks go to the University of California Press, Curbstone Press, University of Georgia Press, University of Massachusetts Press, Harvard University Press, and the University Press of New England.

This book would not have been possible without the vision and inspiration of Leslie Mitchner, who read every work and discussed with me every single entry for this anthology. She had a tremendous belief in my work and in this anthology.

I must also thank Amnesty International for a grant that allowed me to pay the permission fees. My heartful thanks to Bill Schultz, Amnesty International, U.S.A.; and to Florinda Russo, deputy director of the Northeastern region, for their vision and hope, which has allowed this project to happen.

My thanks also go to Nancy Tierney for her careful suggestions of possible authors; to Carmen Larios for researching some of the biographies; to Joy Renjilian-Burgy for her help with the Middle Eastern contributors; to Joan Gillespie for her help in securing the permissions; and to Caroline Wright for her help with Indian writers.

Sites of horror can also be sites of hope. Auschwitz and Rwanda should be remembered for the possibility of goodness and truth amidst the horror. I am grateful to the sites of women's words and courage that have made this world into a true map of hope. I am also grateful for my family and my two children, who are my map of hope.

introduction

When I was a child, I would listen to certain stories told behind closed doors. They appeared to be barely whispers, low intonations of voices. My great-grandmother cried for her sisters, who perished in Auschwitz. At that time, Auschwitz was an unpronounceable word, yet it was very close to my history, my home, and my childhood. As time passed and my lucid yet turbulent childhood and adolescent years receded, I no longer feared the ghosts of my childhood, but I feared the voices of the grown-ups, when they approached the dangerous grounds of usurped memories, of lives violated and transplanted. We were Jews who had traveled from Nazi Europe to South America, a Catholic universe. The pervasive sense of being different, of being surrounded by other histories brought from various countries, was my first contact with literature. From the time I was young, I tried to write about those whispers and cries that lived behind the closed doors of our house. To write was to retake a past that did not belong to me but was mine nonetheless. If childhood left its mark on me as the granddaughter of those who survived the Holocaust, the decade of the 1970s also marked me as part of a generation of young Latin Americans who were exiled, who left the countries they had fought for in search of a more just domicile.

The Holocaust and my exile from Chile, the fact that I was once again a foreigner who did not speak the language —this time, in America—helped me become a writer, but it also helped me feel a great empathy for those with similar destinies, similar pasts replete with silences, doubts, and feelings of alienation. My activism in human rights was born from various conditions that came together: I was Jewish, female, and an exile.

This is how this anthology was born: I have carried inside me many of the voices that appear in *A Map of Hope*. In times of great emotional difficulty, of isolation, I would read the words of other women whose lives seemed like mine. I came to understand that all women share my history—due to abuse, solitude, political violence, sexual violence, and the terror that accompanies these experiences.

1998 marks more than fifty years gone by since the UN's Universal Declaration of Human Rights was declared as a general agreement among Western nations to take responsibility for the destiny of their citizens, especially in the wake of the atrocities of World War II and the Nazi genocide. Regardless of the fact that this declaration was ratified by most Western nations, these human rights have been violated systematically during this century in places like Eastern Europe, Africa, and Latin America. Citizens may wonder how meaningful this declaration is when countries do not respect these declarations and agreements, millions become exiles and refugees, and thousands are tortured. The universality of human rights is constantly undermined by governments that see human rights as secondary to economic and national security. This outlook poses fundamental concerns for women's rights and their relationship to the universality of human rights. Throughout history, women have had almost no chance to exercise their social and cultural rights.

In spite of the advances made in women's rights since 1993, when the UN World Conference on Women stated that the human rights of women and of girl children are inalienably and indivisibly a part of human rights, many world governments pay no attention to the severity of human rights violations that directly involve women, such as direct violence by the state, emotional and psychological violence in the nuclear family, sexual abuse and domestic violence, marital rape, and genital mutilation.

Domestic violence is undoubtedly the primary form of violence against women. In some countries, men have the legal right to beat their wives, and in many other countries domestic violence is not treated as a serious crime. Other forms of abuse are specifically abuses of women—for example, in India, dowry disputes or the ritual of *satī* (widow burning). According to Amnesty International, dowry deaths are also reported in Indian immigrant communities in other countries, and statistics show that the number of reported dowry deaths in 1997 was 4,785. As recently as 1993, 5,000 women were reported to have died in such circumstances.

Another important issue of gender and human rights is the practice of genital mutilation of girls, which now occurs in some twenty countries in Africa, Asia, and the Middle East, as well as in immigrant communities in Europe and the United States. Rape and emotional and psychological abuse have been part of systematic assaults on women. In addition, in both the public and private sectors, girls and women have been caught in the industry of sexual and domestic slavery.

Contrary to what I always thought, slave trade does not only involve Asian women. Some patterns of slave trade are due to economic insecurity. The market focuses on Moscow and Kiev, but it also runs east to Japan and Thailand, where thousands of women are enslaved. This terror reinforces the conditions that affect the human rights of women, who, out of economic desperation, are forced to attempt to survive by doing work that leads to prostitution and mental and physical abuse. According to some reports of the Israeli government, for example, many thousands of women who arrive in Israel from Ukraine disappear as soon as they disembark. A *New York Times* article opens with a chilling scene describing Irina who unknowingly responded to a classified ad in her town's newspaper that promised her financial prosperity.

> She was 21, self-assured and glad to be out of Ukraine. Israel offered her a new world and for a week or two everything seemed possible. Then one morning, she was driven to a brothel where her boss burned her passport before her eyes. "I own you," she recalled him saying. "You are my property and you will work until you earn your way out. Don't try to leave. You have no papers and you don't speak Hebrew. You will be arrested and deported. Then we will get you and bring you back." (*New York Times*, 14 June 1998, pp. 4–5)

This chilling account shows explicitly the relationship between human rights and the rights of women. It is just one piece of specific evidence of violations committed directly against women. Aside from the disappeared, the secretly imprisoned, and the mass-raped women of the world, our robust global economy is apparently up to a few tricks of its own. Trafficking in women is a kind of degradation of the relationship between gender and human rights, but another important variable concerns the relationship between gender and migration. In an important article entitled "The Transitions of Immigration," Carola Suárez Orozco points out that there has been little organized investigation into this situation, but that in general, women emigrate to accompany their husbands, who are escaping political persecution. Their emigration is linked to their affection for their partners, and thus, their other family ties are severed. Orozco concludes that:

> Gender is one of the many factors critical in understanding the immigration experience. However, much of the research on immigration has focused on economic, demographic and sociological factors of work. Very little has been written about the psychological and cultural aspects of immigration. The immigration literature has tended to take a male lens which focuses on the social role of the world of work. (David Rockefeller Center for Latin American Studies, Latin American Studies Newsletter, Harvard University, March 1997, pp. 10–12)

The extent of grave abuses against women throughout the world has prompted many nongovernmental organizations such as Amnesty International, as well as some grassroots movements, to seriously commit their efforts to ending all discrimination and violence against women and to consciousness-raising that will pressure governments and educate civilians on issues of gender and human rights.

This international anthology of women writers and human rights is, to my knowledge, the first to gather the creative, courageous, and committed efforts of women who, through their writing, have engaged in a profound affirmation of women's rights and, through their voices, have participated in the making and unmaking of histories of the world around them.

From the voice of Anna Akhmatova decrying the Stalinist terror to the writings of Nadine Gordimer, the verses of Adrienne Rich, and the diary of Anne Frank, this anthology explores the dimensions of terror and war, as well as the possibility of resistance and refusal amidst the darkness.

Central to the writings in this collection is the courageous effort of each author to create a literary and historical document that speaks of human beliefs, truths, and justice. Their work illuminates the visible as well as the invisible threads of women's histories. Their still small dissenting voices speak out against horror, and their eloquence and imagination speak about social justice through art. Their writing is thus not only an instrument of refusal, but a form of resistance to cultures of fear in which innocent victims—women—are regarded as nonbeings. They reject this status of non-beings and the act of writing becomes a ritual of grief, hope, and freedom.

Theodor Adorno wrote that it would be barbaric to write poetry after

Auschwitz and the damage that was done there to our sense of beauty. Then again, one can also ask: How can we *not* write and pronounce the anger we feel? It seems that, after all, literature grants us the ability to endure and encompass traumatic and horrifying events, to articulate them through writing and the evocative power of memory. While gathering these materials, I have found that writing evokes the universal possibility of surviving; that the voices of Anne Frank, Diana Der-Hovanessian, and Carolina María de Jesus speak to all readers. In the act of telling there is a spirit of survival.

Preparing the materials for *A Map of Hope* has been a surprisingly powerful experience for me. Voices, friendships, letters, and phone calls began to pour in from the most distant and the closest places. All of my correspondents wanted to collaborate, to help, and to tell me of writers I had not known about. This proved to me something I already knew: that literature really matters. It is a way of articulating the self, as well as the soul. A world without writers would be a world lingering in the shadows of silence. This is a collection of creative works into which are deeply woven the themes of human rights and the ways in which these rights—or their absence—affect the daily lives of women. Literature moves us, rescues us from oblivion, and makes us witnesses to our history, here written by the hands of women.

The six parts of *A Map of Hope* address specific issues linked to gender and human rights.

The first part, "War and Remembrance," discusses war as part of women's stories as well as the consequences of war's legacy—the destruction of the self, the dissolution of family and country, and the torture of entire families. Ferida Durakovic's poetry, for example, describes the total physical and spiritual devastation of countries at war.

Part two, "Imprisonment and Censorship," addresses the situation of women in prison, through the works of writers such as Nawal El Sa'adawi, who was arrested in Egypt for her feminist politics; Aung San Suu Kyi, the Nobel Peace Prize–winning activist under house arrest in Burma; and Charlotte Delbo, a French resistance fighter sent to Auschwitz.

Part three, "Childhood," addresses one of the most poignant issues of this anthology: the vulnerability of children, war's most innocent victims. We are carried to the horrific world of Auschwitz, where Nelly Sachs re-creates the voices of dead children, and to war-torn Greece, where Elsa Spartioti, as a child, attempted to understand political violence.

Part four, "Exiles and Refugees," explores the psychological impact on women on becoming refugees and living in exile. Almost 80 percent of all casualties of war involve civilian populations, mostly women and children. They suffer pain and loneliness, the loss of family and home, and the irreversible conditions of displacement, as they endure vulnerability and humiliation. The Japanese-American writers Hisaye Yamamoto and Mitsuye Yamada reveal what is seldom addressed in history books—the existence of internment camps within the United States during World War II. The difficulties of real, as well as invented, nostalgias are described through the voice of Bosnian writer Slavenka Drakulic; and the impossibility of return is portrayed by Alicia Nitecki of Poland. The central focus of the refugee experience is loss: separation, violence, the economic and political deprivation faced by women supporting entire families in nations that have collapsed; and life in territories controlled by soldiers who systematically rape defenseless women refugees.

Part five, "Domestic and Political Violence," addresses these key issues in detail. If displacement is an emblematic condition of women without homes, besieged by civil wars, grieving for family members who have disappeared, political violence is also a fundamental issue of gender and human rights. Domestic violence does not consist only of the physical abuse of women, but includes the voicelessness, due to poverty, to the economic disadvantages closely linked to the fact that they are female. Meena Alexander of India describes the violence felt by an outsider, a female immigrant; Maud Sulter of Ghana depicts her encounters with racial and gender violence; Carolyn Forché addresses this type of violence through the poignant and brutal image of a colonel who devours his own people; and Taslima Nassrin addresses the domestic violence of Islamic fundamentalism.

The mistreatment of women has made women activists attempt to redefine women's rights and their relationship to social and political rights in general, documenting as well as rethinking the particular dichotomies of the private and the public spheres. The concept of women's rights as human rights has allowed for the emergence of a new form of activism worldwide and a new culture of female political imagination and resistance within this theoretical framework that acknowledges the commonality of gender and human rights. This anthology attempts to contribute to this emerging dialogue.

The sixth and last part of this anthology, "Resistance and Refusal," exemplifies the courageous as well as tenacious pursuit of refusal and resistance, by which women say no to despair and fight through the nonviolent power of literature for a more peaceful and safer world for women and their children. It is precisely this resistance to despair that led Nadine Gordimer to fight against apartheid in her native South Africa; that inspired the Chilean Isabel Allende to write *The House of the Spirits*, defying the terror and horror of the Pinochet dictatorship; that led some to find solace, hope, and confidence in the healing and transcending power of literature, as portrayed in Agate Nesaule's "The Reciters." The constant intimidation of and accusations against women whose only crime has been the pursuit of justice and freedom are evoked throughout this book; they link political violence to our everyday lives.

Each poem in this anthology, as well as each memoir, fragment, or narrative, was born at a particular historical moment of exile, war, or imprisonment. All the writers included here have responded to what is essential to art: They create art despite trauma, no matter how heartbreaking. They constantly question the reality in which their texts were born, but above all, they make more beautiful, through words, the failure and pain of existence. These texts not only bear witness to human tragedy; they also present the human need for art—not only in order to survive, but as the only possibility for life. To quote Juan Gelman:

> Nothing human is alien to poetry. There are those who proclaim that poetry must be pure, that art must be pure, but that both must be able to talk about the misery of our humanity. These voices attempt to amputate the registry of poetic and artistic expression and consequently cut down the registry of human passion. Even if he wanted it to be that way, the poet or the artist cannot sustain his creation of reality. Like all the world he has been hurt by reality, from the outside, since his birth. The words have marked all of us forever and that wound will remain open until death. In essence, there is no reality without words, but there are words without reality even if they only exist to deny it. (From an unpublished paper, June 1996; reprinted by permission of the author.)

The writings in this anthology attempt to recover what has often been denied to us: life, love, affection, the possibility of living in our homeland, and freedom. Literature is then more than a witness to the passage of time and its shadows. It is a documentation of the experience of being human in times of adversity and resistance. From the prose of Matilde Mellibovsky, which describes the Plaza de Mayo, to the letters written by Ferida Durakovic in Bosnia during the war, to the fragments of Nuha Al Radi's diary in Iraq, literature binds the voices from the most diverse geographies, makes the experiences of women universal, and gives hope to future generations. Carolina María de Jesus's diary tells us about living in squalor in Brazil, and yet it speaks of hope; she knows she can find more paper to write on, and she writes, conscious of her legacy.

This anthology includes poems, diaries, fragments of novels, and testimonies of those who have resisted totalitarianism and fascism. They describe children for whom the idea of innocence does not exist; they give accounts of women living in exile, isolated from families and communities, empowered only by the language that brings them back home. This home is often a site that exists only in imagination, since their physical home has often been destroyed, and no belongings or tangible mementos remain. Writing, reciting, and speaking are ways to reinvent lost memories as well as the events that caused their destruction.

These writers put a face, an image, and a human dimension on dehumanization and give voice to the voiceless and visibility to what has always been invisible: torture and its sequelae of human rights violations. These women write not only to bear witness, they write to make the readers bear witness to this horror. They do not see writing as an aesthetic diversion; rather, their writing has a purpose: to create a literature of resistance and to bear witness. Such writing as Marguerite Duras's chronicle of the German occupation of Paris, as well as the physical abuse and mutilation of women in Bangladesh and India, described by Taslima Nassrin or Gītā Chattopādhyāy, lends new meaning to the term *resistance*.

This is a collection of voices that seek to acknowledge in literature the universal dimension of horror and its role in the lives of women. The organization of the individual parts focuses on specific goals rather than on specific countries.

The mosaic of voices in a global community of women writers presented here has created a literature of consciousness and of social justice. These voices are united by the universal dimensions of horror and deprivation, as well as a common struggle for social justice and solidarity. Every attempt has been made to include an array of women from a global scope, but this has not always been possible; for example, it has been very difficult to obtain the work of Algerian or African women. Nevertheless, this book goes beyond geographical and ethnic groups and tries to create a unified vision of the problems most relevant to women's struggle.

To my knowledge, this is the first anthology ever to be published that focuses on the way in which specifically women writers have spoken about human rights issues, in which the writers are themselves victims or survivors, or witnesses to their own cultural experience. Their testimony must be heard; it cannot be denied or silenced. From the profoundly moving *Diary of Anne Frank*, to the struggles of Carolina María de Jesus in the favelas of São Paulo, the reader will also become a witness to these acts of courage. The act of writing becomes an act of faith, survival, and transcendence.

This anthology presents the ways in which women writers have written with great lucidity and beauty about horrors they have experienced. Other writers have made an alliance with those witnesses, and they write without condescension or presumption, but out of solidarity and communal justice. This collection includes a myriad of writers who, through the symbolic power of words, have decided to make a difference, to weave poems, stories, letters, and memoirs that speak against tyranny, horror, and brutality.

The women writers who are gathered here speak for peace, justice, and social and political freedom. Each woman addresses fundamental aspects of human rights that have a particular relationship to women, and *A Map of Hope* is framed to address a variety of human rights issues that are linked to gender-based censorship.

The theme of exiles and refugees runs through these pages, but not as a separate category. It is rather a profound interconnection of voices and visions of women and children besieged by war, incarcerated, and living in labor camps. Agate Nesaule takes us into the life of a child in a labor camp, experiencing hunger, poverty, and the humiliations of war. Taslima Nassrin portrays domestic violence and links it to political violence. Slavenka Drakulic reminisces about the power of memory in the life of an exile.

The women in this anthology have woven a tapestry of images through the power of a pen and a scrap of paper. They resist authoritarianism, fascism, and censorship, and they engage the reader through the extraordinary power that literature and imagination have to create transcendent descriptions of fear, torture, disappearance, and despair—and ultimately love, hope, and renewal.

A Map of Hope is intended to reveal to the reader the powerful and global connection that has been an instrumental part of women's voices facing adversity, indifference, and political and domestic violence. These voices—from Baghdad to Amsterdam to Buenos Aires—bear witness to women's conditions, women's hopes, and the memories of these hopes. As Robin Morgan so clearly points out in *Sisterhood Is Global*, those who suffer most from the world's problems are women. "While women represent half the global population and one third of the labor force, they receive only one tenth of the world's income and own less than one percent of the world's property. They are also responsible for two thirds of all working hours" (Robin Morgan, Introduction, *Sisterhood Is Global* [The Feminist Press, 1996]). Two out of three of the world's illiterates are women; while the general level of literacy is increasing, the number of illiterate women is also increasing.

The pieces in this book acknowledge, describe, and celebrate the ways in which women have engaged in the aesthetic representation of gender and human rights: how they speak about evil, political truths, and untruths; how they represent their own vulnerability and subjectivity, and how they write about their own individual freedoms and social freedom. Many of the writers are constantly at risk, persecuted by family, state, government, or their imposed religion. For some of them, the language of poverty is a language of symbols and metaphors. Ultimately, all these writers search for a language that engages both themselves and the reader, as well as future generations. It is no coincidence that this anthology is being published in 1999, a year before the new century begins. In spite of all the horrors and devastation in so many countries, this is a book about hope. According to Nadine Gordimer, "This is a century where we are seeing an end to colonialism in South Africa and, to this I may add, the end of dictatorships in Latin America, but yet, there is Rwanda and the Balkans, wars and homelessness linked to domestic violence in the most wealthy nations of the world" (Nadine Gordimer, Introduction, *Writing and Being* [Harvard University Press, 1995]).

At times of great political repression, literature acquires a powerful function: It legitimizes artistic expression in a totalitarian society whose government prohibits this expression. Women writers, through their words and stories, manage to reaffirm what the greater society has denied. Paradoxically, if patriarchal societies have historically denied the presence of women writers, and also those who write about politics, the existence of extreme conditions due to political and civil violence has allowed these women writers to create and through their texts become visible. The Mothers of Plaza de Mayo, for example, took up public space that had been forbidden to them and gave it life through their search for their missing children. The woman's body has become a place of resistance but also a space that attempts to defy oblivion.

For the women whose writings are collected in these pages, literature alters life. Among the ruins of war or in concentration camps, people write. These writers are the voices that defy fear. As Aung San Suu Kyi says, "The acts of horrors are many times committed due to fear." To write under adversity is to actively resist pain and betrayal, but it is also a form of denying horror. In this anthology, some women have not suffered violations or exile, but they are women, and they are women with a conscience. The privilege of being white does not stop Nadine Gordimer from writing about colonial societies. The privilege of owning land and being educated does not stop Rosario Castellanos from meditating on the condition of the indigenous women of Chiapas. Each voice on this map is the voice of conscience.

A Map of Hope celebrates the UN Universal Declaration of Human Rights and joins the voices of women who for the past fifty years have spoken out in favor of justice, equality, and liberty and whose writings have given a conscience to all of us. *A Map of Hope* is a collection of extraordinary literary works—poems, essays, memoirs, and narratives—that speak of literary responsibility, as well as the vocation of writers who have themselves been victims of political and civil violence or who feel compelled to speak and write about it. The meaning of resistance here takes varied shapes and meanings. This book is intended above all to move, compel, and incite the reader into being there, into thinking: "This could happen to me." More than to convince or to reveal histories, ways of being and becoming, this collection seeks to stir the emotions through the vividness, beauty, and strength of these women's works. Their tenacity inspires us, in turn, to resist and to endure, and to write.

Universal Declaration of Human Rights

PREAMBLE

Whereas recognition of the inherent dignity and of the equal and inalienable rights of all members of the human family is the foundation of freedom, justice and peace in the world.

Whereas disregard and contempt for human rights have resulted in barbarous acts which have outraged the conscience of mankind, and the advent of a world in which human beings shall enjoy freedom of speech and belief and freedom from fear and want has been proclaimed as the highest aspiration of the common people.

Whereas it is essential, if man is not to be compelled to have recourse, as a last resort, to rebellion against tyranny and oppression, that human rights should be protected by the rule of law.

Whereas it is essential to promote the development of friendly relations between nations.

Whereas the peoples of the United Nations have in the Charter reaffirmed their faith in fundamental human rights, in the dignity and worth of the human person and in the equal rights of men and women and have determined to promote social progress and better standards of life in larger freedom.

Whereas Member States have pledged themselves to achieve, cooperation with the United Nations, the promotion of universal respect for and observance of human rights and fundamental freedoms.

Whereas a common understanding of these rights and freedoms is of the greatest importance for the full realization of this pledge.

Now, Therefore, The General Assembly proclaims THIS UNIVERSAL DECLARATION OF HUMAN RIGHTS as a common standard of achievement for all peoples and all nations, to the end that every individual and every organ of society, keeping this Declaration constantly in mind, shall strive by teaching and education to promote respect for these rights and freedoms and by progressive measures, national and international, to secure their universal and effective recognition and observance, both among the peoples of Member States themselves and among the peoples of territories under their jurisdiction.

Article 1. All human beings are born free and equal in dignity and rights. They are endowed with reason and conscience and should act towards one another in a spirit of brotherhood.

Article 2. Everyone is entitled to all the rights and freedoms set forth in this Declaration, without distinction of any kind, such as race, colour, sex, language, religion, political or other opinion, national or social origin, property, birth or other status. Furthermore, no distinction shall be made on the basis of the political, jurisdictional or international status of the country or territory to which a person belongs, whether it be independent, trust, non-self-governing or under any other limitation of sovereignty.

Article 3. Everyone has the right to life, liberty and security of person.

Article 4. No one shall be held in slavery of servitude; slavery and the slave trade shall be prohibited in all their forms.

Article 5. No one shall be subjected to torture or to cruel, inhuman or degrading treatment or punishment.

Article 6. Everyone has the right to recognition everywhere as a person before the law.

Article 7. All are equal before the law and are entitled without any discrimination to equal protection of the law. All are entitled to equal protection against any discrimination in violation of this Declaration and against any incitement to such discrimination.

Article 8. Everyone has the right to an effective remedy by the competent national tribunals for acts violating the fundamental rights granted him by the constitution or by law.

Article 9. No one shall be subjected to arbitrary arrest, detention or exile.

Article 10. Everyone is entitled in full equality to a fair and public hearing by an independent and impartial tribunal, in the determination of his rights and obligations and of any criminal charge against him.

Article 11. (1) Everyone charged with a penal offence has the right to be presumed innocent until proved guilty according to law in a public trial at which he has had all the guarantees necessary for his defence. (2) No one shall be held guilty of any penal offence of any act of omission which did not constitute a penal offence, under national or international law, at the time when it was committed. Nor shall a heavier penalty be imposed than the one that was applicable at the time the penal offence was committed.

Article 12. No one shall be subjected to arbitrary interference with his privacy, family, home or correspondence, nor to attacks upon his honour and reputation. Everyone has the right to the protection of the law against such interference or attacks.

Article 13. (1) Everyone has the right to freedom of movement and residence within the borders of each state. (2) Everyone has the right to leave any country, including his own, and to return to his country.

Article 14. (1) Everyone has the right to seek and to enjoy in other countries asylum from persecution. (2) This right may not be invoked in the case of prosecutions genuinely arising from non-political crimes or from acts contrary to the purposes and principles of the United Nations.

Article 15. (1) Everyone has the right to a nationality. (2) No one shall be arbitrarily deprived of his nationality nor denied the right to change his nationality.

Article 16. (1) Men and women of full age, without any limitation due to race, nationality or religion, have the right to marry and to found a family. They are entitled to equal rights as to marriage, during marriage, and at its dissolution. (2) Marriage shall be entered into only with the free and full consent of the intending spouses. (3) The family is the natural and fundamental group unit of society and is entitled to protection by society and the State.

Article 17. (1) Everyone has the right to own property alone as well as in association with others. (2) No one shall be arbitrarily deprived of his property.

Article 18. Everyone has the right to freedom of thought, conscience and religion; this right includes freedom to change his religion or belief, and freedom, either alone or in community with others and in public or private, to manifest his religion or belief in teaching, practice, worship and observance.

Article 19. Everyone has the right to freedom of opinion and expression; this right includes freedom to hold opinions without interference and to seek, receive and impart information and ideas through any media and regardless of frontiers.

Article 20. (1) Everyone has the right to freedom of peaceful assembly and association. (2) No one may be compelled to belong to an association.

Article 21. (1) Everyone has the right to take part in the government of his country, directly or through freely chosen representatives. (2) Everyone has the right of equal access to public service in his country. (3) The will of the people shall be the basis of the authority of the government; this will shall be expressed in periodic and genuine elections which shall be by universal and equal suffrage and shall be held by secret vote or by equivalent free voting procedures.

Article 22. Everyone, as a member of society, has the right to social security and is entitled to realization, through national effort and international co-operation and in accordance with the organization and resources of each State, of the economic, social and cultural rights indispensable for his dignity and the free development of his personality.

Article 23. (1) Everyone has the right to work, to free choice of employment, to just and favourable conditions of work and to protection against unemployment. (2) Everyone, without any discrimination, has the right to equal pay for equal work. (3) Everyone who works has the right to just and favourable remuneration ensuring for himself and his family an existence worthy of human dignity, and supplemented, if necessary, by other means of social protection. (4) Everyone has the right to form and to join trade unions for the protection of his interests.

Article 24. Everyone has the right to rest and leisure, including reasonable limitation of working hours and periodic holidays with pay.

Article 25. (1) Everyone has the right to a standard of living adequate for the health and well-being of himself and of his family, including food, clothing, housing and medical care and necessary social services, and the right to security in the event of unemployment, sickness, disability, widowhood, old age or other lack of livelihood in circumstances beyond his control. (2) Motherhood and childhood are entitled to special care and assistance. All children, whether born in or out of wedlock, shall enjoy the same social protection.

Article 26. (1) Everyone has the right to education. Education shall be free, at least in the elementary and fundamental stages. Elementary education shall be compulsory. Technical and professional education shall be made generally available and higher education shall be equally accessible to all on the basis of merit. (2) Education shall be directed to the full development of the human personality and to the strengthening of respect for human rights and fundamental freedoms. It shall promote understanding, tolerance, and friendship among all nations, racial or religious groups, and shall further the activities of the United Nations for the maintenance of peace. (3) Parents have a prior right to choose the kind of education that shall be given to their children.

Article 27. (1) Everyone has the right to freely participate in the cultural life of the community, to enjoy the arts and to share in scientific advancement and benefits. (2) Everyone has the right to protection of the moral and material interests resulting from any scientific, literary or artistic production of which he is the author.

Article 28. Everyone is entitled to a social and international order in which the rights and freedoms set forth in this Declaration can be fully realized.

Article 29. Everyone has duties to the community in which alone the free and full development of his personality is possible. (2) In the exercise of his rights and freedoms, everyone shall be subject only to such limitations as are determined by law solely for the purpose of securing due recognition and respect for the rights and freedoms of others and meeting the just requirements of morality, public order and the general welfare in a democratic society. (3) These rights and freedoms may in no case be exercised contrary to the purposes and principles of the United Nations.

Article 30. Nothing in this Declaration may be interpreted as implying for any State, group or person any right to engage in any activity or to perform any act aimed at the destruction of any of the rights and freedoms set forth herein.

a map of

Hope

one

War and Remembrance

Wind and Widow

Lê Thi Mây

Wind widow willowy
off the arms of dawn and grass
full-chested breath
after so much lovemaking in the night

patches of cloud-clothes discarded in the air
lipstick
sunrise
facial cream
aroma moon of the fourteenth day

wind widow after each makeup
backward glances to another time of sadness and laughter

grass
and dawn rises trembling
separated from wind after lovemaking
all night

. . .

wind elegiac-wind
strands of hair from women who died in the bombing
strands of hair from widows who raised orphaned children
the war after ten years have passed—

The Son of Man

Natalia Ginzburg

There has been a war and people have seen so many houses reduced to rubble that they no longer feel safe in their own homes which once seemed so quiet and secure. This is something that is incurable and will never be cured no matter how many years go by. True, we have a lamp on the table again, and a little vase of flowers, and pictures of our loved ones, but we can no longer trust any of these things because once, suddenly, we had to leave them behind, or because we have searched through the rubble for them in vain.

It is useless to believe that we could recover from twenty years like those we have been through. Those of us who have been fugitives will never be at peace. A ring at the door-bell in the middle of the night can only mean the word "police" to us. And it is useless for us to tell ourselves over and over again that behind the word "police" there are now friendly faces from whom we can ask for help and protection. This word always fills us with fear and suspicion. When I look at my sleeping children I think with relief that I will not have to wake them and run off into the night. But it is not a deep, lasting relief. It always seems to me that some day or other we shall once again have to get up and run off in the middle of the night, and leave everything—the quiet rooms, our letters, mementoes, clothes—behind us.

Once the experience of evil has been endured it is never forgotten. Someone who has seen a house collapse knows only too clearly what frail things little vases of flowers and pictures and white walls are. He knows only too well what a house is made of. A house is made of bricks and mortar and can collapse. A house is not particularly solid. It can collapse from one moment to the next. Behind the peaceful little vases of flowers, behind the teapots and carpets and waxed floors there is the other true face of a house—the hideous face of a house that has been reduced to rubble.

We shall not get over this war. It is useless to try. We shall never be people who go peacefully about their business, who think and study and manage their lives quietly. Something has happened to our houses. Something has happened to us. We shall never be at peace again.

We have seen reality's darkest face, and it no longer horrifies us. And there are still those who complain that writers use bitter, violent language, that they write about cruel, distressing things, that they present reality in the worst possible light.

We cannot lie in our books and we cannot lie in any of the things we do. And perhaps this is the one good thing that has come out of the war. Not to lie, and not to allow others to lie to us. Such is the nature of the young now, of our generation. Those who are older than us are still too fond of falsehoods, of the veils and masks with which they hide reality. Our language saddens and offends them. They do not understand our attitude to reality. We are close to the truth of things. This is the only good the war has given us, but it has given it only to the young. It has given nothing but fear and a sense of insecurity to the old. And we who are young are also afraid, we also feel insecure in our homes, but we are not made defenceless by this fear. We have a toughness and strength which those who are older than us have never known.

For some the war started only with the war, with houses reduced to rubble and with the Germans, but for others it started as long ago as the first years of Fascism, and consequently for them the feeling of insecurity and constant danger is far greater. Danger, the feeling that you must hide, the feeling that—without warning—you will have to leave the warmth of your bed and your house, for many of us all this started many years ago. It crept into our childish games, followed us to our desks at school and taught us to see enemies everywhere. This is how it was for many of us in Italy, and elsewhere, and we believed that one day we would be able to walk without anxiety down the streets of our own cities, but now that we can perhaps walk there without anxiety we realize that we shall never be cured of this sickness. And so we are constantly forced to seek out a new strength, a new toughness with which to face whatever reality may confront us. We have been driven to look for an inward peace which is not the product of carpets and little vases of flowers.

There is no peace for the son of man. The foxes and the wolves have their holes, but the son of man hath not where to lay his head. Our generation is a generation of men. It is not a generation of foxes and wolves. Each of us would dearly like to rest his head somewhere, to have a little warm, dry nest. But there is no peace for the son of man. Each of us at some time in his life has had the illusion that he could sleep somewhere safely, that he could take possession of some certainty, some faith, and there rest his limbs. But all the certainties of the past have been snatched away from us, and faith has never after all been a place for sleeping in.

And we are a people without tears. The things that moved our parents do not move us at all. Our parents and those older than us disapprove of the way we bring up our children. They would like us to lie to our children as they lied to us. They would like our children to play with woolly toys in pretty pink rooms with little trees and rabbits painted on the walls. They would like us to surround their infancy with veils and lies, and carefully hide the truth of things from them. But we cannot do this. We cannot do this to children whom we have woken in the middle of the night and tremblingly dressed in the darkness so that we could flee with them or hide them, or simply because the air-raid sirens were lacerating the skies. We cannot do this to children who have seen terror and horror in our faces. We cannot bring ourselves to tell these children that we found them under cabbages, or that when a person dies he goes on a long journey.

There is an unbridgeable abyss between us and the previous generation. The dangers they lived through were trivial and their houses were rarely reduced to rubble. Earthquakes and fires were not phenomena that happened constantly and to everyone. The women did their knitting and told the cook what to make for lunch and invited their friends to houses that did not collapse. Everyone thought and studied and managed his life quietly. It was a different time and probably very fine in its way. But we are tied to our suffering, and at heart we are glad of our destiny as men.

The War

Marguerite Duras

April 20

Today's the day when the first batch of political deportees arrives from Weimar. They phone me from the center in the morning. They say I can come, the deportees won't be there till the afternoon. I go for the morning. I'll stay all day. I don't know where to go to bear myself.

Orsay.[1] Outside the center, wives of prisoners of war congeal in a solid mass. White barriers separate them from the prisoners. "Do you have any news of so and so?" they shout. Every so often the soldiers stop; one or two answer. Some women are there at seven o'clock in the morning. Some stay till three in the morning and then come back again at seven. But there are some who stay right through the night, between three and seven. They're not allowed into the center. Lots of people who are not waiting for anyone come to the Gare d'Orsay, too, just to see the show, the arrival of the prisoners of war and how the women wait for them, and all the rest, to see what it's like; perhaps it will never happen again. You can tell the spectators from the others because they don't shout out, and they stand some way away from the crowds of women so as to see both the arrival of prisoners and the way the women greet them. The prisoners arrive in an orderly manner. At night they come in big American trucks from which they emerge into the light. The women shriek and clap their hands. The prisoners stop, dazzled and taken aback. During the day the women shout as soon as they see the trucks turning off the Solferino Bridge. At night they shout when they slow down just before the center. They shout the names of German towns: "Noyeswarda?"[2] "Kassel?" Or Stalag numbers: "VII A?" "III A Kommando?" The prisoners seem astonished. They've come straight from Le Bourget airport and Germany. Sometimes they answer, usually they don't quite understand what's expected of them, they smile, they turn and look at the Frenchwomen, the first they've seen since they got back.

I can't work properly;[3] of all the names I record none is ever his. Every five minutes I want to give it up, lay down the pencil, stop asking for news, leave

the center for the rest of my life. At about two in the afternoon I go to ask
what time the convoy from Weimar arrives. I leave the circuit and look for
someone to ask. In a corner of the main hall I see about ten women sitting on
the floor and being addressed by a colonel. I go over. The colonel is a tall
woman in a navy blue suit with the cross of Lorraine in the lapel. Her white
hair has been curled with tongs and blue-rinsed. The women look at her. They
look harassed, but listen open-mouthed to what she says. The floor around
them is littered with bundles and cases tied with string. A small child is sleeping on one of the bundles. The women are very dirty and their faces look tired
and shocked. Two of them have enormous bellies. Another woman officer
stands nearby, watching. I go over and ask her what's going on. She looks at me,
lowers her eyes, and says delicately, "STO volunteers."[4] The colonel tells them
to get up and follow her. They rise and follow her. The reason they look so
frightened is that they've just been booed by the wives of the prisoners of war
waiting outside the center. A few days ago I saw some other STO volunteers
arrive. Men, this time. Like the other men they were smiling when they arrived, but gradually they realized and then their faces too looked shocked. The
colonel points to the women and asks the young woman in uniform who's just
told me who they are, "What are we supposed to do with them?" The other
one says, "I don't know." The colonel must have told them they were scum.
Some of them were crying. The pregnant ones stare into space. The colonel
has told them to sit down again. They sit down. Most of them are factory workers, their hands blackened by the oil of German machinery. Two of them are
probably prostitutes, their faces are made up and their hair dyed, but they also
must have worked with machinery, they've got the same grimy hands as the
others. A repatriation officer comes up. "What's all this?" "STO volunteers."
The colonel's voice is shrill, she turns toward the volunteers and threatens,
"Sit down and keep quiet . . . Do you hear? Don't think you're just going to
be let go . . ." She shakes her fist at them. The repatriation officer goes over
to the bunch of volunteers, looks at them, and there, right in front of them, asks
the colonel, "Do you have any orders?" The colonel: "No, do you?" "Someone mentioned six months' detention." The colonel nods her beautiful curly
head: "Serve them right . . ." The officer blows puffs of smoke—Camels—over
the bunch of volunteers, who've been following the conversation with eyes
wild with apprehension. "Right!" he says, and goes off, young, elegant, a born
horseman, his Camel in his hand. The volunteers watch, looking for some in-

dication of the fate awaiting them. There is none. I stop the colonel as she makes off. "Do you know when the convoy from Weimar arrives?" She gives me a searching look. "Three o'clock," she says. She goes on looking at me, weighing me up, and says with just a touch of irritation, "No point in cluttering up the place waiting. It'll only be generals and prefects. Go home." I wasn't expecting this. I think I insult her. I say, "What about the others?" She bridles. "I can't stand that kind of attitude! Go and complain somewhere else, my dear." She's so indignant she goes and tells a small group of other women in uniform, who listen, are also indignant, and look at me. I go up to one of them and say, "Isn't *she* waiting for anyone?" The woman looks at me, scandalized, and tries to calm me down. She says, "The poor thing's got so much to do, her nerves are in shreds." I go back to the Tracing Service at the end of the circuit. Soon afterward I go back to the main hall. D.'s[5] waiting for me there with a forged pass.

About three o'clock there's a rumor: "They're here." I leave the circuit and station myself at the entrance to a little passage opposite the main hall. I wait. I know Robert L. won't be there. D. is beside me. His job is to go and question the deportees to find out if they know Robert L. He's pale. He doesn't pay any attention to me. There's a great commotion in the main hall. The women in uniform fuss around the volunteers and make them sit on the floor in a corner. The main hall is empty. There's a pause in the arrivals of prisoners of war. Repatriation officers go back and forth. The loudspeaker has stopped too. I hear people saying, "The minister," and see Frenay among the officers. I'm still standing at the entrance to the little corridor. I watch the entrance. I know Robert L. can't possibly be there. But perhaps D. will manage to find out something. I don't feel well. I'm trembling, cold. I lean against the wall. Suddenly, there's a hum of voices: "Here they are!" Outside, the women haven't shouted. They haven't applauded. Suddenly, two scouts emerge from the passage carrying a man. He has his arms around their necks. They've joined hands to support his legs. He's in civilian clothes, shaven, he appears to be in great pain. He's a strange color. He must be crying. You couldn't say he's thin, it's something else—there's so little of him left you wonder if he's really alive. But no, he is alive, his face is convulsed by a terrifying grimace. He doesn't look at anything. Not at the minister, not at the hall, not at the flags—nothing. The grimace may be a laugh. He's the first deportee from Weimar to arrive at the center. Without realizing it I've moved forward, I'm in the middle of the hall with my back to the loudspeaker. Two more scouts come in carrying another, an old man. Then another ten or eleven arrive. These appear to be in better condition, they can walk, with help. They're installed on garden benches that have been set out in the hall. The minister goes over to them. The second one to arrive, the old man, is weeping. You can't tell if he's as old as all that, he may be only twenty, you can't tell his age. The minister comes over, takes off his hat, goes up to the old man, holds out his hand. The old man takes it, but doesn't know it's the minister's. A woman in a blue uniform bawls at him: "It's the minister! He's come to meet you!" The old man goes on crying, he hasn't even looked up. Suddenly I see D. sitting down beside him. I'm very cold, my teeth are chattering. Someone comes up to me: "Don't stay here, there's no point, it's making you ill." I know him, he's a fellow from the center. I stay. D. has started to talk to the old man. I go over it all quickly in my head. There's one chance in ten thousand the old man might have met Robert L. In Paris they're beginning to say the army has lists of survivors from Buchenwald. Apart from the old man crying and the rheumatics, the others don't seem in too bad condition. The minister's sitting with them, as are the senior officers. D. talks to the old man at length. I don't look at anything but D.'s face. I feel this is taking a very long time. I move very slowly toward the bench, into D.'s field of vision. He notices, looks at me, and shakes his head to signify, "No, he doesn't know him." I move away. I'm very tired, I feel like lying down on the ground. Now the women in uniform are bringing the deportees mess tins. They eat, and as they eat they answer questions. What's so remarkable is that they don't seem interested in what's said to them. I'll find out next day from the papers that among these people, these old men, are General Challe; his son Hubert Challe, who had been a cadet at Saint-Cyr and who was to die that night, the night of his arrival; General Audibert; Ferrière, head of the state tobacco industry; Julien Cain, director of the Bibliothèque Nationale; General Heurteaux; Marcel Paul; Professor Suard of the faculty of medicine at Angers; Professor Richet; Claude Bourdet; the brother of Teitgen, the minister of information; Maurice Nègre; and others.

I leave the center at about five in the afternoon and go home along the river. The weather's fine, it's a lovely sunny day. I can't wait to get back, to shut myself up with the telephone, be back again in the black ditch. As soon as I leave the embankment and turn into the rue du Bac, the city is far away again and the Orsay center vanishes. Perhaps he will come back after all. I don't know any more. I'm very tired. I'm very dirty. I've been spending part of the night at the center, too. I must make up my mind to take a bath when I get in, it must be a week since I stopped washing. I feel the cold so badly in the spring, the idea of washing makes me shudder, I have a sort of permanent fever that doesn't seem to want to go away. This evening I think about myself. I've never met a woman more cowardly than I am. I go over in my mind other women who are waiting like me—no, none is as cowardly as that. I know some who are very brave. Extraordinary. My cowardice is such that it can't be described, except by D. My colleagues in the Tracing Service think I'm crazy. D. says, "No one has the right to destroy himself like that, ever." He often tells me, "You're sick. You're a madwoman. Look at yourself—you look like nothing on earth." I can't understand what people are trying to say to me. [Even now, transcribing these things from my youth, I can't understand the meanings of those expressions.] Not for a second do I see the need to be brave. Perhaps being brave is my form of cowardice. Suzy is brave for her little boy. The child we had, Robert L. and I, was born dead, he died in the war too: doctors didn't usually go out at night during the war, they hadn't enough gas. So I'm on my own. Why should I husband my strength? There's nothing for me to fight for. No one can know my struggle against visions of the black ditch. Sometimes the vision gets the upper hand and I cry out or leave the house and walk the streets of Paris. D. says, "When you think about it later on you'll be ashamed." People are out in the streets as usual, there are lines outside the shops; there are some cherries already, that's what the women are waiting for. I buy a paper. The Russians are in Strausberg, perhaps even farther, on the outskirts of Berlin. The women standing in line for cherries are waiting for the fall of Berlin. I'm waiting for it too. "Then they'll see, then they'll find out what's what," people say. The whole world is waiting for it. All the governments in the world are agreed. When the heart of Germany stops beating, say the papers, it will be all over. Zhukov has a ring of guns only a hundred yards apart pounding the city from a range of less than forty miles. Berlin is in flames. It will be burned right down to the roots. German blood will flow among its ruins. Sometimes you think you can smell the blood. See it. A prisoner who's a priest brought a German orphan back to the center. He held him by the hand, was proud of him, showed him off, explained how he'd found him and that it wasn't the poor child's fault.

The women looked askance at him. He was arrogating to himself the right to forgive, to absolve, already. He wasn't returning from any suffering, any waiting. He was taking the liberty of exercising the right to forgive and absolve there and then, right away, without any knowledge of the hatred that filled everyone, a hatred terrible yet pleasant, consoling, like a belief in God. So what was he talking about? Never has a priest seemed so incongruous. The women looked away, they spat upon the beaming smile of mercy and light. They ignored the child. A total split, with on the one side the solid, uncompromising front of the women, and on the other just the one man, who was right, but in a language the women didn't understand.

Notes

1. The railroad station, the Gare d'Orsay, was serving as a processing center for prisoners returning to France from Germany—ED.

2. The author's note at this point reads: "I haven't been able to find this name in the atlas. I've probably spelled it as it sounded to me."

3. Duras has been gathering information from returning prisoners about the location of others. She printed this information in a newsletter for deportees' families—ED.

4. STO: The Service du Travail Obligatoire (Forced Labor Service), introduced in February 1943, was an organized deportation of French workers. Some people actually volunteered to work in Germany—TRANS.

5. "D." is Duras's lover—ED.

A Life

Fadwa Tuqan

My life is tears
and a fond heart,
longing, a book of poetry and a lute

My life, my totally sorrowful life,
if its silhouette should vanish tomorrow,
an echo would remain on earth,
my voice repeating:
My life is tears
and a fond heart,
longing, a book of poetry and a lute.

On the sad nights
when silence endlessly deepens,
the phantoms of my loved ones pass
before me like wisps of dreams,
poking the fire alive beneath the ashes
and drenching my pillow with tears,
tears of longing
for ones who have died
and lie, folded in the darkness of the grave.

My orphan heart cries,
"Oh Father, look down on us,
from your immortal horizon
Your death has humiliated us!
We have lived trapped between viper and snake,
exhaled poisons
and defiant enemies
snagged on this world of ingratitude and denial."

At night a phantom appears
My father cleaves the curtain of the unknown,
his eyes shadowed by sorrow,
when my tears pour out,
he leans on me, we weep together
I beg him, "Come back
in your lingering absence—
who'll shelter us?"

On sleepless nights,
I dream of my brother,
that fountain of love,
the fuse for my eyes and heart
till the swirl of death
extinguished his torch
Alone
without his guiding light
I continue, bewildered.

And here's my youth
with all its failed dreams . . .
drenched by sorrow
whenever life embraces it with
thousands of braces and chains.
Pull it back,
that tortured alien youth
that prisoner,
stunted by captivity.

Now I bow my head, desolate.
A lost horizon thunders inside.
Poems alone are my refuge.
In them I describe
my longings
only then can this soul
find calm.

Plucking my lute
in time with my lonesome heart
the throbbing chords
dissolve my grief.
With melody and poetry,
I struggle with the grief of a martyred life.

And here's my song,
song of my life
leaving echoes behind me:
My life is tears
and a fond heart,
longing, a book of poetry and a lute.

An Estate of Memory

Ilona Karmel

(Chapter 7)

The silence must have startled her: the wheels rattled no longer; from the mass huddled against the wall no sound came. Then a bang—the iron bars were being removed, and the door opened on frosty air, on darkness glimmering with snow and on oily yellow light trailing above a row of motionless shapes.

"Do you see anything? SS men, dogs?" the women whispered. Tola began sneaking toward the door but Barbara was faster. "Don't be scared," she called, leaning out. "Ah, look at all this snow."

Timidly the women drew closer to the door, but just then the train moved on and behind it in the yellow light shapes stirred, became figures reaching out as if to beckon them back. They vanished. The train rolled on past glossy darkness, past snow-laden branches, motionless, like paws of white, placid beasts. A jerk. Again the train stopped.

And before the women had time to ask about the SS and dogs, dwarfish figures appeared on the snowy plain, each waving from afar, calling, "Hob nisht moyre, vir senen Yidden!"

"Don't be afraid; we're Jews," Tola was about to translate, when those coming explained themselves by reaching up, by helping the women to scramble out. The engine whistled, steam unfurled against the black sky, and the train moved on until only the last cars were still in view, only the SS men's car, a boot swinging through the open door. It slammed shut. Red sparks burst into the dark. And when they died out the last trace of the Cracow camp was gone—of its nights, its endless Appells, its fear.

Here all was different. No one drove them on, they were allowed to rest, to stretch out their numbed limbs. They walked on, not in a column but in a leisurely crowd, like tourists stopping at whatever delighted their eyes: the full moon shining upon the vast expanse of snow, the arcades of bent bushes; and farther away woods, the impenetrable wall parting at their approach, the white straight road inviting them to come on. The air was quiet except when at times—like a hostess who, guests gone, sets her home aright and then rests—

the breeze stirred, erased the footprints, restored the road to its damask smoothness, then ceased.

"Be glad. You've come to a good place," the dwarfish men—O.D. men they were—repeated. In answer the women smiled, then walked on in an almost festive silence. Throughout the years in ghettos and in camps, dirty slush was the only snow they had known, its purity bestowed only upon the world outside the wires. Now they gained equal rights to joy in winter, to the admiring "How nice, how quiet." "Nice?" Barbara boomed. "It's splendid, the most splendid snow I've ever seen. Ah, it was worth coming here, just for this."

"Don't say such things," Tola was about to warn. Around her shone faces freshened by the frosty air. Barbara laughed, blowing clouds of white breath, until with a sudden extravagance Tola reached up to a branch and shook a flurry of snow into their outstretched arms.

That after such a walk another camp awaited them—the wires, the towers, and a screeching gate—seemed startling at first. But swift to dispel any misapprehension, here was warmth—radiators lining the large hall, blankets on the bunks, and above all, soup. And what soup, hot, thick with parsnips; and the tongue if attentive enough could taste fine strands of meat, so at least Barbara claimed, adding that not even Marta, a jewel among cooks, could have made a better soup.

The women ate in three stages: first out of hunger; next out of prudence, to store supplies; then out of exuberance, out of sheer luxury, so that "I'm full," they could sigh, "I've had enough!"

With the satiated feeling the next day began, and with the sun awakening them instead of a bugle call. The women stretched themselves, looked at the sky, blue outside the windows, then strolled to the barrels of soup, which, though turned a bit sour, was not thick like a pudding.

This was breakfast. After breakfast, as befits a holiday, came guests, the O.D. men met last night. By daylight they appeared a trifle less good-natured, a trifle more shifty-eyed; and all of them, as if this were a requirement of their rank, bandy-legged, the purple collars of their navy blue uniform shining with grease. They brought news about the camp. It was located near the town of Skarzysko-Kamienna and this section of it at least—"Werk A," they called it— was really a good place. To be sure, one was not exactly overfed here; still, with a bit of sense in your head, and with God's help, you could always do some business with the goys in the plant. Of that other section, where dim figures had stood in yellow light, the O.D. men said little; yes, they admitted to some connection between Werk A and that place, but on the whole treated it like a poor relation of whom the less said, the better.

"Not good." They merely shrugged, and began to speak of work in their place, at the plant belonging to Hasag—to Hugo Schneider Aktiengesellschaft. "After Hermann Goering Werke the biggest ammunition plant in Germany," they added, not without a touch of proprietary pride.

"What, ammunition!" Barbara, who until now had been nodding approvingly, jumped up. "Tola, did you hear that?"

"Yes, I heard it."

"But this is terrible, just terrible!"

"You're absolutely right." A greasy blond head popped up from the lower bunk. Another "Absolutely!" and the woman with the gold teeth stood before them. Her long hooked nose too large for her face, her square torso too heavy for her wobbly legs, she looked put together from some odds and ends. "Aurelia Katz," she introduced herself briskly. "And this," she pointed to the freckled girl standing morosely on the side, "this is Alinka—my daughter."

First Tola, then Barbara mumbled something.

"I'm delighted to meet you." Mrs. Katz beamed. "And as I was saying, you are right, eminently so." She reached out, as though to offer Barbara this choice morsel of her vocabulary.

"I won't make ammunition. I'll work like a snail. I'll refuse," Barbara muttered and, brushing Mrs. Katz aside, went off.

Here and there sat the outsiders to the general gaiety, those who had left someone behind. To them Barbara tried to administer comfort, in kind and dosage always the same—an embrace, a fumbling "Oh my dear," then an equally fumbling question to find out what sorrow exactly she was trying to soothe. "Ah, you left a sister in Cracow. A daughter? Oh, my God! But things must be changing for the better, this place shows it. And the war too—it won't last much longer. Soon, in a few months, you'll be together again." Those she comforted gazed at her with half-grateful, half-compassionate looks that Tola, watching on the side, found painful.

At noon barrels of fresh soup were rolled in; and now a feast took place—an orgy of hope. Only a short line formed in front of the barrels, each woman in the line, having been commissioned by others to fetch their soup, juggling a whole cluster of cans. For the majority would not even bother to get down.

They requested "Room service!" They lolled and sprawled on their bunks. Their cheerleader was Seidmanka, an inveterate optimist constantly croaking prophecies of disaster in self-defense against the assault of hope. Now faith took over—in the stomach full forever, in this "find" of a camp, in survival. It shone in her eyes; it lent high adolescent notes to her voice.

"Waiter," she piped. "Waiter, what, soup again? I ordered chicken with mushrooms in wine; and for dessert—"

"Cream puffs. Napoleons!" Barbara clapped her hands. And at last Tola too joined them with her soft, somewhat uneasy laugh.

A new idea struck Seidmanka. To extol the present she would pit it against the past.

"Someone must stand six." In mock fear she rolled her eyes. "Tola, you go."

Tired by her efforts to keep in step with Barbara, Tola stood in the narrow corridor, her cheek leaning against the cool windowpane. Laughter came from the hall. "Let's send a postcard to the Lagerkommandant," someone called. Then steps . . .

A squat, burly man stood before her, his O.D. man's jacket dotted with patches the color of the mud that caked his boots, copper-streaked hair falling upon a face so fleshy that the eyes were almost hidden by the thick folds.

"Tell me," the man gripped her arm, "are they all like you?"

"In what way?" Tola asked.

"Skinny. Flat-chested and skinny. A woman is worth as much as she weighs, Goldberg says. Goldberg, that's me." He pounded his chest, then "Ouch," he winced as she hit his hand still clutching her arm. "Ouch, when they get skinny they get proud."

"It's the other way around. Nowadays when they're proud they get skinny." Guffawing, the man walked into the hall, but soon came back, bringing Barbara along.

"Can you imagine it, Mr. Goldberg says he knows me." Though all smiles Barbara was every inch the lady speaking of her inferior. "He used to deliver something or other to our place."

"Coal, Dziedziczka—twice a year. Yes, it's a small world! If you don't meet someone in Auschwitz you meet them here. If not here then up there." He pointed to the clouds outside the window, and went with Barbara back to the hall.

Tola stayed in the corridor. Outside a group of O.D. men were walking by the wires. Then far off, where gray slush merged with the gray afternoon sky, a tall figure appeared. It was a German, his brown military cloak blown by the wind.

"Six," Tola said coming into the hall.

"Six? What is it? Yes, sure." Barbara laughed.

"It's not a joke. I saw a German coming here."

O.D. men came in and ordered the women to form a column. The tall German who followed them looked almost pitiful—so shyly he stood in the door, so apologetically his faded blue eyes glanced around. Slouching, as though to shrink himself, he approached Goldberg, who addressed him without any excessive deference as Meister Grube.

"Ah, stop whining," Barbara flared up at Mrs. Katz, who with her daughter stood in their four, then leaning backward whispered to Tola that this Kraut looked as if he couldn't count to three.

"Hush," Tola silenced her. Nothing seemed to have changed. Yet she felt something like a chill, then like a presence, as if a courier from the Cracow camp had brought a piece of forgotten luggage—the old familiar fear.

From the door this fear came. There a pimply O.D. man stood, next to him two women: the elder hunched up as though freezing; the other—the bosomy blonde who had whistled during the "ovation"—was slipping something to the O.D. man. Money. The blonde had ransomed herself. Why, those at the column's head must have already found out, for they grew still.

"Tola, wait, we'll go together," Barbara whispered.

"No, stay here!"

Hiding behind the column Tola stole on, then ducked. Light flashed: startled by the glare she looked to the corner where the O.D. men stood. They saw her all the time, yet nobody had bothered to stop her. And she felt afraid of this place where none of the familiar rules held: "six" taken as a joke—she, always the first to warn others, now the last to be warned, and by the Orphan.

"It's bad." The Orphan licked her livid mouth.

"What's happening?"

"We're going to that bad place."

"Everyone?"

"Some will always wriggle out. Rouge, hurry up!" The Orphan nudged the woman next to her.

"Rouge—give rouge" rose from everywhere.

"Yellow" was what Mrs. Katz whimpered.

"Keep quiet," Tola snapped at her. In answer Mrs. Katz smiled. "You'll be sorry you didn't listen to me," this smile said.

"Well, what is it?" asked Barbara.

"Yellow," Mrs. Katz repeated, "the hair turns yellow there, the face, the eyes . . ." And she pointed at her chest, as if in the bad place even the heart turned yellow. It was the lungs she meant. "The lungs just disintegrate," she added softly, like an afterthought.

Barbara opened her mouth, but said nothing. Now everyone was silent, now the familiar rules were being restored by this silence, by the old women clinging to the young, as if their vigor could be borrowed and put on like rouge, by the young shrinking away lest those old would drag them down to the bad place. And at the window Seidmanka was gnawing at the hem of her dress. She kept her money sewn in the hem, she would ransom herself as the blonde had.

Followed by Goldberg and the O.D. men, the Meister approached the column. The blonde stood at its head; the pimply O.D. man whispered with the Meister, who nodded, then ordered the blonde to the other side of the hall. His retinue right behind, he walked on, hastily bypassing those old or no longer too strong, and choosing only the husky young women for the good camp.

"Tolenka—I don't understand. The big wenches, they're going to the bad place?"

"No, they stay here." Tola looked from Barbara's powerful arms to her own, pale, very thin.

"But, Tolenka . . ."

"Mrs. Grünbaum," the Katz woman broke in, "help us, I beg you, not for my sake, but for this child. Criticizing, always criticizing!" She scowled at her daughter, turned back to Barbara, and again it was, "Mrs. Grünbaum, my dear Mrs. Grünbaum."

"For God's sake let me think." Tola shoved her aside. Barbara knows Goldberg, she thought, he may help me to stay, he must . . . But hardly had she glanced at him, when he shook his head.

"Barbara," her mouth could barely move, "stay here, I'll be right back." And this time Barbara did not say "We go together." This time she pressed her fist to her lips.

With a moist "Pst!" and "Here!" Seidmanka was signaling to the pimply

O.D. man. Then, since he still would not respond, she pointed to the money clutched in her hand.

"Seidmanka," Tola began. Only a very few could buy their way into the good camp; she must hurry or she would lose her chance. But she was no good at begging help. "Help me," she cried. "I'll pay every copper back, I'll do anything for you. I—" Tola stopped. Her shaking voice sounded exactly like the Katz woman's whine.

"I beg you," Rubinfeldova took over. "I beg you, listen to Tola." Seidmanka looked at Rubinfeldova, at Tola, then at the crumpled notes.

"Help me—I beg you—I cannot be alone anymore."

"Somehow," Rubinfeldova whispered.

"How? How would we manage? Should we starve for her? Why? What has she ever done for us?"

Discreetly the O.D. man stole toward them; he shoved Seidmanka's money into his boot, then was off.

Tola too walked away. "Ruhe," the Meister shrieked. "Quiet!" the O.D. men echoed, though everyone was quiet, though only eyes dared to beg the Meister for one moment of attention, one glance. But he, turning aside, hurried on to those fit for the good camp.

"Oh, if only you had used your pull and asked Goldberg again to help us." The Katz woman was clutching at Barbara as Tola came back. Barbara raised her fist; she would have struck had Mrs. Katz not moved away. Barbara, for all her courage, was afraid of going to the bad place; Tola saw this fear crumple Barbara's face.

"Stop worrying so much." Tola's calm changed to a bitter delight because she, always the accused, could now accuse in turn. But what for? She would rather make it easy for Barbara to stay in the good camp. "Everything is working out for the best," it seemed as if she were reciting a prepared speech, "really, Barbara."

"Really?"

"Of course. Now, don't tell me you wanted to come along with me."

"I . . ."

"You must stay here, Barbara, because—"

"Connections, Mrs. Grünbaum, you've got such connections," the Katz woman whispered. "Because you'll soon form connections," Tola went on. "You'll help me to transfer back here."

"Really?"

"Of course. Don't look so downcast, Barbara."

"I— When you were gone, I asked that Goldberg for help. 'She can't stay here,' he said. Why not? I don't understand anything."

"The Mae West type is in demand here." So completely did this stale joke drain Tola's strength that she couldn't wait for Barbara to be gone. And soon she was gone. Goldberg, to bring her closer to the Meister, led her away to the center of the column, and behind them Mrs. Katz dragged her daughter along.

So, it was over; now Tola must find herself another four. "Go away, we're already four," she heard wherever she went until, alone again, she stood at the column's end. She didn't mind being alone, only she had to talk to herself, all the time: about Barbara who had learned her lesson amazingly fast, and who would soon join—yes, the "elect"; then about the pimply O.D. man smirking at Rubinfeldova and Seidmanka, like a salesman assuring his customers that they had got their money's worth. Which those two did. "My long-lost relatives," the O.D. man had assured the Meister. He protested, he swore, until they were allowed to join those chosen to stay. Should she go and congratulate them? Not now; later, she decided, and watched the Meister, who was shrinking away—as though anyone would dare to touch a member of the Master Race.

"Aus Deutschland, wir sind aus Deutschland!" the Yekies tried to assert their membership in this race, then, "Zusammen!" they shrieked, clinging to each other, as if there was any reason to separate them—one the spitting image of the other. They drew aside. Leaning forward, the Meister was looking at someone in the second row.

"Zu—zusammen!" Barbara was shouting, was running along the column. As someone pointed toward Tola she stopped, then ran on, all the time shouting "Schwestern! Zusammen!" and looking from Tola to the Meister, who was following her with Goldberg. And behind them trotted Mrs. Katz, pulling her daughter along.

"Zusammen, Schwestern, we're sisters!" Barbara smiled the smile of the simple-minded so delighted by their cunning that they gave themselves away at once. Never before had Tola longed so much to stay together with Barbara, and never before had she wanted so much to be left alone. She could not stand being compared. The Meister and Goldberg were comparing them. They looked at Barbara, and "She deserves the good place," this look said; but her it brushed off.

"Zusammen. Tolenka, I can't speak German. You tell them."

"Yes, I will." And in her excellent German, Tola softly began. First Goldberg, then the Meister drew away from Barbara and closer to her. They listened. Only Barbara, who understood nothing, kept breaking in. "Ja," she muttered. "So! Ja!"

"Herr Meister, as I told you, we're not sisters. We barely know each other. I ask you to use your whole authority to make this woman stay here."

"Ja, so. Ja."

Goldberg strode toward Barbara. It looked as though he would strike, but he laid his hand gently on her neck, and so step by step shoved her on. "Tola!" Barbara stopped suddenly. "Why isn't she coming? Tola, what did you tell them?"

As though to warn her, Goldberg looked at Tola.

"The truth," she spoke, avoiding his stare. "Just the truth."

"Did you hear what she said, did you? Such a slip of a girl, and she came to me, she helped me, and now she is doing everything to make me stay here. Ah, do you think I'd leave her alone? Herr Meister, ich—I—I want to go with her. Goldberg, you tell him. Do you hear me? Goldberg!"

Shrugging, Goldberg said something to the Meister, who looked at Barbara, then gave a slow nod.

"So I can stay with her, can I?" Barbara turned and dashed back so blindly that she collided with Mrs. Katz, who, standing in front of the column, was holding her daughter in front like a buffer.

"This Goldberg," Barbara cried, "he stands up for me, for a woman, like a stove, and here he lets a child go to that dreadful place!" And she stepped aside so that all could see who must go there—a girl of thirteen or so, the long skirt and spiked heels worn to appear more grown-up only making her look like a child dressed up for a masquaerade.

"You, look."

The Meister bent over the girl. "Das Mädel bleibt," he ordered.

"The girls stays," Goldberg translated.

The girl staggered forward; she drew back. And next to her, like a ragdoll loosened at the seams, Mrs. Katz was falling apart, her arms jerking to and from her neck, her head. "No!" Her black arm raked the girl closer. "Together. Mutter, Tochter zusammen!"

The Meister mumbled something and walked on.

"You, what have you done to your daughter?" Barbara gasped.

"I . . . I . . . you're noble, but I . . ." Mrs. Katz sniveled. Then, supported by the girl, she tottered back to her bunk.

Soon afterwards it was over. About fifty women had been chosen to stay, while all the others were to go to the bad place, though when, no one knew. Like an adolescent relieved when the party is over, the Meister stole away. Goldberg and the O.D. men followed, but before leaving one of them had passed the word that not all work in the bad camp made you turn yellow. Was this the truth, or just a comforting lie? If the truth, how many could escape the yellow work, and in what way?

The lights went out. Barbara fell asleep at once, but Tola lay wide awake, while around her the whispers stopped, and only a bunk would squeak as someone tossed in sleep. At last she sat up. "Barbara," she whispered.

"Oh, can't you sleep?" Barbara murmured, barely awake. She herself had slept "wonderfully just like a marmot. But I'm glad you woke up, because I must explain everything."

"Quiet! Let us sleep!" someone muttered.

"I'm terribly sorry. Listen, Tolenka, when this Katz said 'Yellow—'"

"Quiet!"

"If you're tired you can sleep anyhow," Barbara snapped back. "Now where was I? Yes, 'Yellow,' this Katz said; I must admit my heart didn't go out to her at first, and even now I'm not sure; anyhow, she said it, and I . . . I could see myself yellow, all shriveled up, like a lemon gone to rot. And a fear came over me, such fear—" She was silent for a minute, then went on briskly, "Yellow, red, green—no matter what color we turn, we'll just scrub it off when the war is over. Listen," Barbara drew closer, "have you ever imagined—but really, so that you could see it—the end—the end of the war?"

"Yes. Once, I thought . . . I dreamt about it." In the Cracow camp, lying sick with influenza she had dreamed of the end; a sense of welcome had pervaded the dream as though wherever she went she was expected by the sunlit air, the pale green trees, and by the quiet—deep, yet holding the promise of voices just waiting for her call to answer.

"How was it, Tola, how did you imagine it?"

"I was in the park." Barbara's expectant tone made it harder to speak. "There was no one with me, yet I didn't feel lonely."

"And—"

"The trees were in bud, and I felt so free, somehow."

"And then?"

"That's all, Barbara. My dreams are modest."

"No, come on; that was beautiful, just beautiful. Now let me tell you how it will be."

"When the war is over," Barbara began dreamily, like a child whispering "Once upon a time." Tola listened, with the adult's envy of such faith in the world of wonders, yet soon with a twinge of disappointment, for even those wonders were secondhand, each borrowed from some other tale: the rejoicing in the streets, the Germans scurrying around like chickens—this was the Armistice of 1918; Barbara and she herself now in a ramshackle cart, now on foot, going back to the manor—transferred from the beginning of this war to its end. But what came next was new. "And there at home," Barbara said, "there, we'll go down on our knees."

"What?" Tola asked. Then, still casting around for some explanation of Barbara's fearlessness, "Are you a believer?"

"The odd thoughts you can get. To scrub, that's why we'll get down on our knees, so no trace of the Krauts will be left when he comes home, Stefan, my husband." Barbara stopped. Why, Tola did not quite dare to ask.

Yellow, red, green—all will wash off once the war is over, Barbara repeated to herself, like an incantation. The incantation failed. She saw Stefan: he was sitting at the empty table, slouched, his face buried in his hands, a tip of mustache showing through his fingers. He was crying for her, who would never come back. And a shudder passed through her as if only in his grief lay the reality of her death.

A War Letter

Ferida Durakovic

(About the letter from before the war)

The Universe sent darkness to our humble home,
which is gone now. The letter, and every single
                              book,
and dear things: they all burned like Rome.
But it is just an image! Have a look:

We aren't gone! And manuscripts never burn,
they say. It means that I'll read anew
that precious letter, whenever you turn,
whenever only those few syllables

change our agony into an endlessly dull
winter afternoon. In those hours everything's
so simple that I suffer (same old song),
I don't love anyone, and the fear devours

me that passion, which brings back the first day
of love, the re-creation, is finally gone
like the heart grown in a poplar tree! And may
only this flourishing pain stop! May everyone
                              alone

leave for good, to wherever they want: to
water, air, or fire. And us? What fireside
awaits us in the times to come? Here is our home,
where mother can never tire of planting

My War in Four Episodes

Susan Rubin Suleiman

A few summers ago, I returned to Hungary after a thirty-five-year absence. I had left as a child with my parents, crossing on foot into Czechoslovakia (the Communist government had stopped granting exit visas) in August, 1949. I returned with my two sons, age fourteen and seven, as a tourist, in August, 1984. I was spending that summer in Paris, doing research at the Bibliothèque Nationale and working on various writing projects. The trip to Hungary, planned for a while, came as a welcome interruption. My children, who were in the countryside with their father, took the train to Paris and the next day we flew to Budapest. As we got off the plane after an ordinary two-hour flight, I realized with a shock that the journey it had taken me thirty-five years to embark on was shorter in actual time than one of my frequent flights from Boston to Miami, which I had been making for years to visit my mother.

A few months earlier it was my mother who had come to visit us, flying north to consult a specialist at Mass. General Hospital. She was suffering from an old-age disease, temporal arteritis, for which the only effective medication was cortisone. But the drug was killing her, psychologically if not physically. Her fine, beautiful face had become coarse and bloated, her hair had started falling out, soon her skin would become so thin that the slightest bruise would draw blood and create ugly scabs over her arms and legs. She had always been proud of her good looks; she looked on these changes in her body not as a disease to be coped with, but as a death sentence.

The only thing that still cheered her up (later, even that would go) was being around her grandchildren. On that visit in particular, they had a grand time. My older son, in an elated mood, got her to teach him some dirty words in Hungarian, and he and his brother went around the house singing them with glee, mispronouncing all the words. "Csirkeszar, csirkeszar, edd meg csirkeszar." "Chicken shit, chicken shit, go eat chicken shit." My mother, a thing rare for her now, laughed and laughed.

Watching her play Rummi-Kub one night with the boys (she loved the game, it was a version of the gin rummy she and my father had played with friends during the summer evenings in Hungary), I suddenly saw, as clearly as if projected on a screen, my mother as a young woman, holding my hand as we walked down a boulevard in winter, setting our faces against the wind and playing the Multiplication Game. What's eight times seven, what's seven times four, what's three times nine? The questions came faster and faster, until we were both tripping over our tongues and laughing. How I had loved her, my beautiful mother who knew how to play!

I decided before the end of my mother's visit that I had to take my children to the place where I had known that young woman. I told myself that I expected no great revelations from Budapest, but I desired to see again and to let my sons see the city of my childhood, which had suddenly become for me, now that she was dying, also the city of my mother's youth.

To a large degree, my desire was satisfied. We spent several days out of a two-week stay (some of it outside Budapest) roaming the city, visiting the house and neighborhood where I had lived, taking many rolls of photographs. My sons shot pictures of me in the large cobblestone courtyard where I had played as a child—quite shabby now, surrounded by pockmarked walls, with tufts of grass growing between the cobblestones; they snapped me on the fourth floor, leaning over the wrought-iron banister in front of the apartment where I had lived with my parents and grandmother; they took snapshots of me on the steps of the chupah, *the wedding canopy, in the courtyard of the synagogue where my parents were married (the synagogue itself was closed and boarded up). That same courtyard had been the recreation yard of my old religious school, now empty of children (now it was a kosher canteen for the elderly). In a curious way, I felt as if I had occupied all those places of my childhood so that I could return many years later and be photographed there by my children. I became, for a few days, a tour guide of my own life.*

I told my sons about some of the memories stirred up by those stones and streets: the long Sunday walks with my mother and friends in the hills of Buda, the scurrying to ballet lessons along crowded avenues in Pest during weekdays, accompanied by the Viennese lady I called Madame *who taught me French, the visits to the pastry shop where they sold sugar cones filled with whipped chestnut cream in winter, thick and sweet and so smooth to the tongue. My sons listened, mildly interested; but I realized that for them this was a vacation, not a nostalgia trip. I had better not indulge too much in reminiscences.*

One thing I didn't tell them about were my memories, which presented themselves to me chiefly as a series of images, of the last year of the Second World War. I didn't consciously remain silent on that score; simply, it did not occur to me to talk about that year of my life, far back in early childhood, while we were in Budapest. It was only after returning to Paris, emptied of Parisians in the late August heat (my children too had returned to the country), that I decided to write down the episodes I still carried with me from that year, fragmentary, incomplete, but possessing a vividness that surprised me. The experience of seeing again the places of my childhood had restored the sharpness of those images, as well as revealed the desire, long suppressed, to put them into words.

1.

Running

They began rounding up the Jews in Budapest quite late in the war. Spring, 1944, I was four-and-a-half years old.

We lived in an apartment building in a busy part of the city, not far from the Opera House. On the corner of our street stood a large yellow church; a few streets further, the orthodox synagogue and the Jewish Community Bureau, where my father worked as an administrator. In their courtyard, on an upper story, was the elementary school for girls in which I started first grade after the war. The word for "school," ISKOLA, was proudly chiselled into the stone wall. It never occurred to me that one day the school might cease to exist, that one day there might not be enough Jewish girls in Budapest to fill it.

Our apartment building had four stories, with a large inner courtyard bordered on each floor by a gallery with wrought-iron railing. I would run up and down the gallery on our floor, and whenever I stopped and looked down into the courtyard, I felt dizzy. I held on to the wrought iron, my heart pounding with excitement and fear, knowing all the while that I was safe. Then my grandmother would call me in for a snack of buttered bread, thickly sliced rye with a heavy crust, topped by a piece of salted green pepper. ("Oh, gross!" say my children—but they love green pepper, it must be in the blood.)

To the left as you entered the building was the staircase, of noble proportions, with its own wrought-iron railings of complex design. The steps were of smooth whitish stone, worn down in the middle. We lived three flights up, in an apartment with tall windows and a stone balcony overlooking the street. The main room was the dining room: huge square table in the middle, flanked on one side by two shiny pot-bellied buffets; on the other side, a grand piano under which I liked to sit and play. On the same side as the piano, but near the opposite corner, stood a ceramic stove with light green tiles, used for heating, not cooking; facing each other on opposite walls, two double doors opened onto my parents' bedroom on the right, my grandmother's room on the left. At that time, I still slept in my parents' room. After the war, when my grandmother flew off to join my uncle in New York, I inherited her room.

The night the Nazis came, around three or four in the morning, my mother woke me up and dressed me. She and my father and grandmother spoke in whispers, hurrying. After I was dressed, still half asleep, my mother took me by the hand and ran down the stairs with me. Or maybe she picked me up and ran, carrying me. She had torn the yellow star off her coat. At the bottom of the stairs, we slowed down. There were soldiers on both sides of the street door, the concierge standing next to them—a plump, youngish woman, dressed in a heavy coat and felt slippers. It appeared that her job was to identify the Jewish tenants so that none would leave the building on their own.

My mother and I walked past the concierge and the soldiers, out into the street where day was dawning. She held me tightly. We walked up the street toward the church, keeping a steady pace. *Don't look as if you didn't belong here.* After we had turned the corner, we started to run. A mad, panicked dash to the next corner, then a stop, out of breath. Saved.

I have never understood why the concierge let us go. Was she moved by the sight of the woman and child, or had my parents paid her off? Probably they had, for my father succeeded in skipping out a few minutes later. My grandmother stayed behind and was put into a place they called the ghetto, where she lived until the war was over. Later, when I told this story to my friends (everyone in first grade had a story, recounted with melodramatic flourishes on the way home from school), I found it miraculous that she was not taken to Auschwitz, or lined up and shot into the Danube like the people another girl told about. It was at that time, I believe, that I began to conceive of history as a form of luck.

The next scene takes place a few weeks after our escape from the house, on a farm far from Budapest. My parents had decided to leave me with the Christian farmers for my safety, as many other Jewish families were doing. My mother probably explained this to me, although I have no recollection of it. Nor do I remember actually arriving at the farm. I remember being there, scared.

The kitchen of the farmhouse had an earthen floor, a long wooden table in the middle; in one corner stood a massive butter churn. I am standing next to the table with my mother and the farmer's wife. My mother has dressed me in a frilly dress and white leather shoes, like the ones I wear on afternoon visits in town. She kisses me and says it won't be for long. Then she leaves. I cry.

Now I am running across a large dust-covered yard, chased by geese. They are immense, honking furiously, wings aflutter. They're on my heels, stretching their necks to bite me. I run into the kitchen, screaming. The farmer's children laugh and call me a city girl. I can't stop crying, and feel as if I will burn up with shame. As the tears stream down and smear my face, I make a promise to myself: they won't see me cry again.

How long did I stay on the farm? I don't know. It felt like a long time. Since it was summer, I must have turned five while I was there. Meanwhile, back in Budapest, my father managed to get false papers for all three of us. He and my mother decided to take me back, danger or not.

By the time they came for me, I was used to the farm. My mother found me crouching in the dust with the other children, dressed only in a pair of panties, barefooted, busy playing with some broken bits of pottery. I hardly looked up when she ran to me and hugged me.

2.

Snow

Thanks to our false papers, my parents found a job as caretakers on an estate in Buda. The owner of the estate was an old noblewoman, a sculptress. I have no visual memory of her, but I imagine her as a tall, thin, kindly lady with white hair—like the Old Lady in the story of Babar, which I read a few years later. According to my mother, the old lady became very fond of me, even invited my mother to give me an occasional bath in her bathtub. On most days, my mother washed me while I stood in a small enamelled basin on the floor next to the stove in our room. The room was so small that I would bump into the stove and burn myself if I wasn't careful. We had to make fires in the stove by then; it was autumn, turning cold.

My name was Mary. My mother whispered to me every morning not to forget it, never to say my real name, no matter who asked. I told her not to worry, I wouldn't tell. I felt grown-up and superior, carrying a secret like that.

Besides the old lady and us, four other people lived in the house: the lady's young nephew, recently married, with his wife, and an older couple who were also caretakers of some kind. They had been with the lady for many years, and were suspicious of us. One day they asked me what my mother's maiden name was. I said I didn't know, and told my mother. She told them not to ask questions like that: Couldn't they see I was just a baby? Her maiden name was Stern, a Jewish name. I knew that name, it was my grandmother's. Luckily for us, I didn't know what "maiden name" meant.

When winter came, more people arrived, relatives of the old lady. We all lived in one wing of the house to save heat. During the day, the warmest place was the kitchen or the glass-enclosed veranda that received a great deal of sun. The lady's nephew and his wife spent all day on the veranda in wicker armchairs, reading or playing cards. I liked to watch them. The young man especially had a languid, almost petulant air that fascinated me. I recall him as tall and handsome. My mother said he was an "aristocrat," which I understood from her intonation to mean something like "beautiful but weak." Watching him turn the pages of a book or run his fingers through his long wavy hair, I felt totally infatuated with him; at the same time, perhaps because of my mother's intonation as she said the word "aristocrat," his gracefulness filled me with a kind of scorn.

For Christmas, we decorated a tree. I sang "Holy Night" and received presents. My mother had taught me the song during the whole month of December. There was a Christ-child in a cradle beneath the tree. I was fascinated by the lifelike figure of the holy baby and by his mother's golden hair, but most of all I loved the shining colored globes and the streams of glittering silver on the tree. Sometimes I felt sorry that we weren't really Christians—we could have had a tree like that every year.

In January, it turned bitter and cold and snow fell. There were air raids at night, and we all started sleeping on cots in the basement. It soon became clear that my father was the man of the house. He made sure that we all gathered in the basement during air raids, even during the day. He listened to the short-wave radio and told us when the Germans began retreating. When the pipes froze and we had no water, he organized our nocturnal expeditions to gather snow.

How can I describe those winter nights? For years they remained in my memory as an emblem of the war, of the immense adventure that, with hindsight and retelling, the war became for me. Picture a dozen shadows covered by white sheets, flitting across a snow-covered landscape. The sheets prevented us from being seen from the air, blended with the white ground and trees. Mounds of soft snow, darkness and silence—and with all that hushed beauty, a tingling sense of conspiracy. We carried pots and pans, scooping the cleanest snow into them with a spoon. When a pot was full, we took it inside, emptied it into a kettle on the stove, then went back to gather more. Three kettlefuls, my father said, would give us enough water for two days.

I don't know how many times we gathered snow, in fact. Maybe only twice, or once. No matter. I see myself, triumphant, smug, impatient for the boiled snow to cool so that I can drink it. As I bring the glass to my lips, I meet my father's eyes. We exchange a look of pleasure.

I am five years old and I am drinking snow. Outside, bombs are falling. Here in the steamy kitchen, nothing can hurt me.

3.

Liberation

The Russians arrived in Spring. But first, we had German guests. A detachment in retreat invaded the house and set up radio equipment in our kitchen. They were distant, polite, ordinary. I had imagined monsters, like Hitler. (Hitler had horns, he was a giant.) My mother prepared meals for them, listening to their talk—they had no idea that she understood them. She would report their conversations to my father, but there was nothing new. Defeated or not, to us they were still a menace. After a few days, they left. I felt extremely pleased with us, clever Davids outwitting Goliath.

A few nights later, a bomb fell in our backyard. It made a terrific noise, and for a moment we thought it was the end. But when it turned out to have missed the house, we became quite jovial. As soon as there was enough daylight, we trooped out to inspect it. Whose bomb it was, we did not know; but there it sat, less than fifty meters from the house, in the middle of a crater it had made in landing, round and dark green like a watermelon. Somehow it all seemed like a joke, even though we kept repeating how lucky we were, how tragically ironic and ironically tragic it would have been to get killed when the war was almost over.

The Russians arrived huge and smiling, wrapped in large coats with fur on their heads. They were our Liberators, we welcomed them. When they saw my father's gold watch, they laughed delightedly and asked him for it. We didn't understand their words, but their gestures were clear. My father took off the watch and gave it to them. Then they asked my mother to go to their camp and cook for them. They put their arms around her, laughing. She pointed to me, laughing back and shaking her head. Who would take care of the little girl? They insisted, but she held fast. I felt frightened. Finally they let her go.

After that, everything becomes a blur. How much longer did we stay in the house? Did we ever tell the old lady who we were? She was sick, according to my mother's story, and died during the last days of the war. But I have no memory of that.

4.

Home

In 1945, sometime between March and May, we walked back to our house, crossing the Danube on a bridge that had survived the bombings. Walking between my parents, holding each one's hand, I felt madly lucky and absolutely victorious, as if our survival had been wholly our own doing and at the same time due entirely to chance. I was not aware of the paradox then, or if I was aware of it, could certainly not have expressed it. But as I grow older, it occurs to me that I have often felt that way about my life: seeing it, for better or worse, as my own creation, and at the same time, contradictorily, as the product of blind luck.

That day, I mostly stared and tried to register everything—storing it for future use, though I knew not exactly what. I saw a dead horse lying on its side in the street, its legs stretched out; someone had cut a square hole in its flank for meat. From time to time, a bombed-out wall showed where a house had been. We passed empty stores, their doors wide open—looted, said my mother. Inside one, on the floor in front of the counter, a white-haired woman lay dead. I could not take my eyes from her, despite my mother's pulling me away. Who had killed her? Did they do it for money? What did her skin feel like, now that she was dead? Was it cold and leathery? After a while, I stopped thinking and even looking. I concentrated on putting one foot in front of the other.

On our street, all the houses were intact. We walked into ours, through the downstairs door where the soldiers had stood a year before. The courtyard was covered with debris, and there were holes that looked like bullet holes in the walls; otherwise it looked the same. Up the stairs to the third landing: the lock on our apartment door was broken. Inside, the windows were all shattered. Dust lay over everything, stirred occasionally by a breeze. The sky through the glassless window frames looked so near you could almost touch it. I was no longer Mary, but for a moment I could not remember my name.

Conversation with a Stone

Wislawa Szymborska

I knock at the stone's front door.
"It's only me, let me come in.
I want to enter your insides,
have a look round,
breathe my fill of you."

"Go away," says the stone.
"I'm shut tight.
Even if you break me to pieces,
we'll all still be closed.
You can grind us to sand,
we still won't let you in."

I knock at the stone's front door.
"It's only me, let me come in.
I've come out of pure curiosity.
Only life can quench it.
I mean to stroll through your palace,
then go calling on a leaf, a drop of water.
I don't have much time.
My mortality should touch you."

"I'm made of stone," says the stone,
"and must therefore keep a straight face.
Go away.
I don't have the muscles to laugh."

I knock at the stone's front door.
"It's only me, let me come in.

I hear you have great empty halls inside you,
unseen, their beauty in vain,
soundless, not echoing anyone's steps.
Admit you don't know them well yourself."

"Great and empty, true enough," says the stone,
"but there isn't any room.
Beautiful, perhaps, but not to the taste
of your poor senses.
You may get to know me, but you'll never know me
    through.
My whole surface is turned toward you,
all my insides turned away."

I knock at the stone's front door.
"It's only me, let me come in.
I don't seek refuge for eternity.
I'm not unhappy.
I'm not homeless.
My world is worth returning to.
I'll enter and exit empty-handed.

And my proof I was there
will be only words,
which no one will believe.

"You shall not enter," says the stone.
"You lack the sense of taking part.
No other sense can make up for your missing sense of
    taking part.
Even sight heightened to become all-seeing
will do you no good without a sense of taking part.
You shall not enter, you have only a sense of what that
    sense should be,
only its seed, imagination."

I knock at the stone's front door.
"It's only me, let me come in.
I haven't got two thousand centuries,
so let me come under your roof."

"If you don't believe me," says the stone,
"just ask the leaf, it will tell you the same.
Ask a drop of water, it will say what the leaf has said.
And, finally, ask a hair from your own head.
I am bursting with laughter, yes, laughter, vast laughter,
although I don't know how to laugh."

I knock at the stone's front door.
"It's only me, let me come in."

"I don't have a door," says the stone.

Liberation Day

Christa Wolf

I've forgotten what my grandmother was wearing the time that nasty word "Asia" got her back on her feet. The bomber squadrons, which now passed overhead in broad daylight on their way to Berlin, were greatly out of earshot. Someone had pushed open the door of the air-raid shelter, and in the bright triangle of sunlight at the entrance stood a pair of knee-high black military boots, and in them an SS officer, whose blond brain had registered every single word my grandmother had uttered during the long air-raid alarm: "No, no, I'm not budging from here, I don't care if they kill me, one old woman more or less won't matter."

"What?" said the SS officer. "Tired of living? You'd rather fall into the hands of those Asian hordes? Don't you know that the Russians lop women's breasts off?"

That brought my grandmother wheezing to her feet. "Oh, God," she said, "what has humanity done to deserve this?"

"Are you starting up again!" bellowed my grandfather. Now I can see them clearly, walking into the courtyard and taking up their positions alongside our handcart: Grandmother in her fine black coat; on her head the brown striped kerchief which my children still wear when they have a sore throat; Grandfather, wearing a cap with ear flaps and a herring-bone jacket. Time is short, the night is drawing near, closing in along with the enemy, although from a different direction: night from the west and the enemy from the east. In the south, flames rage against the sky. We imagine we can decipher the fiery script. The writing on the sky seems clear and spells out: Go west.

We tried to follow the country road but strayed from it in the darkness, groping about on side paths until we finally came upon a tree-lined drive leading towards a gate and a secluded estate. There was a crooked, slightly shaky man who was limping to the stables in the middle of the night—Kalle, he was called. He was not given to wondering at anything and so addressed the desperate, exhausted little troop in his particular, indifferent manner: Well, folks,

Sodom and Gomorrah? Never mind. There's always room in the smallest cabin for a happy, loving couple.

The man is not so bright, my mother said uneasily, as we followed Kalle across the courtyard, and my grandfather, who never said much, declared with satisfaction, He is pretty crazy in his head. And so he was. Kalle called my grandfather boss, he who had held no higher rank in his lifetime than that of private in the Kaiser's infantry regiment, cobbler's apprentice under Herr Lebüse in Bromberg, and signalman for the German Reich in the administrative district of Frankfurt (Oder). Boss, said Kalle, it's best if you take that cubbyhole back there in the corner. He then disappeared, whistling, "One More Drop for the Road."

Kalle woke us at daybreak and asked my uncle if he knew how to drive a horse and buggy. The owner, Herr Volk, was moving out and needed someone to drive a cart loaded with feed bags.

Herr Volk showed up in person a little later. He was wearing a hunting hat, a loden coat and knickerbockers. And Frau Volk came to bestow a kind and cultured word on the women. I didn't like her because she called me by my first name without asking and allowed her dachshund bitch, Suzie, to sniff at our legs. Then the shooting began right behind us and we headed off at a quick pace. God takes care of his own, said my grandmother.

This is supposed to be a report on *liberation*, the hour of liberation, and I thought nothing could be easier. That hour has been clearly focused in my mind all these years; it has lain ready and waiting, fully completed in my memory. I need only say the word and the machine will start running, and everything will appear on the paper as if of its own accord—a series of accurate, highly defined pictures. But do they add up to anything?

I saw my first corpse at the age of sixteen; rather late for those years. (I don't count the infant I handed in a still bundle from a truck to a refugee woman; I didn't see him, I only heard his mother scream and run away.) Chance had it that Herr Volk's foreman, Wilhelm Grund, was lying dead instead of me, for pure chance alone had kept my uncle with a sick horse in the barn that morning, so that we weren't heading towards the country road alongside Grund's ox cart as usual. We could hear the gunfire from the barn, and the fifteen stabled horses were wild with fear. I have been afraid of horses ever since. But what I have feared more since that moment are the faces of people forced to see what no person should have to see. Wilhelm Grund's son, the young farmhand Gerhard Grund, had such a face as he burst through the barn door, managed a few steps and then collapsed: Herr Volk, what have they done to my father!

Gerhard was my age. His father lay in the dust at the side of the road next to his oxen, eyes staring upwards. Nothing would lower that gaze, not his wife's wailing or the whining of his three other children. This time around, they forgot to tell us that this was not a sight for us children.

"Quick," said Herr Volk. "We've got to get out of here." They grabbed the corpse by the shoulders and legs and dragged him to the edge of the woods and wrapped him in the tarpaulins from the granary of the estate—just as they would have wrapped any of us, myself included. I, too, would have gone to the grave without words and without song—only their wailing—just like Wilhelm Grund the farmhand, and then they would have pushed on. For a long time they would have said nothing, just as we remained silent, and then would have had to ask what they needed to do now to stay alive. They would have torn off large birch branches, just as we did now, to cover the handcarts, as if the foreign pilots would be fooled by this little wandering birch grove. Everything, everything would be like now, only I would no longer be one of them. And the difference, which was everything to me, meant hardly anything to most of the others here. Gerhard Grund was already sitting in his father's seat, driving the oxen forward with his very whip, and Herr Volk nodded to him: "Good boy. Your father died a soldier's death."

I didn't really believe this. It wasn't the way a soldier's death had been described in the textbooks and newspapers, and I told that authority with whom I was continuously in touch and whom I labelled with the name of God— though against my own scruples and reservations—that, in my opinion, a man and father of four children did not deserve an end such as this.

I happened to be on guard at the time. It was my job to signal the next attacks by whistling. There were two American fighters. The birch grove came to a halt. Just as I had figured, it was clearly visible from afar and easy prey on the desolate country road. Everything that had legs jumped out of the handcarts and threw itself in the ditch, myself included. This time I did not bury my head in the sand but lay on my back and continued eating my sandwich. I did not want to die and I certainly was not up to defying death but I did want to see the one who dared shoot at me. First I saw the white stars under the wings, and then the helmet-covered heads of the pilots and, finally, the naked white spots of their faces. I had seen prisoners before, but this was the attacking enemy—face to face. I knew that I was supposed to hate him and it seemed unnatural that I found myself wondering for the space of a second if they were having fun.

When we got back to the wagons, one of our oxen sank to its knees. Blood spurted from its throat. My uncle and grandfather unharnessed it. My grandfather, who had stood alongside the dead Wilhelm Grund without uttering a word, now hurled curses from his toothless mouth. "The innocent creature," he said hoarsely. "Those damned bastards." I was afraid he might begin to cry and hoped he would get everything off his chest by cursing. I forced myself to look at the animal for an entire minute. It couldn't be reproach that I detected in its gaze, so why did I feel guilty? Herr Volk handed his hunting rifle to my uncle and pointed to a spot behind the ox's ear. We were sent away. At the sound of the shot, I looked back. The ox dropped heavily on to its side.

All evening the women were busy cooking the meat. By the time we sat in the straw, sipping broth, it was already dark. Kalle, who had bitterly complained about being hungry, greedily slurped from his bowl, wiped his mouth on his sleeve and began to sing croakingly with contentment, "All dogs bite, all dogs bite, but only hot dogs get bitten . . ."

"To hell with you, you crazy fellow," my grandfather went at him furiously. Kalle fell on to the straw and stuck his head under his jacket.

One need not be afraid when everyone else is afraid. To know this is certainly liberating, but liberation was still to come, and I want to record what today's memory is prepared to yield on the subject. It was the morning of the 5th May, a beautiful day, and once more panic broke out when we heard that we were encircled by Soviet armoured tank troops. Then word came that we should march to Schwerin, where the Americans were. Anyone still capable of asking a question would have found it strange, that surge forward towards the enemy who had been trying to kill us for days now. But no one did. The world stubbornly refused to end and we were not prepared to cope with a world that refused to end. I remember the horrific words uttered by one woman when told that the miracle weapon longed for by the Führer could only exterminate everyone, both the enemy and the Germans. Let them go ahead and use it, she said.

We moved past the last houses of a village along a sandy road. A soldier was washing up at a pump next to a red Mecklenburg farmhouse. He stood there, legs apart, with the sleeves of his white undershirt rolled up, and called out to us, "The Führer is dead," the same way one says, "Nice weather today." I was stunned more at his tone than at the realization that the man was speaking the truth.

I trudged on alongside our cart, heard the coachmen's hoarse shouts, the groaning of the exhausted horses, saw the small fires by the side of the road where the papers of the officers of the Wehrmacht smouldered. There were heaps of guns and anti-tank grenade-launchers sprouting from the ditches, along with typewriters, suitcases, radios and all manner of precious war equipment senselessly lining our way.

Then came the paper. The road was suddenly flooded with paper; they were still throwing it out of the Wehrmacht vehicles in wild anger—forms, induction orders, files, proceedings, documents from the headquarters of a military district, banal routine letters as well as military secrets and the statistics of the dead. As if there were something repulsive about the paper trash, I did not stoop to pick up a page, which I regretted later. I did, however, catch the canned food which a truck driver threw to me. The swing of his arm reminded me of the movement, often performed, with which, in the summer of '39, I had thrown cigarette packs on to the dusty convoys which rolled eastward past our house, day and night. In the six-year interim I had stopped being a child; summer was coming again, but I had no idea how I would spend it.

The supply convoy of a Wehrmacht unit had been abandoned by its escort on a side road. All those who passed by took as much as they could carry. The order of the column dissolved. Many were beside themselves, no longer with fear but with greed. Only Kalle laughed, dragging a large block of butter to our cart, clapping his hands and shouting happily, "Well, I'll be damned! Look at them getting all worked up!"

Then, out of nowhere, we saw the prisoners from the concentration camp nearby. They stood at the edge of the forest and gazed at us. We could have given them a sign that the air was clear, but nobody did. Cautiously, they approached the road. They looked different from all the people I had seen up to then, and I wasn't surprised that we automatically shrank back from them. But it betrayed us, this shrinking back; it showed that, in spite of what we protested to each other and ourselves, we knew. All we unhappy ones who had been driven away from all our possessions, from our farms and our manors, from our shops and musty bedrooms and brightly polished parlours with the pic-

ture of the Führer on the wall—we knew. These people, who had been declared animals and who were slowly coming towards us to take revenge—we
had abandoned them. Now the ragged would put on our clothes and stick their
bloody feet in our shoes, now the starved would seize hold of the flour and the
sausage that we had snatched. And to my horror I felt that it was just, and I
was horrified to feel that it was just, and knew for a fraction of a second that
we were guilty. I forgot it again.

The prisoners pounced not on the bread but on the guns by the side of the
road. They loaded up on ammunition, crossed the road without paying any attention to us, struggled up the opposite slope and mounted sentry there. They
looked down at us. I couldn't bear looking at them. Why don't they scream, I
thought, or shoot into the air, or shoot at us, goddamnit! But they stood there
peacefully. Some of them were reeling and could barely bring themselves to
hold their guns and stand up. Perhaps they had been praying for this moment.
Everything about them was completely foreign to me.

There came a call from the front that everybody except the drivers should
dismount. This was an order. A deep breath went through the convoy, for this
could mean only one thing: the final steps towards freedom lay ahead. Before
we could move on, the Polish drivers jumped off, coiled the reins around the
stanchion of the wagon, formed a small squad and set about going back, eastward. Herr Volk, immediately turning a bluish-red colour, blocked their way.
At first he spoke quietly to them, but soon he began to scream. Conspiracy,
foul play, refusal to work, he shouted. A Polish migrant worker then pushed
Herr Volk aside.

The world had truly turned topsy-turvy, only Herr Volk hadn't noticed yet;
he reached for his whip, but it was stopped in mid-air; someone was holding
his arm. The whip dropped to the ground, and the Poles walked on. His hand
pressed against his heart, Herr Volk leaned heavily against the cart and let himself be comforted by his thin-lipped wife, while Kalle railed at him from above,
shouting, Bastard, bastard. The French people, who stayed with us, called out
farewells to the departing Poles, who understood those farewells no more than
I did, but understood their sound. It hurt being so strictly excluded from their
shouting, waving and the tossing of their caps, from their joy and their language. But it had to be that way. The world consisted of the victors and the van-
quished. The former were free to express their emotions. We had to lock ours
inside us. The enemy should not see us weak.

There he was. I would have preferred a fire-breathing dragon to this light Jeep with its gum-chewing driver and three casual officers. I tried to make an expressionless face and look right through them, and told myself that their unconstrained laughter, their clean uniforms, their indifferent glances, the whole damned victor's pose had probably been planned for our special humiliation.

The people around me began to hide watches and rings. I, too, took my watch off my wrist and carelessly put it in my coat pocket. The guard at the end of the line, a lanky, hulking man, showed the few people carrying arms where to throw their weapons, while he frisked us civilians with a few firm, routine police motions. Petrified with indignation but secretly proud that they believed me capable of carrying a weapon, I let myself be searched, and my overworked sentry routinely asked, "Your watch?"

So he wanted my watch, the victor, but I told him that the other one, "your comrade," his brother officer, had already pocketed it.

It was then that my heightened sense of hearing signalled the rising sound of an airplane engine.

I kept an eye on its approach route out of habit and threw myself to the ground as it swooped down; once more the horrid dark shadow flitting quickly across grass and trees, once more the atrocious sound of bullets pounding into soil. Still? I thought to myself in astonishment, realizing that one can get used to the feeling of being out of danger in a second.

I should be capable of saying how it felt when it became quiet. I stayed put behind the tree. I believe the thought did not occur to me that, from now on, no bomb would be dropped on me again. I wasn't curious about what would happen next. I didn't know how the horned Siegfried is supposed to act if the dragon asks him for his watch rather than gobbling him up, hair and hide. I didn't feel like watching how Herr Siegfried and Herr Dragon would get along as private citizens. I didn't feel like going to the Americans in the occupied mansion for every bucket of water or having a fight with black-haired Lieutenant Davidson from Ohio.

And I felt less up to the talk with the concentration-camp prisoner who sat with us by the fire at night, wearing a pair of bent wire-frame spectacles and mentioning the word "Communism" as if it were a permitted, household word such as "hatred" or "war" or "extermination." No. And least of all did I feel like

War and Memory

June Jordan
Dedicated to Jane Creighton

I

Daddy at the stove or sink. Large
knife nearby or artfully
suspended by his clean hand handsome
even in its menace
slamming the silverware drawer
open and shut/the spoons
suddenly loud as the yelling
at my mother
no (she would say) no
Granville no
about: would he
be late/had she
hidden away the Chinese laundry shirts
again/did she think
it right that he (a man in his own house)
should serve himself a cup of tea a plate
of food/perhaps she thought that he
should cook the cabbage and the pot roast
for himself
as well?
It sure did seem she wanted him to lose
his job because she could not find
the keys
he could not find
and no (she would attempt to disagree)
no Granville no
but was he
trying to destroy her with his mouth

"My mouth?!" my Daddy hunkered down
incredulous and burly now
with anger, "What you mean, 'My mouth'?! You, woman!
Who
you talk to in that way?
I am master of this castle!" Here
he'd gesture with a kitchen fork
around the sagging clutter
laugh and choke the rage tears
watering his eyes: "You no speak to me
like that: You hear?
You damn Black woman!"
And my mother
backing up or hunching smaller
than frail bones should easily allow
began to munch on saltine
crackers
let the flat crumbs scatter on her full lips
and the oilcoth
on the table

"You answer me!" he'd scream, at last:
"I speak to you. You answer me!"
And she might struggle then
to swallow
or to mumble finally out loud:
"And who are you supposed to be? The Queen
of England? Or the King?"
And he
berserk with fury lifted
chair or frying pan
and I'd attack
in her defense: "No
Daddy! No!" rushing for his knees
and begging, "Please
don't, Daddy, please!"

He'd come down hard: My head
break into daylight pain
or rip me spinning crookedly across the floor.
I'd match him fast
for madness
lineage in wild display
age six
my pigtails long enough to hang me
from the ceiling
I would race about for weaponry
another chair a knife
a flowered glass
the radio
"You stop it, Daddy! Stop it!"
brandishing my arsenal
my mother silently
beside the point.
He'd seize me or he'd duck the glass
"You devil child!"
You damn Black devil child!"
"And what are you supposed to be?"
My mother might inquire
from the doorway:
"White? Are you supposed to be a white man
Granville?"
"Not white, but right!" And I would have to bite and kick
or race way
sometimes out the house and racing
still for blocks
my daddy chasing
after me

                              II

Daddy at the table reading
all about the Fiji Islanders or childhood
in Brazil

his favorite National Geographic research
into life beyond our
neighborhood
my mother looking into
the refrigerator
"Momma!" I cried, after staring at the front page
photo of The Daily News.
"What's this a picture of?"
It was Black and White,
But nothing else. No people
and no houses anywhere. My mother
came and took a look above my shoulder.
"It's about the Jews": she said.
"The Jews?"
"It's not! It's more about those Nazis!" Daddy
interjected.
"No, Granville, no!
It's about the Jews. In the war going on,"
my mother amplified, "the German soldiers
take away Jewish families and they make
them march through snow until they die!"
"What kind of ignorant
woman are you?" Daddy shouted out, "It's
not the snow. It's Nazi camps: the concentration
camps!"
"The camps?" I asked them, eagerly: "The Nazis?"
I was quite confused, "But in this picture,
Daddy, I can't see nobody."
"*Any*body," he corrected me: "You can't see
anybody!" "Yes, but what," I persevered, "what is this a
picture of?"
"That's the trail of blood left by the Jewish girls
and women on the snow because the Germans
make them march so long."
"Does the snow make feet bleed, Momma?
Where does the bleeding come from?"

My mother told me I should put away
the papers and not continue to upset myself
about these things I could not understand
and I remember
wondering if my family was a war
going on
and if
there would soon be blood
someplace in the house
and where
the blood of my family would come from

III
The Spanish Civil War:
I think I read about that one.

IV
Joan DeFreitas/2 doors up
she latched onto a soldier
fat cat bulging at the belt
and he didn't look like Hollywood
said he should
so I couldn't picture him defending
me or anyone
but then I couldn't picture war on North
Korea
at that time

V
There was tv
There were buses down to Washington, D.C.
You could go and meet your friends
from everywhere.
It was very exciting.
The tear gas burned like crazy.
The President kept lying to us.

Crowd counts at the rallies.
Body counts on the news.
Ketchup on the steps of universities.
Blood on the bandages around the head of the Vietnamese
women shot between the eyes.
Big guys.

Aerial spray missions.
Little people
Shot at close range
"Hell no! We won't go!"
"Hell no! We won't go!"
Make love
Kill anything that moves.
Kent State.
American artillery unlimited at Jackson State
Who raised these devil children?
Who invented these Americans with pony
tails and Afros and tee shirts and statistical
arguments against the mining of the harbors
of a country far away?

And I remember turning from the footage of the tat-tat-tat-
tat-tat-tat
helicopters
and I wondered how democracy would travel from the graves
at Kent State
to the hidden trenches
of Hanoi

VI

Plump during The War on Poverty
I remember making pretty good
money (6 bucks an hour)
as a city planner and my former
husband married my best

friend and I was never positive
about the next month's rent but
once I left my son sitting
on his lunchbox in the early rain
waiting for a day-care pickup and I went
to redesign low-income housing for the Lower
East Side of Manhattan and three hours after that
I got a phone call from my neighbors
that the pickup never came
that Christopher was waiting
on the sidewalk
in his yellow slicker
on his lunchbox
in the rain.

VII

I used to sometimes call the government
to tell them how my parents
ate real butter or stole sugar
from The Victory Rations
we received

I sometimes called the Operator
asking for Police
to beat my father up for beating me
so bad
but no one listened to
a tattletale
like me:

I think I felt relieved
because the government didn't send a rescue
face or voice to my imagination
and I hated the police
but what else could you do?
Peace never meant a thing to me.

I wanted everyone to mold
the plastic bag for margarine
save stamps
plant carrots
and
(imitating Joe "Brown Bomber" Louis)
fight hard
fight fair
And from the freedom days
that blazed outside my mind
I fell in love
I fell in love with Black men White
men Black
women White women
and I
dared myself to say The Palestinians
and I
worried about unilateral words like Lesbian or Nationalist
and I
tried to speak Spanish when I travelled to Managua
and I
dreamed about The Fourteenth Amendment
and I
defied the hatred of the hateful everywhere
as best I could
I mean
I took long nightly walks to emulate the Chinese
Revolutionaries
and I
always wore one sweater less than absolutely necessary to
keep warm

and I wrote everything I knew how to write against apartheid
and I
thought I was a warrior growing up
and I

buried my father with all of the ceremony all of the music
I could piece together
and I
lust for justice
and I
make that quest arthritic/pigeon-toed/however
and I
invent the mother of the courage I require not to quit

Baghdad Diary

Nuha Al Radi

Last week I went to the Rashid Hotel to pick up a letter which Bob Simpson had brought from Cyprus. He also sent me some packets of seeds for Italian vegetables, a tiny leak in the embargo: useful, if we ever get any water. His room was full of hacks waiting for the big moment. I told him very authoritatively that there would be no war. He said he wished he could believe me. I'm not sure why I was so positive. I should have known better; after all, I witnessed three revolutions in Iraq, the Suez War in Egypt and most of the Lebanese civil war.

DAY ONE.   I woke up at three A.M. to exploding bombs and Salvador Dali, my dog, frantically chasing around the house, barking furiously. I went out on the balcony. Salvador was already there, staring up at a sky lit by the most extraordinary firework display. The noise was beyond description. I couldn't get an answer from Ma and Needles's phone so tried Suha who answered in a hushed voice and said, Put out your lights. Suha was sitting in a shelter she had prepared under the stairs, already stashed with provisions. She'd taped up her windows and doors against nuclear fall-out.

I ventured outside with Salvador to put out the garage light—we were both very nervous. Almost immediately we lost all electricity, so I need not have bothered. The phones also went dead. We are done for, I think: a modern nation cannot fight without electricity and communications. Thank heavens for our ration of Pakistani matches.

With the first bomb, Ma and Needles's windows shattered, those facing the river, and one of poor Bingo's pups was killed in the garden by flying glass—our first war casualty.

DAY TWO.   Amal and Munir also lost their windows, so they've moved in here. Ma and Suha will stay here at night. Needles prefers to stay with Menth. M.A.W. only joins us for dinner. Said came by and picked us up to have lunch with Taha—kebabs and beer, delicious. Said has a good supply of petrol (which he's not prepared to share). There were no air raids, and everything seemed normal. Today, all over Baghdad, bread was thrown from government trucks to thronging crowds.

Day Three.   Suha and I spent the day merrily painting while the war was going on full blast outside. I wonder how we manage to feel so detached. This afternoon we saw a SAM missile explode in the sky. I caught Mundher Baig on his grandson's tricycle, his legs scrunched up under his chin, pedalling round and round his garage. He is convinced he will not see his grandchildren again.

At night there was a fire in the orchard, which I thought was from a bomb but in fact had been started by Flayih. He had been burning some dry wood near the dead core of a palm tree, trying to produce coal. It took the whole water supply from Dood's house and mine, plus the fire extinguisher from the car, to put out the fire. Now we have no water. Flayih still has no coal.

Day Four.   I woke to an air raid at five and went round to Zaid's house. He was there with his two aunts, both about 110 years old. One was bent double over the stove; the other never stopped chattering. Because of the constant air raids they are afraid to go upstairs to their bedrooms so they sleep in their clothes in the sitting-room. They seem oblivious to the enormity of what's happening around them and concentrate only on the immediate things; that's why, though they are so old and frail, they're so alive and entertaining. Zaid's phone still works so I tried to call Asia and Suha: no answer. Their house is on the river, directly opposite Dora refinery. There is a huge black cloud hanging over that part of Baghdad.

Mundher Baig has made a generator for his house using precious petrol. Ten of us stood gaping in wonder at this machine and the noise it made. Only four days have passed since the start of the war but already any mechanical thing seems totally alien.

Suha is experimenting with a recipe for basturma. The meat in our freezers is thawing so it's a good thing the weather is cold.

In the evening, we cook potatoes in the fireplace. M.A.W. says you can almost taste the potato through the charcoal; admittedly they are burnt. I make a dynamite punch with Aquavit, vodka and fresh orange juice.

DAY FIVE.   Munir gave me a calendar today; it's the twenty-first of January. My painting of Mundher Baig and family is nearly finished. I got my bicycle fixed. Although it's new we've been unable to inflate the tyres for days. They both turn out to have punctures. I told the guy mending it that it was new, and he said they always come like this. He thought someone punctures them before they leave the factory. The bike is called Baghdad. At least it's not called Ishtar, the name of our goddess of war that already honours fridges, freezers, soap, matches, heaters and hotels.

We are all now going to the loo in the orchard, fertilizing it and saving water. Janette, who now comes by every day, says that everyone else has gone off to the countryside because it's the best place to be during a war. Then she added that our house is like being in the country anyway. She is looking for someone to share her bed today, quite crazed; I said it wasn't uppermost in my mind right now.

Apparently people take off for the countryside with their freezers loaded on their pick-up trucks and barbecue the food as it defrosts. Only Iraqis would escape from a war carrying freezers full of goodies. We've always been hoarders. Now we have to eat our hoard.

Basil is cooking up all the food from his freezer and feeding it to his cats.

DAY SIX.   Got up for the regular five o'clock air raid, which finished an hour later. We went to queue for our petrol ration—twenty litres. Amal, who never remembers to wear her glasses, backed into a wall. The entire country has collapsed and disintegrated in a few days. They say that outside Baghdad everything goes on as normal. I wonder how long we can survive this kind of bombardment. Perhaps we will get water tomorrow.

DAY SEVEN.   The worst has happened: we have to drink warm beer. I cleaned out the freezer and removed a ton of different kinds of bread. All I ever had in my freezer was bread, ice and bones for Salvador. Asam had so much chicken in hers that she gave away some and grilled the rest; now Nofa goes around chewing on chicken rather than her usual chocolate bars. She is saving those for harder times, she says. We have to eat everything that will spoil. This means we all shit so much more, all in the garden. If we use the bathroom they say the sewage will back up on us—I have only now discovered an electric pump takes it to the sewage plant. One takes so much for granted. I wonder whether the Allies thought of these things when they planned the bombing. I fear it will be a long time until we have electricity.

Ma began making her own basturma following Suha's recipe. She stuffed the meat and spices into nylon stockings—there are no animal intestines to hand—and hung them in Dood's empty house, in posh marble surrounds. We started burning the rubbish today, clearing the orchard of dead matter. Amal insisted on wearing her high heels, even for collecting brambles.

Rumour had it that there was a difficult night ahead, the seventh, but it clouded over, so maybe God was on our side. I like the idea that some of our Scuds are decoys, probably crafty Russian training. I'd rather we didn't hit civilians but I suppose accuracy is asking too much.

We got some water today, although there wasn't enough pressure to push it up to the roof tank. Still I'm not complaining.

I finished Mundher's painting and we had a little party to celebrate its unveiling. We opened a bottle of champagne and ate *meloukhia* and a million other things. I wish that our stock of food would finish so we could eat a little less. M.A.W.'s sister and brother-in-law fled their house in Fahama and have come to live with him: two more for dinner. His sister left dressed in a green suit, which is all she has now. She is sweet, but hardly says a word; the brother never stops talking and is deaf as a post. He is probably the last surviving communist in the country. In his youth he was well-known for singing old Iraqi songs. He lulled us to sleep with his pleasant voice—dozing heads lolling in different directions.

DAY EIGHT.   Silence. It's six in the morning and there's no air raid. I ate so much last night that I couldn't sleep. Depression has hit me with the realization that the whole world hates us. It is not a comforting thought. We have bitten off more than we can chew. Ma's theory is that the world now is ruled by the two smallest powers: Kuwait with its money and oil, and Israel with its power and intellect. It's an unfair world. Other countries do wrong: look what Russia did in Afghanistan, or Turkey invading Cyprus, or Israel taking over Palestine and Lebanon. Nobody bombed them senseless. They were not even punished. Perhaps we have too much history. At least Baghdad is now on the map: I will no longer have to explain where I come from.

I had a recurrent dream before the start of the war: Americans in battle fatigues jogging down Haifa Street, lining up in the alley, kissing each other.

They were led by a girl dressed in red. Then suddenly I was on my own and everything was dry as dust, and all I could see was bare earth. What bothered me was the loneliness of the dream. Am I going to be the only survivor?

DAY NINE.   Since the war began I have been unable to read a word, not even a thriller. Ma, who usually never stops knitting, can't knit; while Suha and Amal, who have no talent for knitting, have now started. Fastidious Asam, who normally changes her clothes twice a day, now sleeps in the same clothes for two days running. She has hidden all the scissors in her house in case someone breaks in and attacks her with them. She has also wrapped her jewellery in plastic bags, boxed them, and buried them in the garden—hoping that she will remember the exact spot.

I'm trying to get M.A.W. to use his time constructively. I gave him my wall clock to repair. He complained endlessly, then started to fiddle with it and got it to work. He's excellent at mending things, having an endless supply of patience for machines but almost none for life and people. He says if we defeat Israel he'll eat a spoonful of shit—sometimes it's a plateful depending on how good or bad the news. Today he says if we retain Kuwait he'll eat ten platefuls.

Basil came by and I told him to put his mind to basic agriculture. Now that we are back in the Dark Ages we have to figure out a way to haul water up from the river. People have taken to doing their washing in the Tigris, but the river is fast flowing and dangerous. The water situation is bad.

They captured an island in the Gulf that appeared suddenly at low tide: we did not even know its name.

DAY TEN.   "Read my Lips," today is the tenth day of the war and we are still here. Where is your three-to-ten-days-swift-and-clean kill? Mind you, we are ruined. I don't think I could set foot in the West again. Maybe I'll go to India: they have a high tolerance level and will not shun us Iraqis.

Suha mended her bike today. Hers was also new and its tyres were also punctured. We rode out together and caused a sensation in the streets. All very friendly. One guy on a bike sidled by and said he had a Mercedes at home. "Are we in Paris?" said another. One sour man shouted: "We don't like girls that ride bikes," and we yelled at him, "More fool you," and rode away. Nofa says I look like ET because I'm wrapped in a hundred scarves and they fly behind me; more like a witch, I'd say. Tomorrow I'll be fifty years old. I feel very depressed. Who the hell ever wanted Kuwait anyway?

M.A.W. says we can get electricity in one minute if we attach ourselves to Turkey or Jordan, because we have a connected circuit. Yesterday we heard we may be getting it from Iran. But what can they connect it to if they bombed the stations?

Everyone talks endlessly about food. While eating lunch the conversation is about what we are having for dinner. We have cooked up all the meat we had. The basturmas we hung in Dood's house are beginning to stink—the whole house reeks.

Hala says she will give me a bucket of water as my birthday present.

DAY ELEVEN.   I had great hopes for my birthday. Lots of people were invited, and they all came and more. Drinks flowed in buckets. Someone peed on my bathroom floor (I'm sure it was that horrid Mazin who came uninvited). Fuzzle stayed the night. She said to Yasoub, "Take me out to pee," and they went out into the garden arm in arm, so romantic after all these years of marriage. There was a lovely full moon. Fuzzle later entertained us with stories about her air-raid shelter. She goes there every night with Mary, her Indian maid, from six in the evening till seven the next morning. There are three tiers of bunks; the lower one is the most coveted. Fuzzle gets very nervous when the bombing starts, and being diabetic her blood count shoots up. It was a particularly bad night and we had to take her mind off the noisy bombing outside— she was used to the quiet of the shelter and the soldiers singing to Mary. We must all have the hides of rhinos here in this house; no one seems afraid.

DAY TWELVE.   We got water from the taps today. Drew endless buckets up to the tank on the roof. I filled them up below and Munir pulled them up with a rope, eighty buckets in all. Very hard work, and I got soaked in the process.

DAY THIRTEEN.   I'm typing by candlelight and can see very little: maybe this won't be legible tomorrow. Ma and Suha went to the souk today to buy more lanterns, and an air raid started. No one bothered to shelter or go home, but just went on with their usual business. In fact there was such a crush that Ma and Suha managed to lose each other. They were bombing the bridge at Southgate. The shock caused all the doors of the buildings in the vicinity to blow open, and all the windows went—broken glass everywhere. Amal's shop, which is right beside the bridge, also got blown up. So now both her house and shop are destroyed. She never complains.

It was Suhub's birthday so we all met there for lunch. Driving across the Adhamiya Bridge we could see black columns of smoke rising in all directions. They are burning tyres to confuse the enemy. Some confusion. Samih said that an unexploded rocket had fallen in the garden of the Rashid Hotel, and there was a mad scrabble for mementoes before the security forces sealed it off.

Are we in for a nuclear war? I must say I don't feel there is a risk of death, at least not for myself—I know that I will survive. Twenty-seven thousand bombing raids so far. Is the world mad? Do they not realize what they are doing? I think Bush is a criminal. This country is totally ruined. Who gives the Americans the licence to bomb at will? I can understand Kuwait wanting to destroy us, but not the rest of the world.

The peasant's life that we now lead is very hard, and the work never stops. I get up, come downstairs, collect firewood, clean the grate and make up the evening fire. I clean the kitchen and boil water for coffee. Suha and Amal cook the meals; Ma makes the bread and cakes. I do the soups and salads. I grow all the raw materials for it, lettuce, radishes, celery, parsley and rocca in the orchard. Lunch is a simple snack; dinner—our one meal—is eaten between seven and eight, sometimes accompanied by bombing, other times not.

I have learned to do a lot of things in the dark, except sleep through the night. In fact, we all sleep very little; adrenalin keeps us going.

Salvador has got a new girlfriend. She is horrible. He bit Said yesterday. Salvador is not a dog you can stroke.

DAY FOURTEEN.   Mundher Baig died in his sleep. He had a bad heart and yesterday chased up nine floors to check the damage to our building. But he really died of sorrow: he could not comprehend why the world wanted to destroy us. He kept asking Ma yesterday why they were doing it. Somehow I knew while painting his portrait that it would never hang in his house. That was why I finished it in such a hurry, unveiling it before the paint was dry. He was not made for death, so lively and full of energy, good for laughter and for fights. We are going to miss him.

We each chose a section of Baghdad and drove around to inform friends and relatives of the funeral. I went to Mansur, crossing the Adhamiya Bridge during a full-scale air raid. Sirens were going off, rockets and bombs were falling, I was unmoved. Lubna says she saw a plane come down in Karrada; it turned out to be a cruise missile.

Day Fifteen.   All the water that Munir and I hauled up to the roof-tank yesterday disappeared through a leak in the downstairs toilet. A tragedy. I have lived in this house for three years and have had to change that loo twice already. It must be jinxed.

I went to help Amal clean up her shop, a mess of broken glass. The holes in Jumhuriya Bridge were neat and precise, with a lot of metal hanging underneath. The bridge was packed with people looking down through the holes. A siren was sounding but nobody moved.

Object Permanence

Dzvinia Orlowsky

Even a grave can be bulldozed
to give up what it hides.

For years Grandmother saved her money.
Yet when her brother's remains

arrived, she may for all she knew
have been crying

into the bones of a large dog.

. . .

Father may seem dead
but it's you that's changed.

That sheet placed over his body—
his stillness,

were all just to fool you.
You're the child again,

and the game is to test you,
to see how well you remember.

You lift the sheet, cry out.
Each time his face is locked

into another.
Each time he shows you how

he never left.

Blind Chinese Soldiers

Taiko Hirabayashi

On March 9, 1945, a day when by coincidence one of the biggest air raids took place, the sky over Gumma Prefecture was clear. An airplane, which might have taken off from Ota, flew along with the north wind.

Taking the road from Nashiki in the morning, I (a certain intellectual-turned-farmer) came down from Mount Akagi, where the snow in the valleys of the mountain was as hard as ice. From Kamikambara I took the Ashino-line train to Kiryu, transferred to the Ryoge-line, and got off at Takasaki. I was to transfer again to the Shingo-line to go to Ueno.

It was around four-thirty in the afternoon. Although the sky was still so light as to appear white, the dusty roofs of this machinery-producing town and the spaces among the leaves of the evergreen trees were getting dark. The waiting room on the platform was dark and crowded with people who had large bamboo trunks or packages of vegetables on their shoulders or beside them on the floor. It reverberated with noise and commotion.

After taking a look at the large clock hanging in front of me, I was about to leave the waiting room. Just at that moment, a group of policemen with straps around their chins crossed a bridge of the station and came down to the platform. Among them were the police chief and his subordinate, carrying iron helmets on their backs and wearing white gloves. The subordinate was talking about something with the station clerk who accompanied them, but it seemed that the word of the police chief, who interrupted their talk, decided the matter. The clerk crossed the bridge and then returned from the office with a piece of white chalk in his hand. Pushing people aside, he started drawing a white line on the platform.

I was standing in front of the stairway with one leg bent; I had sprained it when someone dropped a bag of nails in the crowded Ryoge-line train. The clerk came up to me, pushed me back aggressively, and drew a white line. As was usual in those days, the train was delayed considerably. The passengers, quite used to the arrogance of the clerks, stepped aside without much resistance and, to pass the time, watched what was happening with curiosity.

Shortly, a dirty, snow-topped train arrived. Before I noticed it, the policemen, who had been gathered together in a black mass, separated into two groups. They stood at the two entrances of the car that I was planning to board. The white lines had been drawn right there.

The car seemed quite empty, but when I tried to enter I found myself forcibly prevented by a policeman. I then realized that in the center of the car there was a young, gentle-looking officer sitting and facing another young officer who was obviously his attendant. With his characteristic nose, he was immediately recognizable as Prince Takamatsu.

With the strange, deep emotion that one might experience upon recognizing an existence hitherto believed to be fictitious, I gazed at this beautiful young man. My natural urge was to shout and tell everyone out loud, "The Prince is in there. He's real!" Yet it was not the time, either for myself or for the other passengers, for such an outburst. Unless one managed to get into one of the cars—at the risk of life and limb—one would have to wait additional long hours; how long, no one knew.

I rushed to one of the middle cars immediately. Yet my motion was slowed by the wasteful mental vacuum that the shock of seeing the Prince had created. I stood at the very end of the line of passengers, looking into the center of the car and trying to see whether there was some way I could get in.

After glimpsing the pleasant and elegant atmosphere in the well-cleaned car with blue cushions, I found myself reacting with a particularly strong feeling of disgust to the dirtiness and confusion of this car. Shattered window glass, the door with a rough board nailed to it instead of glass, a crying child, an old woman sitting on her baggage, a chest of drawers wrapped in a large *furoshiki* cloth, an unwrapped broom—a military policeman appeared, shouting that there was still more space left in the middle of the car, but no one responded to his urging.

I gave up trying to get into this car and ran to the last car. There were no passengers standing there. A soldier, possibly a lower-ranking officer, was counting with slight movements of his head the number of the plain soldiers in white clothes who were coming out of the car. An unbearable smell arose from the line of the soldiers who, carrying blankets across their shoulders, had layers of filth on their skin—filth which one could easily have scraped off.

I was looking up at the doorway wondering what this could mean; then my legs began trembling with horror and disgust.

Looking at them carefully, I could see that all of these soldiers were blind; each one stretched a trembling hand forward to touch the back of the soldier ahead. They looked extremely tired and pale; from their blinking eyes tears were falling and their hair had grown long. It was hard to tell how old they were, but I thought they must be between thirty-five and fifty years old. On further examination, I observed that there was one normal person for every five blind men. The normal ones wore military uniforms which, although of the same color as Japanese uniforms, were slightly different from them. They held sticks in their hands.

Judging from the way they scolded the blind soldiers or watched how the line was moving, I guessed they must be caretakers or managers of the blind soldiers.

"Kuai kuaide! Kuai kuaide!" [Quickly, quickly] a soldier with a stick shouted, poking the soldier in front of him. I realized then that all the soldiers in this group were Chinese. I understood why, even aside from the feeling evoked by their extreme dirtiness, they looked strange and different.

All the soldiers who were led out of the car were left standing on the platform. There were about five hundred of them. I doubted my own eyes and looked at them again carefully. All of them half-closed their eyes as if it were too bright, and tears were dripping from every eye. It was certain that every one of them was blind.

The supervising soldiers who were not blind saluted suddenly, and a Japanese officer with a saber at his waist appeared from one of the cars.

"What about the others?" he asked, passing by a soldier who was busy counting the number of blind soldiers.

"They will come later, sir, on such and such a train," the lower officer answered.

"What on earth is this all about?" the sympathetic yet suspicious expressions of the passengers seemed to ask. A middle-aged woman even started crying, holding her hand-towel to her eyes. It was obvious that both the commander and the lower officer wanted to hide the blind soldiers from the passengers, but it took a long time to get the rest off the train, and the number of onlookers gathering behind the fence gradually increased.

At last those at the head of the line began climbing up the stairs of the station, while the train started moving slowly. I was standing on the steps of the car in front of the one which had just been emptied and was holding on with all my might. I could see the policemen who were guarding the soldiers whispering to each other.

"I guess they were used for a poison gas experiment or they are the victims of some sort of explosion," said a man with an iron helmet on his back, standing four or five persons ahead of me.

"They don't have to carry out poison gas experiments in the motherland," a man who appeared to be his companion objected. Following up the companion's comment, I asked a woman of about forty who was standing next to me,

"When did those soldiers get on the train?"

"Let's see, I think at around Shinonoi."

"Then they must have come from around the Nagoya area," I said to myself, although it did not give me a clue to understand anything.

Soon the passengers forgot about it and began to converse.

"I came from Echigo. I am on my way to Chiba with my daughter." The woman whom I had just come to know started talking in a friendly manner. She told me that she was bringing her daughter to report for duty in the women's volunteer army and that her departure had been delayed for a week because her daughter had had an ugly growth on her neck. Since they could not get through tickets to Chiba, they would go as far as they could, then stay in the place they had reached, standing in line until they could buy tickets to continue their journey. They had come this far, she said, but the hardships they had been through were beyond description.

I had been offended a moment ago by the unconcerned way in which this woman had answered my question about the Chinese soldiers, but I now thought I could understand it. The Japanese were too involved in their own affairs to be moved by such an incident.

When the train left a station some time later, I went into the car which had been occupied by the Chinese soldiers, hoping to sit down and rest. I returned soon, however, because the smell there was intolerable.

The conductor came from the end of the train, announcing "Jimbobara next, Jimbobara next," as he passed among the passengers. By that time, the windows on the west side were burning with the rays of the setting sun, and the huge red sun was setting with the sanctity of the apocalypse. I realized that the car occupied by the Chinese had been taken away and that my car had become the last of the train.

Yes, there was the Prince, still in the car ahead of us, I remembered. But I was too tired to tell anyone.

After the war was over, I asked the merchants who had their shops in front of the Takasaki station whether they had seen the group of Chinese soldiers boarding the train again. They all said they had never seen them again. Perhaps they never returned from that place.

Deadline

Barbara Kingsolver

January 15, 1991

The night before the war begins, and you are still here.
You can stand in a breathless cold
ocean of candles, a thousand issues of your same face
rubbed white from below by clear waxed light.
A vigil. You are wondering what it is
you can hold a candle to.

You have a daughter. Her cheeks curve
like aspects of the Mohammed's perfect pear.
She is three. Too young for candles but
you are here, this is war.
Flames cover the gold-sparked ends of her hair,
her nylon parka laughing in color,
inflammable. It has taken your whole self
to bring her undamaged to this moment,
and waiting in the desert at this moment
is a bomb that flings gasoline in a liquid sheet,
a laundress's snap overhead, wide as the ancient Tigris,
and ignites as it descends.

The polls have sung their opera of assent: the land
wants war. But here is another America,
candle-throated, sure as tide.
Whoever you are, you are also this granite anger.
In history you will be the vigilant dead
who stood in front of every war with old hearts
in your pockets, stood on the carcass of hope
listening for the thunder of its feathers.

The desert is diamond ice and only stars above us here
and elsewhere, a thousand issues of a clear waxed star,
a holocaust of heaven
and somewhere, a way out.

two

Imprisonment
and Censorship

Dedication

Anna Akhmatova

The mountains bow before this anguish,
The great river does not flow.
In mortal sadness the convicts languish;
The bolts stay frozen. There's someone who
Still feels the sunset's glow,
Someone who can still distinguish
Day from night, for whom the fresh
Wind blows. But we don't know it, we're obsessive,
We only hear the tramp of boots, abrasive
Keys scraping against our flesh.
Rising as though for early mass,
Through the capital of beasts we'd thread.
Met, more breathless than the dead,
Mistier Neva, lower sun. Ahead,
Hope was still singing, endlessly evasive.
The sentence! and now at last tears flood.
She'd thought the months before were loneliness!
She's thrown down like a rock.
The heart gives up its blood.
Yet goes . . . swaying . . . she can still walk.
My friends of those two years I stood
In hell—oh all my chance friends lost
Beyond the circle of the moon, I cry
Into the blizzards of the permafrost:
Goodbye. Goodbye.

Prologue

Anna Akhmatova

In those years only the dead smiled,
Glad to be at rest:
And Leningrad city swayed like
A needless appendix to its prisons.
It was then that the railway-yards
Were asylums of the mad;
Short were the locomotives'
Farewell songs.
Stars of death stood
Above us, and innocent Russia
Writhed under bloodstained boots, and
Under the tyres of Black Marias.

1

They took you away at daybreak. Half wak-
ing, as though at a wake, I followed.
In the dark chamber children were crying,
In the image-case, candlelight guttered.
At your lips, the chill of an ikon,
A deathly sweat at your brow.
I shall go creep to our wailing wall,
Crawl to the Kremlin towers.

2

Gently flows the gentle Don,
Yellow moonlight leaps the sill,

Leaps the sill and stops astonished as it sees the shade

Of a woman lying ill,
Of a woman stretched alone.

Son in irons and husband clay.
Pray. Pray.

3

No, it is not I, it is someone else who is suffering.
I could not have borne it. And this thing which has
   happened,
Let them cover it with black cloths,
And take away the lanterns . . .
Night.

4

Someone should have shown you—little jester,
Little teaser, blue-veined charm-
er, laughing-eyed, lionised, sylvan-princessly
Sinner—to what point you would come:
How, the three hundredth in a queue,
You'd stand at the prison gate
And with your hot tears
Burn through the New-Year ice.
How many lives are ending there! Yet it's
Mute, even the prison-poplar's
Tongue's in its cheek as it's swaying.

5

For seventeen months I've called you
To come home, I've pleaded
—O my son, my terror!—grovelled
At the hangman's feet.
All is confused eternally—
So much, I can't say who's
Man, who's beast any more, nor even
How long till execution.
Simply the flowers of dust,
Censers ringing, tracks from a far
Settlement to nowhere's ice.

And everywhere the glad
Eye of a huge star's
Still tightening vice.

6

Lightly the weeks are flying,
What has happened, I can't take in.
Just as, my dearest, the white
Nights first watched you in prison,
So they again gaze down
With their warm aquiline eyes and
Of your cross transcendent
And of death I hear them speak.

7

The Sentence

Then fell the word of stone on
My still existing, still heaving breast.
Never mind, I was not unprepared, and
Shall manage to adjust to it somehow.

Thank God, I've many things to do today—I
Need to kill and kill again
My memory, turn my heart to stone, as
Well as practise skills gone rusty, such

As to live, for instance . . . Then there's always
Summer, calling out my Black Sea dress!
Yes, long ago I knew this day:
This radiant day, and this empty house.

8

To Death

You will come in any case, so why not now?
Life is very hard: I'm waiting for you.
I have turned off the lights and thrown the door wide open
For you, so simple and so marvellous.

Take on any form you like.
Why not burst in like a poisoned shell,
Or steal in like a bandit with his knuckleduster,
Or like a typhus-germ?
Or like a fairy-tale of your own invention—
Stolen from you and loathsomely repeated,
Where I can see, behind you in the doorway,
The police-cap and the white-faced concierge?
I don't care how. The Yenisei is swirling,
The Pole Star glittering. And eyes
I love are closing on the final horror.

9

Already madness trails its wing
Decisively across my mind;
I drink its fiery wine and sink
Into the valley of the blind.

I yield to it the victory:
There is no time, there is no room
Except to sue for peace with my
—However strange—delirium.

I fall upon my knees, I pray
For mercy. It makes no concession.
Clearly I must take away
With me not one of my possessions—

Not the stone face, hollow blanks
Of eyes, my son's, through pain's exquisite
Chisel; not the dead's closed ranks
In the hour of prison visits;

Not the dear coolness of his hands;
Nor, dimmed in distance's elision,
Like limetrees' shady turbulence,
His parting words of consolation.

Freedom from Fear

Aung San Suu Kyi

It is not power that corrupts but fear. Fear of losing power corrupts those who wield it and fear of the scourge of power corrupts those who are subject to it. Most Burmese are familiar with the four *a-gati*, the four kinds of corruption. *Chanda-gati*, corruption induced by desire, is deviation from the right path in pursuit of bribes or for the sake of those one loves. *Dosa-gati* is taking the wrong path to spite those against whom one bears ill will, and *moga-gati* is aberration due to ignorance. But perhaps the worst of the four is *bhaya-gati*, for not only does *bhaya*, fear, stifle and slowly destroy all sense of right and wrong, it so often lies at the root of the other three kinds of corruption.

Just as *chanda-gati*, when not the result of sheer avarice, can be caused by fear of want or fear of losing the goodwill of those one loves, so fear of being surpassed, humiliated or injured in some way can provide the impetus for ill will. And it would be difficult to dispel ignorance unless there is freedom to pursue the truth unfettered by fear. With so close a relationship between fear and corruption it is little wonder that in any society where fear is rife corruption in all forms becomes deeply entrenched.

Public dissatisfaction with economic hardships has been seen as the chief cause of the movement for democracy in Burma, sparked off by the student demonstrations of 1988. It is true that years of incoherent policies, inept official measures, burgeoning inflation and falling real income had turned the country into an economic shambles. But it was more than the difficulties of eking out a barely acceptable standard of living that had eroded the patience of a traditionally good-natured, quiescent people—it was also the humiliation of a way of life disfigured by corruption and fear. The students were protesting not just against the death of their comrades but against the denial of their right to life by a totalitarian regime which deprived the present of meaningfulness and held out no hope for the future. And because the students' protests articulated the frustrations of the people at large, the demonstrations quickly grew into a nationwide movement. Some of its keenest supporters were businessmen who had developed the skills and the contacts necessary not only to survive but to prosper within the system. But their affluence offered them no genuine sense of security or fulfilment, and they could not but see that if they and their fellow citizens, regardless of economic status, were to achieve a worthwhile existence, an accountable administration was at least a necessary if not a sufficient condition. The people of Burma had wearied of a precarious state of passive apprehension where they were "as water in the cupped hands" of the powers that be.

> Emerald cool we may be
> As water in cupped hands
> But oh that we might be
> As splinters of glass
> In cupped hands.

Glass splinters, the smallest with its sharp, glinting power to defend itself against hands that try to crush, could be seen as a vivid symbol of the spark of courage that is an essential attribute of those who would free themselves from the grip of oppression. Bogyoke Aung San regarded himself as a revolutionary and searched tirelessly for answers to the problems that beset Burma during her times of trial. He exhorted the people to develop courage: "Don't just depend on the courage and intrepidity of others. Each and every one of you must make sacrifices to become a hero possessed of courage and intrepidity. Then only shall we all be able to enjoy true freedom."

The effort necessary to remain uncorrupted in an environment where fear is an integral part of everyday existence is not immediately apparent to those fortunate enough to live in states governed by the rule of law. Just laws do not merely prevent corruption by meting out impartial punishment to offenders They also help to create a society in which people can fulfil the basic requirements necessary for the preservation of human dignity without recourse to corrupt practices. Where there are no such laws, the burden of upholding the principles of justice and common decency falls on the ordinary people. It is the cumulative effect on their sustained effort and steady endurance which will change a nation where reason and conscience are warped by fear into one where legal rules exist to promote man's desire for harmony and justice while restraining the less desirable destructive traits in his nature.

In an age when immense technological advances have created lethal weapons which could be, and are, used by the powerful and the unprincipled to dominate the weak and the helpless, there is a compelling need for a closer relationship between politics and ethics at both the national and international levels. The Universal Declaration of Human Rights of the United Nations proclaims that "every individual and every organ of society" should strive to promote the basic rights and freedoms to which all human beings regardless of race, nationality or religion are entitled. But as long as there are governments whose authority is founded on coercion rather than on the mandate of the people, and interest groups which place short-term profits above long-term peace and prosperity, concerted international action to protect and promote human rights will remain at best a partially realized struggle. There will continue to be arenas of struggle where victims of oppression have to draw on their own inner resources to defend their inalienable rights as members of the human family.

The quintessential revolution is that of the spirit, born of an intellectual conviction of the need for change in those mental attitudes and values which shape the course of a nation's development. A revolution which aims merely at changing official policies and institutions with a view to an improvement in material conditions has little chance of genuine success. Without a revolution of the spirit, the forces which produced the iniquities of the old order would continue to be operative, posing a constant threat to the process of reform and regeneration. It is not enough merely to call for freedom, democracy and human rights. There has to be a united determination to persevere in the struggle, to make sacrifices in the name of enduring truths, to resist the corrupting influences of desire, ill will, ignorance and fear.

Saints, it has been said, are the sinners who go on trying. So free men are the oppressed who go on trying and who in the process make themselves fit to bear the responsibilities and to uphold the disciplines which will maintain a free society. Among the basic freedoms to which men aspire that their lives might be full and uncramped, freedom from fear stands out as both a means and an end. A people who would build a nation in which strong, democratic institutions are firmly established as a guarantee against state-induced power must first learn to liberate their own minds from apathy and fear.

Always one to practise what he preached, Aung San himself constantly demonstrated courage—not just the physical sort but the kind that enabled him to speak the truth, to stand by his word, to accept criticism, to admit his faults, to correct his mistakes, to respect the opposition, to parley with the enemy and to let people be the judge of his worthiness as a leader. It is for such moral courage that he will always be loved and respected in Burma—not merely as a warrior hero but as the inspiration and conscience of the nation. The words used by Jawaharlal Nehru to describe Mahatma Gandhi could well be applied to Aung San: "The essence of his teaching was fearlessness and truth, and action allied to these, always keeping the welfare of the masses in view."

Gandhi, that great apostle of non-violence, and Aung San, the founder of a national army, were very different personalities, but as there is an inevitable sameness about the challenges of authoritarian rule anywhere at any time, so there is a similarity in the intrinsic qualities of those who rise up to meet the challenge. Nehru, who considered the instillation of courage in the people of India one of Gandhi's greatest achievements, was a political modernist, but as he assessed the needs for a twentieth-century movement for independence, he found himself looking back to the philosophy of ancient India: "The greatest gift for an individual or a nation . . . was *abhaya*, fearlessness, not merely bodily courage but absence of fear from the mind."

Fearlessness may be a gift but perhaps more precious is the courage acquired through endeavour, courage that comes from cultivating the habit of refusing to let fear dictate one's actions, courage that could be described as "grace under pressure"—grace which is renewed repeatedly in the face of harsh, unremitting pressure.

Within a system which denies the existence of basic human rights, fear tends to be the order of the day. Fear of imprisonment, fear of torture, fear of death, fear of losing friends, family, property or means of livelihood, fear of poverty, fear of isolation, fear of failure. A most insidious form of fear is that which masquerades as common sense or even wisdom, condemning as foolish, reckless, insignificant or futile the small, daily acts of courage which help to preserve man's self-respect and inherent human dignity. It is not easy for a people conditioned by fear under the iron rule of the principle that might is right to free themselves from the enervating miasma of fear. Yet even under the most crushing state machinery courage rises up again and again, for fear is not the natural state of civilized man.

The wellspring of courage and endurance in the face of unbridled power is generally a firm belief in the sanctity of ethical principles combined with a historical sense that despite all setbacks the condition of man is set on an ultimate course for both spiritual and material advancement. It is his capacity for self-

The Border Patrol State

Leslie Marmon Silko

I used to travel the highways of New Mexico and Arizona with a wonderful sensation of absolute freedom as I cruised down the open road and across the vast desert plateaus. On the Laguna Pueblo reservation, where I was raised, the people were patriotic despite the way the U.S. government had treated Native Americans. As proud citizens, we grew up believing the freedom to travel was our inalienable right, a right that some Native Americans had been denied in the early twentieth century. Our cousin old Bill Pratt used to ride his horse three hundred miles overland from Laguna, New Mexico, to Prescott, Arizona, every summer to work as a fire lookout.

In school in the 1950s, we were taught that our right to travel from state to state without special papers or threat of detainment was a right that citizens under Communist and totalitarian governments did not possess. That wide open highway told us we were U.S. citizens; we were free . . .

Not so long ago, my companion Gus and I were driving south from Albuquerque, returning to Tucson after a book promotion for the paperback edition of my novel *Almanac of the Dead*. I had settled back and gone to sleep while Gus drove, but I was awakened when I felt the car slowing to a stop. It was nearly midnight on New Mexico State Road 26, a dark, lonely stretch of two-lane highway between Hatch and Deming. When I sat up, I saw the headlights and emergency flashers of six vehicles—Border Patrol cars and a van were blocking both lanes of the highway. Gus stopped the car and rolled down the window to ask what was wrong. But the closest Border Patrolman and his companion did not reply; instead, the first agent ordered us to "step out of the car." Gus asked why, but his question seemed to set them off. Two more Border Patrol agents immediately approached our car, and one of them snapped, "Are you looking for trouble?" as if he would relish it.

I will never forget that night beside the highway. There was an awful feeling of menace and violence straining to break loose. It was clear that the uniformed men would be only too happy to drag us out of the car if we did not speedily comply with their request (asking a question is tantamount to resistance, it seems). So we stepped out of the car and they motioned for us to stand on the shoulder of the road. The night was very dark, and no other traffic had come down the road since we had been stopped. All I could think about was a book I had read—*Nunca Más*—the official report of a human rights commission that investigated and certified more than twelve thousand "disappearances" during Argentina's "dirty war" in the late 1970s.

The weird anger of these Border Patrolmen made me think about descriptions in the report of Argentine police and military officers who became addicted to interrogation, torture, and the murder that followed. When the military and police ran out of political suspects to torture and kill, they resorted to the random abduction of citizens off the streets. I thought how easy it would be for the Border Patrol to shoot us and leave our bodies and car beside the highway, like so many bodies found in these parts and ascribed to drug runners.

Two other Border Patrolmen stood by the white van. The one who had asked if we were looking for trouble ordered his partner to "get the dog," and from the back of the van another patrolman brought a small female German shepherd on a leash. The dog apparently did not heel well enough to suit him, and the handler jerked the leash. They opened the doors of our car and pulled the dog's head into it, but I saw immediately from the expression in her eyes that the dog hated them and that she would not serve them. When she showed no interest in the inside of our car, they brought her around back to the trunk, near where we were standing. They half-dragged her up into the trunk, but still she did not indicate any stowed-away human beings or illegal drugs.

Their mood got uglier; the officers seemed outraged that the dog could not find any contraband, and they dragged her over to us and commanded her to sniff our legs and feet. To my relief, the strange violence the Border Patrol agents had focused on us now seemed shifted to the dog. I no longer felt so strongly that we would be murdered. We exchanged looks—the dog and I. She was afraid of what they might do, just as I was. The dog's handler jerked the leash sharply as she sniffed us, as if to make her perform better, but the dog refused to accuse us; she had an innate dignity that did not permit her to serve the murderous impulses of those men. I can't forget the expression in the dog's eyes; it was as if she were embarrassed to be associated with them. I had a small amount of medicinal marijuana in my purse that night, but she refused to expose me. I am not partial to dogs, but I will always remember the small German shepherd that night.

Unfortunately, what happened to me is an everyday occurrence here now. Since the 1980s, on top of greatly expanding border checkpoints, the Immigration and Naturalization Service and the Border Patrol have implemented policies that interfere with the rights of U.S. citizens to travel freely within our borders. INS agents now patrol all interstate highways and roads that lead to or from the U.S.-Mexico border in Texas, New Mexico, Arizona, and California. Now, when you drive east from Tucson on Interstate 10 toward El Paso, you encounter an INS check station outside Las Cruces, New Mexico. When you drive north from Las Cruces up Interstate 25, two miles north of the town of Truth or Consequences, the highway is blocked with orange emergency barriers, and all traffic is diverted into a two-lane Border Patrol checkpoint—ninety-five miles north of the U.S.-Mexico border.

I was detained once at Truth or Consequences, despite my and my companion's Arizona driver's licenses. Two men, both Chicanos, were detained at the same time, despite the fact that they too presented ID and spoke English without the thick Texas accents of the Border Patrol agents. While we were stopped, we watched as other vehicles—whose occupants were white—were waved through the checkpoint. White people traveling with brown people, however, can expect to be stopped on suspicion they work with the sanctuary movement, which shelters refugees. White people who appear to be clergy, those who wear ethnic clothing or jewelry, and women with very long hair or very short hair (they could be nuns) are also frequently detained; white men with beards or men with long hair are likely to be detained, too, because Border Patrol agents have profiles of "those sorts" of white people who may help political refugees. (Most of the political refugees from Guatemala and El Salvador are Native American or mestizo because the indigenous people of the Americas have continued to resist efforts by invaders to displace them from their ancestral lands.) Alleged increases in illegal immigration by people of Asian ancestry mean that the Border Patrol now routinely detains anyone who appears to be Asian or part Asian, as well.

Once your car is diverted from the interstate highway into the checkpoint area, you are under the control of the Border Patrol, which in practical terms exercises a power that no highway patrol or city patrolman possesses: they are willing to detain anyone, for no apparent reason. Other law-enforcement officers need a shred of probable cause in order to detain someone. On the books, so does the Border Patrol; but on the road, it's another matter. They'll order you to stop your car and step out; then they'll ask you to open the trunk. If you ask why or request a search warrant, you'll be told that they'll have to have a dog sniff the car before they can request a search warrant, and the dog might not get there for two or three hours. The search warrant might require an hour or two past that. They make it clear that if you force them to obtain a search warrant for the car, they will make you submit to a strip search as well.

Traveling in the open, though, the sense of violation can be even worse. Never mind high-profile cases like that of former Border Patrol agent Michael Elmer, acquitted of murder by claiming self-defense, despite admitting that as an officer he shot an illegal immigrant in the back and then hid the body, which remained undiscovered until another Border Patrolman reported the event. (Last month, Elmer was convicted of reckless endangerment in a separate incident, for shooting at least ten rounds from his M-16 too close to a group of immigrants as they were crossing illegally into Nogales in March 1992.) Never mind that in El Paso, a high school football coach driving a vanload of his players in full uniform was pulled over on the freeway and a Border Patrol agent put a cocked revolver to his head. (The football coach was Mexican-American, as were most of the players in his van; the incident eventually caused a federal judge to issue a restraining order against the Border Patrol.) We've a mountain of personal experiences like that that never make the newspapers. A history professor at UCLA told me she had been traveling by train from Los Angeles to Albuquerque twice a month doing research. On each of her trips, she had noticed that the Border Patrol agents were at the station in Albuquerque scrutinizing the passengers. Since she is six feet tall and of Irish and German ancestry, she was not particularly concerned. Then one day when she stepped off the train in Albuquerque, two Border Patrolmen accosted her, wanting to know what she was doing, and why she was traveling between Los Angeles and Albuquerque twice a month. She presented identification and an explanation deemed suitable by the agents and was allowed to go about her business.

Just the other day, I mentioned to a friend that I was writing this article and he told me about his seventy-three-year-old father, who is half Chinese and had set out alone by car from Tucson to Albuquerque the week before. His father had become confused by road construction and missed a turnoff from Interstate 10 to Interstate 25; when he turned around and circled back, he missed the turnoff a second time. But when he looped back for yet another try, Border Patrol agents stopped him and forced him to open his trunk. After they satisfied themselves that he was not smuggling Chinese immigrants, they sent him on his way. He was so rattled by the event that he had to be driven home by his daughter.

This is the police state that has developed in the southwestern United States since the 1980s. No person, no citizen, is free to travel without the scrutiny of the Border Patrol. In the city of South Tucson, where 80 percent of the respondents were Chicano or Mexicano, a joint research project by the University of Wisconsin and the University of Arizona recently concluded that one out of every five people there had been detained, mistreated verbally or nonverbally, or questioned by INS agents in the past two years.

Manifest Destiny may lack its old grandeur of theft and blood—"lock the door" is what it means now, with racism a trump card to be played again and again, shamelessly, by both major political parties. "Immigration," like "street crime" and "welfare fraud," is a political euphemism that refers to people of color. Politicians and media people talk about "illegal aliens" to dehumanize and demonize undocumented immigrants, who are for the most part people of color. Even in the days of Spanish and Mexican rule, no attempts were made to interfere with the flow of people and goods from south to north and north to south. It is the U.S. government that has continually attempted to sever contact between the tribal people north of the border and those to the south.

Now that the "Iron Curtain" is gone, it is ironic that the U.S. government and its Border Patrol are constructing a steel wall ten feet high to span sections of the border with Mexico. While politicians and multinational corporations extol the virtues of NAFTA and free trade (in goods, not flesh), the ominous curtain is already up in a six-mile section at the border crossing at Mexicali; two miles are being erected but are not yet finished at Naco; and at Nogales, sixty miles south of Tucson, the steel wall has been all rubber-stamped and awaits construction, likely to begin in March. Like the pathetic multimillion-dollar antidrug border surveillance balloons that were continually deflated by high winds and made only a couple of meager interceptions before they blew away, the fence along the border is a theatrical prop, a bit of pork for contractors. Border entrepreneurs have already used blowtorches to cut passageways through the fence to collect "tolls" and are doing a brisk business. Back in Washington, the INS announces a $300 million computer contract to modernize its record keeping and Congress passes a crime bill that shunts $255 million to the INS for 1995, $181 million earmarked for border control, which is to include seven hundred new partners for the men who stopped Gus and me in our travels, and the history professor, and my friend's father, and as many as they could from South Tucson.

It is no use; borders haven't worked, and they won't work, not now, as the indigenous people of the Americas reassert their kinship and solidarity with one another. A mass migration is already under way; its roots are not simply economic. The Uto-Aztecan languages are spoken as far north as Taos Pueblo near the Colorado border, all the way south to Mexico City. Before the arrival of the Europeans, the indigenous communities throughout this region not only conducted commerce; the people shared cosmologies, and oral narratives about the Maize Mother, the Twin Brothers, and their grandmother, Spider Woman, as well as Quetzalcoatl, the benevolent snake. The great human migration within the Americas cannot be stopped; human beings are natural forces of the earth, just as rivers and winds are natural forces.

Deep down the issue is simple: the so-called Indian Wars from the days of Sitting Bull and Red Cloud have never really ended in the Americas. The Indian people of southern Mexico, of Guatemala, and those left in El Salvador, too, are still fighting for their lives and for their land against the cavalry patrols sent out by the governments of those lands. The Americas are Indian country, and the "Indian problem" is not about to go away.

One evening at sundown, we were stopped in traffic at a railroad crossing in downtown Tucson while a freight train passed us, slowly gaining speed as it headed north to Phoenix. In the twilight I saw the most amazing sight: dozens of human beings, mostly young men, were riding the train; everywhere, on flatcars, inside open boxcars, perched on top of boxcars, hanging off ladders on tank cars and between boxcars. I couldn't count fast enough, but I saw fifty or sixty people headed north. They were dark young men, Indian and mestizo; they were smiling and a few of them waved at us in our cars. I was reminded of the ancient story of Aztlán, told by the Aztecs but known in other Uto-Aztecan communities as well. Aztlán is the beautiful land to the north, the origin place of the Aztec people. I don't remember how or why the people left Aztlán to journey farther south, but the old story says that one day, they will return.

Auschwitz

Charlotte Delbo

This city we were passing through
was a strange city.
Women wore hats
perched on curly hair.
They also wore shoes and stockings
as is done in town.
None of the inhabitants of this city
had a face
and in order to hide this
all turned away as we passed
even a child who was carrying in his hand
a milk can as tall as his legs
made of violet enamel
and who fled when he saw us.
We were looking at these faceless beings
and it was we who were amazed.
We were disappointed as well
hoping to see fruits and vegetables in the shops.
Indeed, there were no shops
only display windows
wherein I would have liked to recognize myself
amid the ranks sliding over the glass panes.
I raised an arm
but all the women wished to recognize themselves
all raised an arm
and not one found out which one she was.
The face of the station clock registered the time
we were happy to look at it
it was the real time

and relieved to arrive at the beet silos
where we were taken to work
on the other side of the town
we had walked through like a wave of morning sickness.

The Legend of Miss Sasagawara

Hisaye Yamamoto

Even in that unlikely place of wind, sand, and heat, it was easy to imagine Miss Sasagawara a decorative ingredient of some ballet. Her daily costume, brief and fitting closely to her trifling waist, generously billowing below, and bringing together arrestingly rich colors like mustard yellow and forest green, appeared to have been cut from a coarse-textured homespun; her shining hair was so long it wound twice about her head to form a coronet; her face was delicate and pale, with a fine nose, pouting bright mouth, and glittering eyes; and her measured walk said, "Look, I'm *walking!*" as though walking were not a common but a rather special thing to be doing. I first saw her so one evening after mess, as she was coming out of the women's latrine going toward her barracks, and after I thought she was out of hearing, I imitated the young men of the Block (No. 33), and gasped, "Wow! How much does *she* weigh?"

"Oh, haven't you heard?" said my friend Elsie Kubo, knowing very well I had not. "That's Miss Sasagawara."

It turned out Elsie knew all about Miss Sasagawara, who with her father was new to Block 33. Where had she accumulated all her items? Probably a morsel here and a morsel there, and, anyway, I forgot to ask her sources, because the picture she painted was so distracting: Miss Sasagawara's father was a Buddhist minister, and the two had gotten permission to come to this Japanese evacuation camp in Arizona from one further north, after the death there of Mrs. Sasagawara. They had come here to join the Rev. Sasagawara's brother's family, who lived in a neighboring Block, but there had been some trouble between them, and just this week the immigrant pair had gotten leave to move over to Block 33. They were occupying one end of the Block's lone empty barracks, which had not been chopped up yet into the customary four apartments. The other end had been taken over by a young couple, also newcomers to the Block, who had moved in the same day.

"And do you know what, Kiku?" Elsie continued. "Oooh, that gal is really temperamental. I guess it's because she was a ballet dancer before she got stuck in camp, I hear people like that are temperamental. Anyway, the Sasakis, the new couple at the other end of the barracks, think she's crazy. The day they all moved in, the barracks was really dirty, all covered with dust from the dust storms and everything, so Mr. Sasaki was going to wash the whole barracks down with a hose, and he thought he'd be nice and do the Sasagawaras' side first. You know, do them a favor. But do you know what? Mr. Sasaki got the hose attached to the faucet outside and started to go in the door, and he said all the Sasagawaras' suitcases and things were on top of the Army cots and Miss Sasagawara was trying to clean the place out with a pail of water and a broom. He said, 'Here let me flush the place out with a hose for you; it'll be faster.' And she turned right around and screamed at him, 'What are you trying to do? Spy on me? Get out of here or I'll throw this water on you!' He said he was so surprised he couldn't move for a minute, and before he knew it, Miss Sasagawara just up and threw that water at him, pail and all. Oh, he said he got out of that place fast, but fast. Madwoman, he called her."

But Elsie had already met Miss Sasagawara, too, over at the apartment of the Murakamis, where Miss Sasagawara was borrowing Mrs. Murakami's Singer, and had found her quite amiable. "She said she was thirty-nine years old—imagine, thirty-nine, she looks so young, more like twenty-five; but she said she wasn't sorry she never got married, because she's had her fun. She said she got to go all over the country a couple of times, dancing in the ballet."

And after we emerged from the latrine, Elsie and I, slapping mosquitoes in the warm, gathering dusk, sat on the stoop of her apartment and talked awhile, jealously of the scintillating life Miss Sasagawara had led until now and nostalgically of the few ballets we had seen in the world outside. (How faraway Los Angeles seemed!) But we ended up as we always did, agreeing that our mission in life, pushing twenty as we were, was first to finish college somewhere when and if the war ever ended and we were free again, and then to find good jobs and two nice, clean young men, preferably handsome, preferably rich, who would cherish us forever and a day.

My introduction, less spectacular, to the Rev. Sasagawara came later, as I noticed him, a slight and fragile-looking old man, in the Block mess hall (where I worked as a waitress, and Elsie, too) or in the laundry room or going to and from the latrine. Sometimes he would be farther out, perhaps going to the post office or canteen or to visit friends in another Block or on some business to the Administration buildings, but wherever he was headed, however doubtless his destination, he always seemed to be wandering lostly. This may have been because he walked so slowly, with such negligible steps, or because he wore perpetually an air of bemusement, never talking directly to a person, as though, being what he was, he could not stop for an instant his meditation on the higher life.

I noticed, too, that Miss Sasagawara never came to the mess hall herself. Her father ate at the tables reserved for the occupants, mostly elderly, of the end barracks known as the bachelors' dormitory. After each meal, he came up to the counter and carried away a plate of food, protected with one of the pinkish apple wrappers we waitresses made as wrinkleless as possible and put out for napkins, and a mug of tea or coffee. Sometimes Miss Sasagawara could be seen rinsing out her empties at the one double-tub in the laundry that was reserved for private dishwashing.

If any one in the Block or in the entire camp of 15,000 or so people had talked at any length with Miss Sasagawara (everyone happening to speak of her called her that, although her first name, Mari, was simple enough and rather pretty) after her first and only visit to use Mrs. Murakami's sewing machine, I never heard of it. Nor did she ever willingly use the shower room, just off the latrine, when anyone else was there. Once, when I was up past midnight writing letters and went for my shower, I came upon her under the full needling force of a steamy spray, but she turned her back to me and did not answer my surprised hello. I hoped my body would be as smooth and spare and well-turned when I was thirty-nine. Another time Elsie and I passed in front of the Sasagawara apartment, which was really only a cubicle because the once-empty barracks had soon been partitioned off into six units for families of two, and we saw her there on the wooden steps, sitting with her wide, wide skirt spread splendidly about her. She was intent on peeling a grapefruit, which her father had probably brought to her from the mess hall that morning, and Elsie called out, "Hello there!" Miss Sasagawara looked up and stared, without recognition. We were almost out of earshot when I heard her call, "Do I know you?" and I could have almost sworn that she sounded hopeful, if not downright wistful, but Elsie, already miffed at having expended friendliness so unprofitably, seemed not to have heard, and that was that.

Well, if Miss Sasagawara was not one to speak to, she was certainly one to speak of, and she came up quite often as topic for the endless conversations which helped along the monotonous days. My mother said she had met the late Mrs. Sasagawara once, many years before the war, and to hear her tell it, a sweeter, kindlier woman there never was. "I suppose," said my mother, "that I'll never meet anyone like her again; she was a lady in every sense of the word." Then she reminded me that I had seen the Rev. Sasagawara before. Didn't I remember him as one of the three bhikshus who had read the sutras at Grandfather's funeral?

I could not say that I did. I barely remembered Grandfather, my mother's father. The only thing that came back with clarity was my nausea at the wake and the funeral, the first and only ones I had ever had occasion to attend, because it had been reproduced several times since—each time, in fact, that I had crossed again the actual scent or suspicion of burning incense. Dimly I recalled the inside of the Buddhist temple in Los Angeles, an immense, murky auditorium whose high and huge platform had held, centered in the background, a great golden shrine touched with black and white. Below this platform, Grandfather, veiled by gauze, had slept in a long grey box which just fitted him. There had been flowers, oh, such flowers, everywhere. And right in front of Grandfather's box had been the incense stand, upon which squatted two small bowls, one with a cluster of straw-thin sticks sending up white tendrils of smoke, the other containing a heap of coarse, grey powder. Each mourner in turn had gone up to the stand, bowing once, his palms touching in prayer before he reached it; had bent in prayer over the stand; had taken then a pinch of incense from the bowl of crumbs and, bowing over it reverently, cast it into the other, the active bowl; had bowed, the hands praying again; had retreated a few steps and bowed one last time, the hands still joined, before returning to his seat. (I knew the ceremony well from having been severely coached in it on the evening of the wake.) There had been tears and tears and here and there a sudden sob.

And all this while, three men in black robes had been on the platform, one standing in front of the shining altar, the others sitting on either side, and the entire trio incessantly chanting a strange, mellifluous language in unison. From time to time there had reverberated through the enormous room, above the singsong, above the weeping, above the fragrance, the sharp, startling whang of the gong.

So, one of those men had been Miss Sasagawara's father. . . . This information brought him closer to me, and I listened with interest later when it was told that he kept here in his apartment a small shrine, much more intricately constructed than that kept by the usual Buddhist household, before which, at regular hours of the day, he offered incense and chanted, tinkling (in lieu of the gong) a small bell. What did Miss Sasagawara do at these prayer periods, I wondered; did she participate, did she let it go in one ear and out the other, or did she abruptly go out on the steps, perhaps to eat a grapefruit?

Elsie and I tired one day of working in the mess hall. And this desire for greener fields came almost together with the Administration annoucement that henceforth the wages of residents doing truly vital labor, such as in the hospital or on the garbage trucks that went from mess hall to mess hall, would be upped to nineteen dollars a month instead of the common sixteen.

"Oh, I've always wanted to be a nurse!" Elsie confided, as the Block manager sat down to his breakfast after reading out the day's bulletin in English and Japanese.

"What's stopped you?" I asked.

"Mom," Elsie said. "She thinks it's dirty work. And she's afraid I'll catch something. But I'll remind her of the extra three dollars."

"It's never appealed to me much, either," I confessed. "Why don't we go over to garbage? It's the same pay."

Elsie would not even consider it. "Very funny. Well, you don't have to be a nurse's aide, Kiku. The hospital's short all kinds of help. Dental assistants, receptionists. . . . Let's go apply after we finish this here."

So, willy-nilly, while Elsie plunged gleefully into the pleasure of wearing a trim blue-and-white striped seersucker, into the duties of taking temperatures and carrying bedpans, and into the fringe of medical jargon (she spoke very casually now of catheters, enemas, primiparas, multiparas), I became a relief receptionist at the hospital's front desk, taking my hours as they were assigned. And it was on one of my midnight-to-morning shifts that I spoke to Miss Sasagawara for the first time.

The cooler in the corridor window was still whining away (for that desert heat in summer had a way of lingering intact through the night to merge with the warmth of the morning sun), but she entered bundled in an extraordinarily long black coat, her face made petulant, not unprettily, by lines of pain.

"I think I've got appendicitis," she said breathlessly, without preliminary.

"May I have your name and address?" I asked, unscrewing my pen.

Annoyance seemed to outbalance agony for a moment, but she answered soon enough, in a cold rush, "Mari Sasagawara, Thirty-three-seven C."

It was necessary also to learn her symptoms, and I wrote down that she had chills and a dull aching at the back of her head, as well as these excruciating flashes in her lower right abdomen.

"I'll have to go wake up the doctor. Here's a blanket, why don't you lie down over there on the bench until he comes?" I suggested.

She did not answer, so I tossed the Army blanket on the bench, and when I returned from the doctors' dormitory, after having tapped and tapped on the door of young Dr. Moritomo, who was on night duty, she was still standing where I had left her, immobile and holding onto the wooden railing shielding the desk.

"Dr. Moritomo's coming right away," I said. "Why don't you sit down at least?"

Miss Sasagawara said, "Yes," but did not move.

"Did you walk all the way?" I asked incredulously, for Block 33 was a good mile off, across the canal.

She nodded, as if that were not important, also as if to thank me kindly to mind my own business.

Dr. Moritomo (technically, the title was premature; evacuation had caught him with a few months to go on his degree), wearing a maroon bathrobe, shuffled in sleepily and asked her to come into the emergency room for an examination. A short while later, he guided her past my desk into the laboratory, saying he was going to take her blood count.

When they came out, she went over to the electric fountain for a drink of water, and Dr. Moritomo said reflectively, "Her count's all right. Not appendicitis. We should keep her for observation, but the general ward is pretty full, isn't it? Hm, well, I'll give her something to take. Will you tell one of the boys to take her home?"

This I did, but when I came back from arousing George, one of the ambulance boys, Miss Sasagawara was gone, and Dr. Moritomo was coming out of the laboratory where he had gone to push out the lights. "Here's George, but that girl must have walked home," I reported helplessly.

"She's in no condition to do that. George, better catch up with her and take her home," Dr. Moritomo ordered.

Shrugging, George strode down the hall; the doctor shuffled back to bed; and soon there was the shattering sound of one of the old Army ambulances backing out of the hospital drive.

George returned in no time at all to say that Miss Sasagawara had refused to get on the ambulance.

"She wouldn't even listen to me. She just kept walking and I drove alongside and told her it was Dr. Moritomo's orders, but she wouldn't even listen to me."

"She wouldn't?"

"I hope Doc didn't expect me to drag her into the ambulance."

"Oh, well," I said. "I guess she'll get home all right. She walked all the way up here."

"Cripes, what a dame!" George complained, shaking his head as he started back to the ambulance room. "I never heard of such a thing. She wouldn't even listen to me."

Miss Sasagawara came back to the hospital about a month later. Elsie was the one who rushed up to the desk where I was on day duty to whisper, "Miss Sasagawara just tried to escape from the hospital!"

"Escape? What do you mean, escape?" I said.

"Well, she came in last night, and they didn't know what was wrong with her, so they kept her for observation. And this morning, just now, she ran out of the ward in just a hospital nightgown and the orderlies chased after her and caught her and brought her back. Oh, she was just fighting them. But once they got her back to bed, she calmed down right away, and Miss Morris asked her what was the big idea, you know, and do you know what she said? She said she didn't want any more of those doctors pawing her. *Pawing* her, imagine!"

After an instant's struggle with self-mockery, my curiosity led me down the entrance corridor after Elsie into the longer, wider corridor admitting to the general ward. The whole hospital staff appeared to have gathered in the room to get a look at Miss Sasagawara, and the other patients, or those of them that could, were sitting up attentively in their high, white, and narrow beds. Miss Sasagawara had the corner bed to the left as we entered and, covered only by a brief hospital apron, she was sitting on the edge with her legs dangling over the side. With her head slightly bent, she was staring at a certain place on the floor, and I knew she must be aware of that concentrated gaze, of trembling old Dr. Kawamoto (he had retired several years before the war, but he had been drafted here), of Miss Morris, the head nurse, of Miss Bowman, the nurse in charge of the general ward during the day, of the other patients, of the nurse's aides, of the orderlies, and of everyone else who tripped in and out abashedly on some pretext or other in order to pass by her bed. I knew this by her smile, for as she continued to look at that same piece of the floor, she continued, unexpectedly, to seem wryly amused with the entire proceedings. I peered at her wonderingly through the triangular peephole created by someone's hand on hip, while Dr. Kawamoto, Miss Morris, and Miss Bowman tried to persuade her to lie down and relax. She was as smilingly immune to tactful suggestions as she was to tactless gawking.

There was no future to watching such a war of nerves as this; and besides, I was supposed to be at the front desk, so I hurried back in time to greet a frantic young mother and father, the latter carrying their small son who had had a hemorrhage this morning after a tonsillectomy yesterday in the out-patient clinic.

A couple of weeks later on the late shift I found George, the ambulance driver, in high spirits. This time he had been the one selected to drive a patient to Phoenix, where special cases were occasionally sent under escort, and he was looking forward to the moment when, for a few hours, the escort would permit him to go shopping around the city and perhaps take in a new movie. He showed me the list of things his friends had asked him to bring back for them, and we laughed together over the request of one plumpish nurse's aide for the biggest, richest chocolate cake he could find.

"You ought to have seen Mabel's eyes while she was describing the kind of cake she wanted," he said. "Man, she looked like she was eating it already!"

Just then one of the other drivers, Bobo Kunitomi, came up and nudged George, and they withdrew a few steps from my desk.

"Oh, I ain't particularly interested in that," I heard George saying.

There was some murmuring from Bobo, of which I caught the words, "Well, hell, you might as well, just as long as you're getting to go out there."

George shrugged, then nodded, and Bobo came over to the desk and asked for pencil and paper. "This is a good place. . . ." he said, handing George what he had written.

Was it my imagination, or did George emerge from his chat with Bobo a little ruddier than usual? "Well, I guess I better go get ready," he said, taking leave. "Oh, anything you want, Kiku? Just say the word."

"Thanks, not this time," I said. "Well, enjoy yourself."

"Don't worry," he said. "I will!"

He had started down the hall when I remembered to ask, "Who are you taking, anyway?"

George turned around. "Miss Sa-sa-ga-wa-ra," he said, accenting every syllable. "Remember that dame? The one who wouldn't let me take her home?"

"Yes," I said. "What's the matter with her?"

George, saying not a word, pointed at his head and made several circles in the air with his first finger.

"Really?" I asked.

Still mum, George nodded in emphasis and pity before he turned to go.

How long was she away? It must have been several months, and when, towards late autumn, she returned at last from the sanitarium in Phoenix, everyone in Block 33 was amazed at the change. She said hello and how are you as often and easily as the next person, although many of those she greeted were surprised and suspicious, remembering the earlier rebuffs. There were some who never did get used to Miss Sasagawara as a friendly being.

One evening when I was going toward the latrine for my shower, my youngest sister, ten-year-old Michi, almost collided with me and said excitedly, "You going for your shower now, Kiku?"

"You want to fight about it?" I said, making fists.

"Don't go now, don't go now! Miss Sasagawara's in there," she whispered wickedly.

"Well," I demanded. "What's wrong with that, honey?"

"She's scary. Us kids were in there and she came in and we finished, so we got out, and she said, 'Don't be afraid of me. I won't hurt you.' Gee, we weren't even afraid of her, but when she said that, gee!"

"Oh, go home and go to bed," I said.

Miss Sasagawara was indeed in the shower and she welcomed me with a smile. "Aren't you the girl who plays the violin?"

I giggled and explained. Elsie and I, after hearing Menuhin on the radio, had in a fit of madness sent to Sears and Roebuck for beginners' violins that cost five dollars each. We had received free instruction booklets, too, but unable to make heads or tails from them, we contented ourselves with occasionally taking the violins out of their paper bags and sawing every which way away.

Miss Sasagawara laughed aloud—a lovely sound. "Well, you're just about as good as I am. I sent for a Spanish guitar. I studied it about a year once, but that was so long ago I don't remember the first thing and I'm having to start all over again. We'd make a fine orchestra."

That was the only time we really exchanged words and some weeks later I understood she had organized a dancing class from among the younger girls in the Block. My sister Michi, becoming one of her pupils, got very attached to her and spoke of her frequently at home. So I knew that Miss Sasagawara and her father had decorated their apartment to look oh, so pretty, that Miss Sasagawara had a whole big suitcase full of dancing costumes, and that Miss Sasagawara had just lots and lots of books to read.

The fruits of Miss Sasagawara's patient labor were put on show at the Block Christmas party, the second such observance in camp. Again, it was a gay, if odd, celebration. The mess hall was hung with red and green crepe paper streamers and the grayish mistletoe that grew abundantly on the ancient mesquite surrounding the camp. There were even electric decorations on the token Christmas tree. The oldest occupant of the bachelors' dormitory gave a tremulous monologue in an exaggerated Hiroshima dialect; one of the young boys wore a bow-tie and whispered a popular song while the girls shrieked and pretended to be growing faint; my mother sang an old Japanese song; four of the girls wore similar blue dresses and harmonized on a sweet tune; a little girl in a grass skirt and superfluous brassiere did a hula; and the chief cook came out with an ample saucepan and, assisted by the waitresses, performed the familiar *dojosukui*, the comic dance about a man who is merely trying to scoop up a few loaches from an uncooperative lake. Then Miss Sasagawara shooed her eight little girls, including Michi, in front, and while they formed a stiff pattern and waited, self-conscious in the rustly crepe paper dresses they had made themselves, she set up a portable phonograph on the floor and vigorously turned the crank.

Something was past its prime, either the machine or the record or the needle, for what came out was a feeble rasp but distantly related to the Mozart minuet it was supposed to be. After a bit I recognized the melody; I had learned it as a child to the words,

When dames wore hoops and powdered hair,
And very strict was e-ti-quette,
When men were brave and ladies fair,
They danced the min-u-et. . . .

And the little girls, who might have curtsied and stepped gracefully about under Miss Sasagawara's eyes alone, were all elbows and knees as they felt the Block's one-hundred-fifty or more pairs of eyes on them. Although there was sustained applause after their number, what we were benevolently approving was the great effort, for the achievement had been undeniably small. Then Santa came with a pillow for a stomach, his hands each dragging a bulging burlap bag. Church people outside had kindly sent these gifts, Santa announced, and every recipient must write and thank the person whose name he would find on an enclosed slip. So saying, he called by name each Block child under twelve and ceremoniously presented each eleemosynary package, and a couple of the youngest children screamed in fright at this new experience of a red and white man with a booming voice.

At the last, Santa called, "Miss Mari Sasagawara!" and when she came forward in surprise, he explained to the gathering that she was being rewarded for her help with the Block's younger generation. Everyone clapped and Miss Sasagawara, smiling graciously, opened her package then and there. She held up her gift, a peach-colored bath towel, so that it could be fully seen, and everyone clapped again.

Suddenly I put this desert scene behind me. The notice I had long awaited, of permission to relocate to Philadelphia to attend college, finally came, and there was a prodigious amount of packing to do, leave papers to sign, and goodbyes to say. And once the wearying, sooty train trip was over, I found myself in an intoxicating new world of daily classes, afternoon teas, and evening concerts, from which I dutifully emerged now and then to answer the letters from home. When the beautiful semester was over, I returned to Arizona, to that glowing heat, to the camp, to the family; for although the war was still on, it had been decided to close down the camps, and I had been asked to go back and spread the good word about higher education among the young people who might be dispersed in this way.

Elsie was still working in the hospital, although she had applied for entrance into the cadet nurse corps and was expecting acceptance any day, and the long conversations we held were mostly about the good old days, the good old days when we had worked in the mess hall together, the good old days when we had worked in the hospital together.

"What ever became of Miss Sasagawara?" I asked one day, seeing the Rev. Sasagawara go abstractedly by. "Did she relocate somewhere?"

"I didn't write you about her, did I?" Elsie said meaningfully. "Yes, she's re-located all right. Haven't seen her around, have you?"

"Where did she go?

Elsie answered offhandedly. "California."

"California?" I exclaimed. "We can't go back to California. What's she do-ing in California?"

So Elsie told me: Miss Sasagawara had been sent back there to a state in-stitution, oh, not so very long after I had left for school. She had begun slip-ping back into her aloof ways almost immediately after Christmas, giving up the dancing class and not speaking to people. Then Elsie had heard a couple of very strange, yes, very strange things about her. One thing had been told by young Mrs. Sasaki, that next-door neighbor of the Sasagawaras.

Mrs. Sasaki said she had once come upon Miss Sasagawara sitting, as was her habit, on the porch. Mrs. Sasaki had been shocked to the core to see that the face of this thirty-nine-year-old woman (or was she forty now?) wore a beatific expression as she watched the activity going on in the doorway of her neigh-bors across the way, the Yoshinagas. This activity had been the joking and loud laughter of Joe and Frank, the young Yoshinaga boys, and three or four of their friends. Mrs. Sasaki would have let the matter go, were it not for the fact that Miss Sasagawara was so absorbed a spectator of this horseplay that her head was bent to one side and she actually had one finger in her mouth as she gazed, in the manner of a shy child confronted with a marvel. "What's the matter with you, watching the boys like that?" Mrs. Sasaki had cried. "You're old enough to be their mother!" Startled, Miss Sasagawara had jumped up and dashed back into her apartment. And when Mrs. Sasaki had gone into hers, adjoining the Sasagawaras', she had been terrified to hear Miss Sasagawara begin to bang on the wooden walls with something heavy like a hammer. The banging, which sounded as though Miss Sasagawara were using all her strength on each blow, had continued wildly for at least five minutes. Then all had been still.

The other thing had been told by Joe Yoshinaga who lived across the way from Miss Sasagawara. Joe and his brother slept on two Army cots pushed to-gether on one side of the room, while their parents had a similar arrangement on the other side. Joe had standing by his bed an apple crate for a shelf, and he was in the habit of reading his sports and western magazines in bed and throwing them on top of the crate before he went to sleep. But one morning he had noticed his magazines all neatly stacked inside the crate, when he was sure he had carelessly thrown some on top the night before, as usual. This happened several times, and he finally asked his family whether one of them had been putting his magazines away after he fell asleep. They had said no and laughed, telling him he must be getting absent-minded. But the mystery had been solved late one night, when Joe gradually awoke in his cot with the feeling that he was being watched. Warily he had opened one eye slightly and had been thoroughly awakened and chilled in the bargain by what he saw. For what he saw was Miss Sasagawara sitting there on his apple crate, her long hair all undone and flowing about her. She was dressed in a white nightgown and her hands were clasped on her lap. And all she was doing was sitting there watching him, Joe Yoshinaga. He could not help it, he had sat up and screamed. His mother, a light sleeper, came running to see what had happened, just as Miss Sasagawara was running out the door, the door they had always left unlatched or even wide open in summer. In the morning Mrs. Yoshinaga had gone straight to the Rev. Sasagawara and asked him to do something about his daughter. The Rev. Sasagawara, sympathizing with her indignation in his benign but vague manner, had said he would have a talk with Mari.

And, concluded Elsie, Miss Sasagawara had gone away not long after. I was impressed, although Elsie's sources were not what I would ordinarily pay much attention to, Mrs. Sasaki, that plump and giggling young woman who always felt called upon to explain that she was childless by choice, and Joe Yoshinaga, who had a knack of blowing up, in his drawling voice, any incident in which he personally played even a small part (I could imagine the field day he had had with this one). Elsie puzzled aloud over the cause of Miss Sasagawara's derangement and I, who had so newly had some contact with the recorded explorations into the virgin territory of the human mind, sagely explained that Miss Sasagawara had no doubt looked upon Joe Yoshinaga as the image of either the lost lover or the lost son. But my words made me uneasy by their glibness, and I began to wonder seriously about Miss Sasagawara for the first time.

Then there was this last word from Miss Sasagawara herself, making her strange legend as complete as I, at any rate, would probably ever know it. This came some time after I had gone back to Philadelphia and the family had joined me there, when I was neck deep in research for my final paper. I happened one day to be looking through the last issue of a small poetry magazine that had suspended publication midway through the war. I felt a thrill of recognition at the name, Mari Sasagawara, signed to a long poem, introduced as ". . . the first published poem of a Japanese-American woman who is, at present, an evacuee from the West Coast making her home in a War Relocation center in Arizona."

It was a *tour de force*, erratically brilliant and, through the first readings, tantalizingly obscure. It appeared to be about a man whose lifelong aim had been to achieve Nirvana, that saintly state of moral purity and universal wisdom. This man had in his way certain handicaps, all stemming from his having acquired, when young and unaware, a family for which he must provide. The day came at last, however, when his wife died and other circumstances made it unnecessary for him to earn a competitive living. These circumstances were considered by those about him as sheer imprisonment, but he had felt free for the first time in his long life. It became possible for him to extinguish within himself all unworthy desire and consequently all evil, to concentrate on that serene, eight-fold path of highest understanding, highest mindedness, highest speech, highest action, highest livelihood, highest recollectedness, highest endeavor, and highest meditation.

This man was certainly noble, the poet wrote, this man was beyond censure. The world was doubtless enriched by his presence. But say that someone else, someone sensitive, someone admiring, someone who had not achieved this sublime condition and who did not wish to, were somehow called to companion such a man. Was it not likely that the saint, blissfully bent on cleansing from his already radiant soul the last imperceptible blemishes (for, being perfect, would he not humbly suspect his own flawlessness?) would be deaf and blind to the human passions rising, subsiding, and again rising, perhaps in anguished silence, within the selfsame room? The poet could not speak for others, of course; she could only speak for herself. But she would describe this man's devotion as a sort of madness, the monstrous sort which, pure of itself, might possibly bring troublous, scented scenes to recur in the other's sleep.

The Censors

Luisa Valenzuela

Poor Juan! One day they caught him with his guard down before he could even realize that what he had taken to be a stroke of luck was really one of fate's dirty tricks. These things happen the minute you're careless, as one often is. Juancito let happiness—a feeling you can't trust—get the better of him when he received from a confidential source Mariana's new address in Paris and knew that she hadn't forgotten him. Without thinking twice, he sat down at his table and wrote her a letter. The letter. The same one that now keeps his mind off his job during the day and won't let him sleep at night (what had he scrawled, what had he put on that sheet of paper he sent to Mariana?).

Juan knows there won't be a problem with the letter's contents, that it's irreproachable, harmless. But what about the rest? He knows that they examine, sniff, feel, and read between the lines of each and every letter, and check its tiniest comma and most accidental stain. He knows that all letters pass from hand to hand and go through all sorts of tests in the huge censorship offices and that, in the end, very few continue on their way. Usually it takes months, even years, if there aren't any snags; all this time the freedom, maybe even the life, of both sender and receiver is in jeopardy. And that's why Juan's so troubled: thinking that something might happen to Mariana because of his letter. Of all people, Mariana, who must finally feel safe there where she always dreamt about living. But he knows that the *Censor's Secret Command* operates all over the world and cashes in on the discount in air fares; there's nothing to stop them from going as far as that obscure Paris neighborhood, kidnapping Mariana, and returning to their cozy homes, certain of having fulfilled their noble mission.

Well, you've got to beat them to the punch, do what every one tries to do: sabotage the machinery, throw sand in its gears, that is to say get to the bottom of the problem to try to stop it.

This was Juan's sound plan when he, along with many others, applied for a censor's job—not because he had a calling like others or needed a job: no, he applied simply to intercept his own letter, an idea none too original but comforting. He was hired immediately, for each day more and more censors are needed and no one would bother to check on his references.

Ulterior motives couldn't be overlooked by the *Censorship Division*, but they needn't be too strict with those who applied. They knew how hard it would be for the poor guys to find the letter they wanted and even if they did, what's a letter or two compared to all the others that the new censor would snap up? That's how Juan managed to join the *Post Office's Censorship Division*, with a certain goal in mind.

The building had a festive air on the outside that contrasted with its inner staidness. Little by little, Juan was absorbed by his job, and he felt at peace since he was doing everything he could to retrieve his letter to Mariana. He didn't even worry when, in his first month, he was sent to *Section K* where envelopes are very carefully screened for explosives.

It's true that on the third day a fellow worker had his right hand blown off by a letter, but the division chief claimed it was sheer negligence on the victim's part. Juan and the other employees were allowed to go back to their work, though feeling less secure. After work, one of them tried to organize a strike to demand higher wages for unhealthy work, but Juan didn't join in; after thinking it over, he reported the man to his superiors and thus he got promoted.

You don't form a habit by doing something once, he told himself as he left his boss's office. And when he was transferred to *Section J*, where letters are carefully checked for poison dust, he felt he had climbed a rung in the ladder.

By working hard, he quickly reached *Section E* where the job became more interesting, for he could now read and analyze the letters' contents. Here he could even hope to get hold of his letter to Mariana, which, judging by the time that had elapsed, would have gone through the other sections and was probably floating around in this one.

Soon his work became so absorbing that his noble mission blurred in his mind. Day after day he crossed out whole paragraphs in red ink, pitilessly chucking many letters into the censored basket. These were horrible days when he was shocked by the subtle and conniving ways employed by people to pass on subversive messages; his instincts were so sharp that he found behind a simple "the weather's unsettled" or "prices continue to soar" the wavering hand of someone secretly scheming to overthrow the Government.

His zeal brought him swift promotion. We don't know if this made him happy. Very few letters reached him in *Section B*—only a handful passed the other hurdles—so he read them over and over again, passed them under a magnifying glass, searched for microdots with an electron microscope, and tuned his sense of smell so that he was beat by the time he made it home. He'd barely manage to warm up his soup, eat some fruit, and fall into bed, satisfied with having done his duty. Only his darling mother worried, but she couldn't get him back on the right track. She'd say, though it wasn't always true: Lola called, she's at the bar with the girls, they miss you, they're waiting for you. Or else she'd leave a bottle of red wine on the table. But Juan wouldn't indulge: any distraction could make him lose his edge and the perfect censor had to be alert, keen, attentive, and sharp to nab cheats. He had a truly patriotic task, both self-sacrificing and uplifting.

His basket for censored letters became the best fed as well as the most cunning in the whole *Censorship Division*. He was about to congratulate himself for having finally discovered his true mission, when his letter to Mariana reached his hands. Naturally, he censored it without regret. And just as naturally, he couldn't stop them from executing him the following morning, one more victim of his devotion to his work.

A Window on Soweto

Joyce Sikakane

Detention

I was detained on May 10, 1969 at about 2 A.M. We heard knocking and woke to the flashing of torches outside and shouts of "Police! Police! Open the door!" We all got up—my mother, myself and my two brothers—and the police came in. There were three white policemen, one white policewoman and an African policeman, all in plain clothes.

They demanded Joyce Sikakane and I said it was myself and they produced a warrant of arrest under Section 6 of the Terrorism Act. They said they wanted to search the house. They were all brandishing their guns about and so they searched the house and took away whatever documents and personal papers— all my letters for example—they wished. The policewoman was guarding me the whole time.

After about two hours they told me to get dressed, as I was still in my nightie; I did so and was escorted to the car. I was afraid to wake Nkosinathi who was still sleeping, so I left him without saying goodbye.

On the way out of Soweto the car dropped off the African policeman in Meadowlands. I remember him saying, "Thank you, my baas, you caught the terrorist. I hope you get the information you want out of her."

We drove off to John Vorster Square (Security Police HQ), where another policeman got out, and then on again. When I asked where we were going, the only reply was that I was being detained under the Terrorism Act. I was terrified: I didn't see myself as a terrorist and didn't know why I should be detained under the Terrorism Act.

I was taken to Pretoria Central Prison. They knocked on the big door, the guard looked out and then opened the gate and I was led in. First we went to the office; they spoke to the matron and papers were signed. My engagement ring was taken from me—I was upset about that. Then we crossed the prison yard to another part of the prison. In the yard were about a hundred African women, some with babies on their backs, some sitting on the ground, some with vegetable baskets full of onions, pumpkins and so on, whom I could see were vendors who had been arrested for illegally selling vegetables in the street. As I came into the yard, the policeman shouted to the women to shut their eyes. This was because I was a Terrorism Act detainee, to be held incommunicado, which meant no one should know who or where I was. I was taken past and up some stairs, where the two policemen escorting me greeted another man as Colonel Aucamp.

He told the matron to take me to a cell. And I heard her ask, "Is she a condemned woman?" as I was shown into a cell with a bright blinding light that made me see sparks.

Aucamp immediately said, "No, no, not that one, I made a mistake." So I was taken out and led along to the common shower room, where there were lots of women prisoners, some naked under the showers, some undressing, some waiting their turn. The matron told me to undress, which I did, and got under the cold shower. I could tell the other women knew there was something special about me, being under escort and alone and jumping the queue like that.

After the cold shower I picked up my paper bag of clothes—the matron told me not to dress—and I was led to a cell. It was narrow and high, situated in what I later discovered was the isolation wing. The outer steel door was opened and then the inner barred door; I went in and the matron locked first one and then the other.

So there I was, in this tall narrow empty cell, gazing around. There was a small high hole covered with mesh, for ventilation. And it was very cold: May is the beginning of winter in South Africa and we had already had some frost. Suddenly I heard women's voices coming from outside in the yard, talking. I was horrified to hear them talking about their love affairs inside prison—the experienced women telling the freshers what to expect, how some were chosen as husbands and some as wives, and generally describing the whole scene to them. It gave me a real fright, standing there naked. I at once got my paper bag and put my panties on!

When I looked around at the contents of the cell all I saw was a damp sisal mat, rolled up, and three grey blankets, also damp and smelling of urine. That was all. I just sat down on the mat and waited.

It wasn't until 7 o'clock that evening that the cell door opened. There was a white wardress and an African woman prisoner in prison uniform, who shoved a plate of food through the door, along the floor, together with a galvanized bucket. All the time the wardress stood between me and the prisoner, so I should not be seen. Then they left, locking the doors behind them. But I heard them open the next cell and then I knew I wasn't alone: if the next cell was occupied I wasn't the only woman detainee.

From then on the pattern of prison life was always the same. In the morning at about 7 A.M. the cell door was opened, the shit bucket and empty plate taken out and a plate of porridge and cup of coffee put in. There was a bucket of sometimes warm water too, to wash oneself and one's underclothes. Lunch was usually about noon, though it could be earlier—on Sundays it was about 10:30—and consisted of izinkobe or dry mealies—corn kernels—which had been boiled but were still dry and hard. There was a beverage too, some sort of drink, which the prisoners used to call puza'mandla—drink power! Then at about 2 P.M. came supper, which was soft maize porridge with one or two pieces of meat, possibly pork, in it. That was all until the next day.

For the first few days I didn't eat anything. I was frightened, angry, depressed, wondering why I had been detained, scared of what might happen, and crying most of the time. By the third day, I had cried all my tears out. At least, I think it was the third day. Two huge policemen, with layers and layers of chin, came for me. I asked where they were taking me and they said, to give an account of your sins.

I was driven in a big Cadillac, with a policeman on either side of me and two more in front. We went to the Compol building (police HQ) in Pretoria. Knock, knock again, the police escort identify themselves and we drive in.

Down corridors to an office. It looks like any other office except it has these wooden partitions. Right facing me is a stone sink; and then there's a desk and a few chairs. I can see it's a work room. All along the walls is this wooden partitioning, covering the windows but capable of being drawn back. It kind of encloses the room, insulates it from outside. And just off this room is a sort of gym closet with punch bags—and a huge African policeman with fierce red eyes standing there. While I was being interrogated policemen kept trooping in to practice boxing on the punch bags.

Interrogation

There was a constant stream of policemen, about fifteen or twenty, coming into the room, as if they were going on stage. They were brandishing guns, holding documents, smoking cigarettes, greeting me, some scowling at me.

They all looked different, some like bulldogs, some like Alsatians, some like timid cats. Some of them behaved with great politeness, like perfect gentlemen. I think this performance was just put on to confuse me, for the next thing was Major Swanepoel coming in. He is the most sadistic and most feared of all the police interrogators: several people have died as a result of his "questioning."

"Have you heard of Major Swanepoel?" he said. "I am Major Swanepoel." All the other policemen gave way to him, treating him very deferentially. Then interrogation began.

They fired questions and statements at me; all of a sudden they were all talking about me and my personal life—all my experiences, which they seemed to know better than I did! As they did so they incidentally revealed the extent of their informer network: I found they knew about all sorts of incidents in my career—the story about the Malawian air hostesses being allowed to stay in an all-white hotel, for instance, that I had been working on when I was detained. I also discovered, from things they said, who else had been questioned: Winnie Mandela, wife of ANC leader Nelson Mandela, and Rita Ndzanga, for instance. They had interrogated many other people I knew, and from what they knew I could see they had been tortured to extract the information.

From me they wanted confirmation: that certain things had been done, that I had knowingly participated, and whatever else I could add. From what they know one has to judge what to admit and what to hide and what one might not manage to hide—because it flashes into your mind what risk to others is involved, and also the possibility of being tortured yourself and whether the type of information you have is worth dying for. I knew that in our case what we had been doing was something that would not, in any other country, be considered "terroristic": we were involved with the welfare of political prisoners, helping to make arrangements for families of prisoners to visit their husbands or parents. And so why not admit it? Yes, I did that—so what? We hadn't been involved in anything connected with violence or arms—that would have called for other methods of interrogation. As far as I was concerned they were more interested in getting information about the underground communication network.

The interrogation lasted right through until the following day. They took turns, and took breaks. I was just standing there. I would be tired, I would squat down, I would jump about a bit. I was shown the bricks—the torture bricks on which the men detainees are made to stand. The questioning went on, without food, without anything, till the following morning. Then I was taken back to my cell.

It was about ten days before I was taken again for interrogation. This time it lasted for three whole days because this time they were concerned with taking a statement. Under the Terrorism Act a detainee may be held until a statement to the satisfaction of the Commissioner of Police has been given, and the purpose of the interrogation is to obtain such a statement which can then be used against you or someone else. They still ask questions: anything you admit goes down on the statement.

This time my interrogation took place on the third floor of Compol building, and the interrogators were Major Botha and Major Coetzee. They were trained and experienced political officers. Oh, they were courteous gentlemen, but I could sense hatred—they hated every bit of me. But they had to get what they wanted from me.

They put the proposal that I should be a state witness, giving evidence for the state against the others. I asked why should I do that? and they said, well, you're young, you're an intelligent girl, you have a fiancé outside the country. If you are afraid to give evidence because of what your organization will do to you, we can always give you another name and find a job in one of our embassies abroad—say in Malawi or London, where you can join your fiancé!

All the time, because of what they wanted out of me, they were at pains to explain that they were not against Africans or black people in general. They were only against communists. They argued that people like myself, young, intelligent, pretty, etc., were being misled by communists. They, on the other hand, were offering me a chance. I found this insulting. How could they sit there, admit that apartheid was a repressive system, which they did while maintaining that racism occurred all over the world. What hypocrites, I said inside me, to say communists had misled me into wanting to change the system. I didn't need any communists to tell me apartheid is evil. I know. Nor would I join the enemy camp for the sake of self-preservation.

So I told Major Botha and Major Coetzee I was not interested in their offer. They said in that case you are going to be here a long time. Others had given evidence, they said. If you refuse we have lots of other evidence we can use, the others are willing. . . .

. . . That same afternoon the cells were opened, first mine, and then four others, and we were taken out. I'll never forget the feelings of that moment, a kind of muted consternation, when we five women all saw each other. There was Winnie Mandela, Rita Ndzanga, Martha Dhlamini, Thokozile Mngoma—and of course we each half expected, as our interrogators had said, that the others had agreed to give evidence. But they hadn't. I remember we hugged each other hard: it was too good to be true. We felt this was a moment of victory and we were together. . . .

North American Time

Adrienne Rich

When my dreams showed signs
of becoming
politically correct
no unruly images
escaping beyond borders
when walking in the street I found my
themes cut out for me
knew what I would not report
for fear of enemies' usage
then I began to wonder

II

Everything we write
will be used against us
or against those we love.
These are the terms,
take them or leave them.
Poetry never stood a chance
of standing outside history.
One line typed twenty years ago
can be blazed on a wall in spraypaint
to glorify art as detachment
or torture of those we
did not love but also
did not want to kill

We move   but our words stand
become responsible
for more than we intended

and this is verbal privilege

III

Try sitting at a typewriter
one calm summer evening
at a table by a window
in the country, try pretending
your time does not exist
that you are simply you
that the imagination simply strays
like a great moth unintentional
try telling yourself
you are not accountable
to the life of your tribe
the breath of your planet

IV

It doesn't matter what you think.
Words are found responsible
all you can do is choose them
or choose
to remain silent.   Or, you never had a choice,
which is why the words that do stand
are responsible

and this is verbal privilege

V

Suppose you want to write
of a woman braiding
another woman's hair—
straight down, or with beads and shells
in three-strand plaits or corn-rows—
you had better know the thickness
the length   the pattern
why she decides to braid her hair
how it is done to her

what country it happens in
what else happens in that country

You have to know these things

VI

Poet, sister: words—
whether we like it or not—
stand in a time of their own.
No use protesting   *I wrote that*
before Kollontai was exiled
Rosa Luxemburg, Malcolm,
Anna Mae Aquash, murdered,
before Treblinka, Birkenau,
Hiroshima, before Sharpeville,
Biafra, Bangladesh, Boston,
Atlanta, Soweto, Beirut, Assam
—those faces, names of places
sheared from the almanac
of North American time

VII

I am thinking this in a country
where words are stolen out of mouths
as bread is stolen out of mouths
where poets don't go to jail
for being poets, but for being
dark-skinned, female, poor.
I am writing this in a time
when anything we write
can be used against those we love
where the context is never given
though we try to explain, over and over
For the sake of poetry at least
I need to know these things

VIII

Sometimes, gliding at night
in a plane over New York City
I have felt like some messenger
called to enter, called to engage
this field of light and darkness.
A grandiose idea, born of flying.
But underneath the grandiose idea
is the thought that what I must engage
after the plane has raged onto the tarmac
after climbing my old stairs, sitting down
at my old window
is meant to break my heart and reduce me to silence.

IX

In North America time stumbles on
without moving, only releasing
a certain North American pain.
Julia de Burgos wrote:
That my grandfather was a slave
is my grief;   had he been a master
that would have been my shame.
A poet's words, hung over a door
in North America, in the year
nineteen-eighty-three.
The almost-full moon rises
timelessly speaking of change
out of the Bronx, the Harlem River
the drowned towns of the Quabbin
the pilfered burial mounds
the toxic swamps, the testing-grounds

and I start to speak again

Piercing the Blockade

Nawal El Saadawi

As I stood behind the door, I could see dawn breaking through the covering of night. Pressing my nose between the thick black bars, I sniffed a breeze of fresh air. I remembered the sight of the imprisoned lion in the Cairo Zoo . . . thrusting his large head between the steel columns, then pacing round and round inside the bars without cease. I recalled, too, the sight of the wolf inside his steel cage and the tiger and all the other animals.

I look at my fingers, clutching the steel bars. My fingernails have grown and lengthened—they look like claws now. I haven't cut them since I came to prison. Scissors are among the prohibited items, since they are considered sharp implements. I contemplate my fingers in astonishment. I've never had such fingernails, ever! Are they my own fingernails or the claws of an animal?

My hair has grown, too; it touches my neck and shoulders by now. Thick, tousled hair like a lion's mane. I probe my face; under my hand, I feel my nose extending between the steel bars, as if it has lengthened to become like an elephant's trunk! I have forgotten the shape of my face; I haven't seen it in a mirror since I entered prison. Mirrors are among the prohibited items, since they are considered sharp implements.

I touch my arms and legs. The skin is dark brown, and across it run lines of red and blue, like fingernail marks. Do I scratch at night, while I'm asleep? Has scabies infection been transmitted to me?

I stretch my nose outside the bars . . . through it I escape far from the odour of burnt gas, the rotting garbage in the corners, and the dampness of the cement floor and tiles. I remain standing behind the bars; I sense the fatigue in my body due to standing for so long. I bend my body to sit upon the hard ground. I rest my body against the bars. I remain sealed, still like the wall. Time, too is like the wall.

I feel tired due to such a long period of sinking. I unroll my body and get to my feet. I stroll around the cell. All of my cellmates are asleep. Dawn prayer has not yet been announced. Boduur is still sleeping, her features given over to sadness. All the bodies have gone lax, faces pale and faded in a complete submission to a long, sad sleep.

My heart is heavy . . . how long will time stretch on for us in this grave? Time does not budge, like this mangy ceiling over my head from which dangles an electric light, flaming day and night like a bulging red eye, with a black rope wound round its neck on to which cling flies—sleeping or dead.

How long have I been in this steel cage? When was the first night? Since Sunday, 6 September, and what is today? I don't know the day of the week, or the date, or the hour. In prison one loses one's sense of the date, and of time itself.

I've been here for a long time . . . for a century . . . a thousand years . . . since I was born and since I became aware of something called time . . . Ever since they broke down the door by force and carried me off in the van on this unknown voyage through the darkness.

Since that day I've been here and no one has told me why. No one has directed any charges at me, and the only answer I have had to any of my questions is: "We are awaiting instructions from above. We are awaiting new orders."

What are the old orders, then? The Precautionary Detention Order! And what does "the Precautionary Detention Order" signify? It means imprisonment inside a cell, behind bars, without an investigation, without letters from home or visits, without newspapers or radio or going out into the prison courtyard. Complete, absolute imprisonment without human or legal rights. Absolute imprisonment which will end no one knows when, except one man, the one who issued the Precautionary Detention Order. And he is the sole person able to cancel or alter it.

For the first time, the meaning of "autocracy" is embodied before me. For the first time, dictatorship takes tangible form before my eyes. Previously, I had rejected it as an idea, a style, and a system of organization. But now I came to reject it with my entire being, with all the longing I feel for life and freedom, with my soul and body alike. Yet how does such a rejection begin to assume the form of positive action? How do I break through the blockade thrown up around my mind and body? I cannot pull my body out between the steel bars . . . but I can extract my mind.

The idea of breaking through the blockade began to take me captive. I whispered to Fathiyya-the-Murderess: "Fathiyya, I want to send a letter to my family . . . is that possible?"

"Everything is possible," she whispered.

"Inside prison?" I said out loud, in astonishment.

She laughed. "Inside prison is just like outside prison. Everything is possible . . . what's important is the determination to do it."

"I am determined!" I said.

"Your will is like mine," she said, laughing again. "When I decide to do something . . . Oh God . . ."

I spent an entire night writing a letter to my family—to my husband, son, and daughter. It was a long letter, into which I emptied all that was in my head.

The days and nights went by, and still I received no reply. My eyes would meet Fathiyya's gaze, and I would say nothing. The *shawisha*'s eyes were always observant, and her ears were sharp. In her eyes was a look of suspicion and doubt . . . and Fathiyya avoided looking my way. Why was she afraid to look me in the eye? Had I put my confidence in the wrong place? Had Fathiyya given my letter to the *shawisha*, or to the administrators of the prison?

It is not my nature to harbour suspicions. As far as I am concerned, a person is innocent until proven guilty. Whenever I looked into Fathiyya's eyes, I felt that she was sincere; she was a woman of courage and decency. Were my perceptions deceptive? I've always trusted my subconscious perceptions, and I don't distinguish between intellect and feelings. Sound feelings mean a sound mind. Sometimes the intellect errs, knowing only numbers and the circumscribed logical thinking which we inherit and to which we become accustomed. But sound feelings represent the more profound mind—that which comprises human sentiment, emotional feelings, perception and discernment and the accumulation of knowledge and experience.

Day after day, though, the doubt was growing in my mind. Perhaps I had sketched features from my imagination to place over the real Fathiyya. Maybe, after all, she was a spy!

The blood rushed to my face. I felt sudden terror. I lost confidence in my ability to judge people and things.

I sensed myself falling, disintegrating, my heart pounding, my throat dry. My fingers were trembling. Fawqiyya smiled triumphantly and whispered in my ear: "I told you she was a spy. Everyone who comes into our cell here is a spy. Don't trust anyone."

The walls and steel bars were folding in on me from all sides. Doubt and burnt gas choked me. I did not see human faces, but only expanses of blackness, holes from which gazed eyes as red as those of devils. The face of Fathiyya came to resemble Satan's countenance. Murderess, daughter of a murderess, as the *shawisha* would say. For me, she'd injected poison into her honeyed words.

I tossed and turned upon the wooden board, unable to close an eyelid. I became aware that torture in prison does not take place by means of the bars, or the walls, or the stinging insects, or hunger or thirst or insults or beating.

Prison is doubt. And doubt is the most certain of tortures. It is doubt that kills the intellect and body—not doubt in others, but doubt in oneself . . . The teaming, crushing question for the mind: was I right or wrong? Had Fawqiyya been correct in her doubts? Had my judgement been in error?

I opened my eyes in the morning to the sound of the key turning three times in the door. I did not get out of bed; I did not carry out my daily exercises; I did not take a shower or drink tea. I stayed in bed, bitterness in my throat and a painful lump in my heart.

"How odd!" my astonished cellmates remarked. "Are you ill?"

"If the doctor has got sick," someone said, "this is the end."

"We've all been sick except you," another called out, "so your turn has come now!"

Not one of them really believed that I was ill. But no sooner did they glance at my face than silence fell. I did not know what my face looked like.

"Shall we call the doctor?" I heard a sympathetic voice ask. "Can I make a cup of tea?" inquired another voice, even gentler.

Even Boduur and Fawqiyya—I saw them at my side. For the first time, I saw a kind smile on Boduur's face, a smile like that of a mother to her child. I heard her say, "I'll give you a blanket of mine, you must have caught a cold."

And the deep furrow in Fawqiyya's forehead all but disappeared as she said gently, "I told you to keep up your health more carefully! It's that cold shower every day that has made you ill."

And *Shawisha* Nabawiyya placed her thin hand on my head. "Looks like we've put the evil eye on you, by God. I'll say the Verse of Yasin for you."

And I saw Fathiyya's face. I shut my eyes.

I don't want to see her.

But she drew near and whispered in my ear. "I have a letter for you."

I leapt out of bed.

The Prisoner

Angelina Muñiz-Huberman

My tears have been my meat
day and night, while they
continually say unto me,
Where is thy God?
Psalm 42:3

Here in the corner of the cell, my fingernails wrenched out and my body battered and bruised, I know that I have reached the limits of pain.

Pain bursts cells and twists nerves. In the beginning, it brings fear, then total oblivion. In the end, nothing matters anymore and courage is reborn. There is nothing to lose if everything has already been lost. There is no longer any fear of speaking, because words are empty. Only the constant pain remains, from one end of the body to the other.

When I feel my body disintegrating swiftly, pore by pore, in dreamed strokes of the whip, I become fully aware of it.

Time does not exist: an eye swollen shut by blows does not need to know if it is day or night; a broken leg does not take one anywhere; mutilated sex does not recognize the moment of pleasure.

I do not need anything now. Everything is superfluous. To think about going back is not to think. If, like a stroke of lightning, the light of her face appears to me, I am not surprised and do not recognize her.

Because if I recognized her, I would weep, and the salt of my tears would burn the places where my nails once were.

But I do recognize her, and the light of her face is there on the wall, where I no longer see the blood stains or the crushed insects. She smiles, and then I remember her.

Her eyes. Her hair. Her hand caressing me.

No, I do not want to remember. To remember is to smile, to pardon. I do not want to.

Better the stupor of delirium. The opaque eyes of the executioners. The languid mouths of the torturers. The sticks, the whips, the knives. Everything hard and sharp.

Not her face, or her smooth skin. Nothing. Do not remember her.

Do not even speak. Forget language altogether. Only screams. Return to the primitive, to the darkness of the cave, to the tenacious rock.

But here again is light, a kind of dawn which battles against thick and obstinate shadows. A confused, slow, almost unseeing light, as when I began to open my swollen eye.

It is not a light that marks time, not a light which clarifies. It is a luminous hole inside me, visceral, radiating out toward all the points of pain in my body. It is a light which calms me. It is the certainty that suffering touches bottom, that it can reach no deeper, that it is covered by sand and washed by the sea.

It is the light of goodness which gilds the space of the cell and denies the roots of evil.

My body, bathed in light, stops aching. I believe that I smile. I believe that I rest. I believe that I sleep. I believe that when I wake, I will recover my lost hope. I believe that then I will know how to tell where God is.

Gemütlich

Maria Banus

Gemütlich, the German word
translated, flickers and fades.
Pleasant? Familiar? Easy? Agreeable?
No. In German it has a different shade.

Gemütlich has cottage curtains, flowers,
napkins edged in lace.
The tick-tock of an old clock,
coffee klatsches in a cozy place.

Gemütlich after a brisk walk
through wind and fog
finds you at home in your
castle with your dog.

They gave you orders you obeyed.
Canary, dog, wife, are still.
You are the master here,
and you relax to pay your bills.

Gemütlich—the little graveyard
on the hill
with angels, and old willows
all sun-filled.

You listen to the ticking clock.
The nearby marketstalls
are being taken down.
Twilight falls.

I travel through one
German town and then the rest
and think of Germans lost
who sleep east and west

under strange skies, vanished,
crushed where they went.
Over their graves foreign winds
and bitter mint.

They sleep badly under cold clods
in an unsheltered place
with no canary nearby
no curtain made of lace.

They went to distant places.
They ordered. They obeyed.
They killed. And they sleep
in the bed they made.

Gemütlich—a kind of painting
on pottery cups and plates.
Light flickers on the pitchers,
on the window panes and grate.

A woman grinds the coffee.
The clock strikes. Tall
shadows pass in the white enamel,
bloodied shadows, one and all.

Block 4 Barrack 4 "Apt" C

Mitsuye Yamada

The barbed fence
protected us
from wildly twisted
sagebrush.
Some were taken
by old men with gnarled
hands.
These sinewed branches
were rubbed and polished
shiny with sweat and body oil.

They creeped on
under and around our coffee table
with apple crate stands.

Lives spilled over us
through plaster walls
came mixed voices.
Bared too
a pregnant wife
while her man played *go*
all day
she sobbed alone
and a barracksful
of ears shed tears.

Threads Drawn from the Heart

Sheila Cassidy

And what is it to work without love?
It is to weave the cloth with threads drawn from your
heart, even as if your beloved were to wear that
cloth.

Kahlil Gibran
The Prophet

Every night we were in bed by eleven for, glorying in the little power given to them, the wardresses were strict in their enforcement of the prison rules. Anyone found out of bed, or talking or smoking, was punished by the suspension of the visit of their family, or if they dared to protest, a day in the *calabozo*, a punishment cell.

As I lay in the dark on the first night and watched the glow of forbidden cigarettes, I tried to digest the experiences of the day and I was thankful that no one could see the tears of self-pity that flowed unbidden down my cheeks. After supper I had spoken at length to Francisca and when I had told her that I was certain that I would only be in the camp for a few days she had shaken her head and told me gently that it was the general opinion that I would be detained for two or three months. I stared at her unbelieving as she told me that they had come to the conclusion that the Chilean government would never risk setting me at liberty until the New Year hearings of the United Nations at Geneva were over. The last hearing, in which the Junta had been publicly condemned for the "flagrant disregard of human rights," had been given wide publicity in Chile, and my release, they thought, would therefore be delayed until after the next hearing.

Smiling, she told me that three months was a very short time, and that most of them would be in prison for a year or more. Finally, with the seriousness that characterized these youthful world-changers, she said that experience of life in the community would be very good for me as, like all of them, I had much to learn.

I began to experience that night a sense of conflict that was to torment me for the whole of my stay in Tres Alamos, and which even in England does not let me rest. Fêted and loved as the *"gringa"* who had suffered for their cause, and thus accepted as one of them, I longed to be as other-centred and self-disciplined as they, and yet I found myself naturally expecting the preferential treatment, love and respect that was accorded to me. To be told that I could benefit from a period of this spartan community life with the unspoken implication that I had to learn about the war with self-indulgence filled me with an anguish that shamed me because I knew that they were right.

In bed that night I fought the battle which always seems so absurdly difficult: the fight to be reasonable. I knew that I was incredibly lucky to be alive, and that the experience of living with and getting to know these girls was a privilege that money could not buy. I knew, too, that unless something very unexpected happened, I was safe, and that I would ultimately be released. I realized that, much as I liked to see myself as one of this brave band of women, mine was nothing more than a temporary and superficial participation in their situation, for I would return to my country and my loved ones and pick up the threads of my life. Not for me was the anguish of fears for a missing brother or sweetheart or the knowledge that my family was going hungry to keep me alive. For me release would signify permanent reunion with my family; for my companions it meant freedom but also heart-rending farewells to parents whom they would never see again, as they set off to rebuild their lives in whatever country would accept them. The knowledge of how lucky I was gave me small comfort that night and I could have lain on the ground and screamed like a spoilt child, "I want to go home."

Sleep magically reknit the ravell'd sleave of my care, and I rose in the morning resolved to learn all that I could from my new friends. We breakfasted at the long wooden tables which were ranged round the patio and the standard prison breakfast was greatly improved by the addition of Nescafé to the nondescript hot liquid sent from the kitchen and of margarine for the bread. I found myself sitting opposite the girl who had given me her hairclip. This was Lucinda, a girl of rare artistic ability whom I soon grew to love for her deep sensitivity, unfailing good humour and kindness.

Breakfast was served by a team of girls whose turn it was to work that day. There were six or eight of them and, under the direction of one of the older members of the community and the "economist," they prepared and served the meals and washed up afterwards. It was a good system for, although it meant a day of very hard work, it only came every eight or ten days as everyone took their turn according to the rota.

After breakfast there was quiet activity while beds were made and teeth cleaned then, promptly at nine o'clock, the "workshops" began. Three of the four long wooden tables were occupied, each by a group of girls doing a different type of craft work. At first I thought this was occupational therapy until it was explained to me that the goods made were sold and each worker was paid a wage after new materials had been purchased. Many of the girls were married and had small children; some of their husbands were unemployed, but a greater proportion of them were also in detention, and some of them had disappeared. The children therefore were cared for by the girls' parents or by their in-laws, and in many cases there was a real need for the small contributions they were able to make by selling their work.

There were five workshops which produced in turn sandals, fine leather goods, articles of crochet, soft toys and embroidered blouses. I learned much from the girls who ran these workshops because shortage of money and materials had taught them to improvise in a way that we, in our affluent society, have forgotten. Most important of all, however, I learned about working in a team. Always inordinately proud of my achievements I like to make things on my own, and "all me own work" has long been a saying in my family. It was therefore totally alien to me to finish off something begun by someone less skilled, unless, of course, *I* was bountifully assisting *them*. Likewise, I did not like to have someone else touch my work, for if their help was skilled I could not claim the finished article as my own, and if they were less skilled, then I feared that my handiwork would be spoiled.

This attitude was outside my friends' comprehension. Each of them worked happily, apparently uncomplicated by such emotions, doing that part of the work that they did best or which was allotted to them by the team supervisor. Thus in the embroidery workshop my friend Lucinda worked in the design section, inventing and modifying designs to be embroidered on the blouses, while a myriad of other workers painstakingly washed the material, ironed it, cut it out and made the blouses, and then traced the patterns on the fabric. All over the outside patio (for we were allowed outside at the discretion of the wardress) girls sat in groups meticulously embroidering the peasant-style blouses with fine brightly-coloured wools. Each Friday morning the finished garments were once more washed and ironed and given to the visiting families so that they could be sold among the tight circle of friends of the families of the detainees. In 1976 many of these blouses were exported and sold at exhibitions in support of the prisoners in different countries. They are a true example of the artistic work produced in bleak detention camps throughout the length of Chile, a flowering in the desert that bears witness to the unquenchable flame of the human spirit.

The urge to create something lovely burned like a fire in all the prisons. Underfed and lonely in the snows of Dawson Island the first political prisoners of the Junta, lawyers, doctors, professors and cabinet ministers produced engraved pendants of a haunting loveliness from the finely polished stones that they picked up from the ground under their feet. Later, the men of Chacabuco, the big concentration camp in the northern desert of Chile, produced copper rings made from the wire that had imprisoned them, and engraved pendants from worthless coins.

Perhaps the most fascinating and original of the prison arts was the work in bone. The Chilean national dish is *cazuela*, a beef stew in which a piece of meat is served on the bone in the stock in which it has been cooked, accompanied by a potato and a piece of pumpkin. The prisoners found that it was possible to work with the dried bones and thereafter families were commissioned to bring in the bones from the Sunday *cazuela* and they were carefully washed and dried in the sun and stored until they were needed. It was a skilled art, requiring much patience. The object to be "carved" was drawn on the bone and then cut out with a fine saw. This could take an hour or more, depending upon the hardness of the bone and the skill of the worker. It was then filed smooth and finally sandpapered and lastly polished with an abrasive paste made from zinc oxide powder or, if there was none available, toothpaste. Only certain prisoners found this work to their taste, but they produced the most lovely pendants of which the favourite designs were the dove of peace, or the clenched fist that signified the resistance of the Chilean people. I joined the bone carvers and made a number of crosses which I gave away to my friends. The last and most successful I could not bring myself to give away and when I was interviewed at the airport one of the newspapers reported that I was wearing two crosses, one gold and the other ivory!

The art of the detention camps was fired by two deep human needs: the desire to give to loved ones, and the need to express the multitude of feelings of sorrow and joy, anger, despair and an ever-flowering hope. Because of the constant repression there developed a highly symbolic art, and hidden away because of the intermittent raids were drawings and poetry in which the deepest emotions were allowed to cry out. So strict was the self-imposed emotional discipline to maintain morale that no tears were shed or loved ones publicly mourned, but hearts were poured out on paper and anger exhausted in carving symbols of the fight for freedom.

Many of the poems have been smuggled out and they are a poignant testimony of the anguish in which they were composed. The following poem was written in July 1974 in the public gaol in Santiago where men were herded into dark cells where it is hard not to succumb to bitterness and despair:

> There,
> where the light of the sun
> lost itself
> more than a century ago,
> where all gaiety
> is impossible
> and any smile
> is a grimace of irony,
> where the stone stench of darkness
> inhabits those corners
> even the spiders
> have abandoned as inhospitable,
> and where human pain eludes
> that which can be called human
> and enters the category
> of the unprintable . . .
> There, I am writing.

From the scorched, disused saltpetre mine of the desert camp of Chacabuco comes the cry of a coal miner, over a thousand miles from his wife and children in the green southern town of Lota near Concepción.

> I want my bread, I want the air beyond this wall of wire.
> I look out into the distance over the white roofs of earth
> and can just barely see
> cars crossing the nitrous pampa
> from north to south and from south to north,
> the frontier train on the small tracks
> like a child's toy on the hillside . . .

My hope!
I turn to look at everything:
the gay travelling couple,
the son encountering his mother
the father who is returning,
the blind one who is singing for money
and who never sees the combat planes
quickly devour space, soldiers of the air at war.
I want to return to my earth:
to drink in my hand
the water which has surrendered itself
to the tranquillity of raindrops,
to contemplate the forest,
to stretch out on the grasses
to listen to the trill of birds
to kiss the wheat,
to smell herbs freshly nibbled off branches
by the goat on the rocky crag,
to hear the barking of a dog
or the mooing of a cow.
Such joy!
The afternoon arrives whistling tranquil tunes
and singing songs of freedom.
Walking in the streets without concealing my face
I, miner of Lota, with joyous steps,
lift my sooty face
and with my breast warmed by the heat
extracted from the inner recesses of the earth
by my fist and my soul
reach my home
and joyfully encounter my wife waiting at the door
the children catching at her hem
her smile and her awaited kiss
without room for a tear.
May the darkness be not so dark
and may hatred not close our souls.

So much of this poetry is written in blood and tears for children, husbands and wives. This is a message to his children from a man who like so many was imprisoned because he taught that all men are created equal.

SPEAKING WITH THE CHILDREN

It so happens that I won't be home tomorrow either
and I'll continue beneath the night

that eclipses and erodes
the profiles of the world I know.

If it comes to pass
that I get lost during the night
and don't find the road back home,
I want you to know the reasons for my absence.

I have learned and I have taught that a person is free,
and now I awaken to the rattling of irons and bolts,
Because I loved culture
and humanity's inheritance
the flames have fed themselves with my books.

I did not stain my spirit with hatred,
but I have seen the anguish
of the epileptic terror
of naked men being electrocuted.
I returned to the roads the peasants used,
speaking of a life without miseries.
I explained that work brings dignity
that there is no bread at all
without a sheaf of wheat made noble
by the planting of a seed into the earth
by a simple hand.
For this, among other things,
it so happens,
that I won't be home again tomorrow either
but continue beneath the night.

Doctors, lawyers, teachers, and all the other professional people who had taught "that work brings dignity" now turned their hands and their hearts to manual labour, and almost overnight intellectuals became craftsmen. I was fascinated by the sandal workshop not only because the finished products were charming, but because of the improvisation with materials. The soles of the sandals were made from old car tyres, and the designs on the leather drawn with felt pens. Greek designs taken from some old book were adapted and tooled on to the leather and then the colours picked out in brilliant reds and greens. When the pens ran dry they were refuelled with cologne for the girls had found that the spirit was a solvent for the dye.

Although the majority of the prisoners worked, there was no obligation and some of those who had no need to earn money preferred to work on their own.

When I had settled in I was delighted at the wide range of crafts, for I have always loved to work with my hands. After years of being too busy either studying or working to be creative I threw myself into a multitude of activities. In the first few days I was severely frustrated by lack of materials, for though I was surrounded by a wealth of fabric, wool and leather, I quickly found that it was all spoken for, and when I pleaded for left-over scraps I found that in this economical society there were no leftovers. The instruments, too, were in great demand, and were jealously guarded by the workshop chiefs against careless or inexpert users. It wasn't until I had proved myself as an able worker in bone and various other materials that I was allowed to borrow the precious leather knives and punches to make miniscule Christmas gifts with the remnants that fell from the cobbler's last.

On my first day as I set up "house" in the small place alloted to me I made a bag in which to guard my various treasures. It was made in the style of old-fashioned shoe holders, and had several different sized pockets, in the depths of which I repeatedly lost small treasures such as hair grips or pencil stubs. With my name and a large flower brightly if irregularly appliquéd on it I nailed it firmly to the only bare piece of wall and christened it the *guardahuifa*, a name which is really only funny in Spanish, but means a repository for bits and pieces.

As I surveyed my new home I felt a great need for a crucifix. Not usually a devotee of religious objets d'art, perhaps I sensed that my life here would be so full that in my new happiness I risked neglecting the God to whom I had turned so instinctively in my pain.

I set out, therefore, to mark by bunk with the sign of the cross and eventually found two narrow strips of wood which I glued together and stained with dye purloined from the sandal makers; upon it I hung with fragments of red wool a copper Christ fashioned out of a piece of discarded telephone wire. I nailed it firmly to the bottom of the top bunk so that I faced it when lying in my bed.

> You pray in your distress and in your need;
> would that you might pray also in the fullness
> of your joy and in your days of abundance.
> Kahlil Gibran
> *The Prophet*

three

Childhood

A Dead Child Speaks

Nelly Sachs

My mother held me by my hand.
Then someone raised the knife of parting:
So that it should not strike me,
My mother loosed her hand from mine.
But she lightly touched my thighs once more
And her hand was bleeding—

After that the knife of parting
Cut in two each bite I swallowed—
It rose before me with the sun at dawn
And began to sharpen itself in my eyes—
Wind and water ground in my ear
And every voice of comfort pierced my heart—

As I was led to death
I still felt in the last moment
The unsheathing of the great knife of parting.

Indian Mother

Rosario Castellanos

She always walks with a load on her shoulders: her baby and, then, her simple wares.

Wearily she crosses the mountains that imprison her and descends to the hostile city below.

Once her goods are sold (or pilfered or despoiled), the Indian mother seeks rest. From the streets she is expelled by the insolence of passersby and the profusion and speed of vehicles. She takes refuge instead in the trees—her ancient, trusted friends—in the park. There she remains, in silence. She speaks only with her gods in the church. Weeping, she utters her prayer of humble complaint, her sorrowful imploring and utmost submission.

When the Indian mother returns to her village, she can be seen shepherding her flock, weaving the coarse cloth that will protect her family from the cold, preparing their meager repast.

In her brief moments of repose, she holds her baby on her lap. She hovers over him with a solicitude as anxious as it is useless. She contemplates him with eyes filled with love and guilt. The shadowy depth of her gaze has a name: despair.

For the Indian mother knows that tomorrow's horizons will be the same as today's: misery, ignorance, humiliation. Her hands (hands that motherhood should have filled with gifts) are empty. They will never be fully able to stifle her child's hungry cries, nor pour oil on wounds made by the burdens he must bear. The sorrow of dignity offended will not be forgotten.

Behold, then, a pair of empty hands. Beggar's hands, victim's hands, stalk our consciences with the obsessive tenacity of remorse. No, there is no room for bewilderment. For if anyone has taken from these hands what is rightly theirs, it is we. And who, besides us, can make restitution and fill them once more?

Oh, may sleep elude our brows, may friendship pierce our hearts like thorns, and may songs offend our mouths, as long as the hands of this woman, this Indian mother, remain unable to give her child bread, light, and justice.

On the Road at Night There Stands the Man

Dahlia Ravikovitch

On the road at night there stands the man
Who once upon a time was my father.
And I must come to the place where he stands
Because I was his eldest daughter.

And night after night he stands there alone in his place
And I must go down to his place and be there.
And I want to ask the man how long will I have to,
And I know, even as I ask, I will always have to.

In the place where he stands there is a fear of danger
Like the day he was walking along and a car ran him over.
And that's how I knew him and I found ways to remember
That this was the man who once was my father.

And he doesn't tell me one word of love
Though once upon a time he was my father.
And even though I was his eldest daughter
He cannot tell me one word of love.

My City: A Hong Kong Story

Xi Xi

—and what did you see there
mother asks.

Mother is sitting in a rocking-chair. I tell her I saw cannons. I saw cannons lining the fortress wall. When the time comes for them to go off, I believe they will shake the whole city. I tell her that the cannons I saw were black in colour. Although it is summer, and it was noon, they were warm to the touch, like a sleeping volcano. Though there seemed to be boiling lava inside, the volcano was asleep.

The cannons mother had known were not warm, they were red hot. The cannons mother had known were not sleeping volcanos, they were wide awake. Those cannons blasted basin-shaped holes in the Olympic stadium; those cannons turned a whole plain of peach blossoms into scorching flames. At the railway station the whole floor was littered with single shoes. (If you had come from south station, you would know.)

A mother called out the name of a little girl. The girl was carrying her own little bag on her back, with her clothes and a few days' rations inside. Sewn to her clothes was a square of white cloth on which names were written in black ink. The child's name, and her parents' names. And also her date of birth, her native province, and an address as unpredictable as fate. (If you had come from south station, you would know.)

—did you see the sunrise
mother asks.

I did not. I did not go up the mountain to see the sun rise. That was because the sky had darkened. I can never predict my own fortune. When we left the ancient fortress, we said goodbye to the group of cannons and took a path that goes up another mountain. We walked on for four whole hours. It started to rain. It was a drizzle, like a wet net hanging over our heads. It was because of the rain that we did not go up to a higher peak to see the sunrise.

Looking at the sunrise is like searching for hope, mother says. Those who go to see the sunrise always get up at shortly after three in the morning. All around them is a blur of emptiness. They group together, flashlights in hand, and follow the leader on the trek up the mountain. Though they all have thick clothes on, they still say: Oh, it's so cold. And it is August, the height of summer.

Everyone waits on the peak. If it is a peak surrounded by mountain ranges, and the clouds in the distance brighten first, you would think that these are the colours of sunset. When all the clouds are aglow with bright colours, suddenly, there is the sun, floating in a mountain gorge.

No one can make out the shape of the sun, whether it is round or square; its brilliance is so dense and so blinding that no one can take a good look at it. All one has is a feeling of what the sun looks like. It is like a rapidly revolving, brilliant colour mixer.

Mother likes the sunrise on the ocean. A morning on the embankment, looking at the white sky, so white it was almost transparent. It was already dawn, around six in the morning. A white ball rose out of the distant sea. All of a sudden it shot up from the water as though it had kicked its way out, whipping up a considerable spray. Or perhaps it was like someone taking a dumpling out of a bowl of sweet soup. The white ball was not bright at all; it was rather like snow, or a lump of dough ready for the oven. The white ball was also like the moon rising slowly from the ocean: a series of stills run together. The white ball floating in the sky was so fragile, so pale, and then suddenly it shone forth with the utmost brilliance, and the eye could see it no more.

I did not see the sunrise. We camped on a sizable piece of flat land on the peak. That day we cooked some vegetables which we had picked from the fields we walked past. We also picked some papayas. It was drizzling, and we took a stroll. In the tea fields nearby, the tea shrubs stretched out many tiny twigs. The new tea leaves washed by the rain were like fresh green vegetables, but the old tea leaves were dark.

—what else did you see

asks mother.

Mother gently fans herself with a straw fan. I tell her I saw the convicts. They had on dark blue tops and shorts, and some were naked from the waist up. They were working on the road. I saw them planting trees—digging holes, and then putting the seedlings into the earth. I saw them paving the road, pushing a two-handled wheelbarrow.

When we came down the mountain we walked along the catchwater into a forestation area where there were no roads, and we almost got lost. There were so many trees. Their many leaves could have made up a thick specimen album.

I do not remember how we came out of the forestation area. It was a maze, but it was beautiful. If I had not been able to make my way out, I would have had no regrets. Yet we saw the path outside, charged towards it, and out we came. We walked past a prison, a no-security one. The convicts were working near the catchwater. As we watched them work, some of them asked: Got any cigarettes? Those who did offered them all their cigarettes, and they lit up at once. When they were given cigarettes, they said thank you to us.

Mother recalls two faces. When she walked out of a bakery, she was holding a long stick of bread. Before she had walked down to the end of the street, a black hand appeared before her eyes, grabbed the bread, and disappeared. She looked at the empty paper bag in her hand, dazed for a while. Then she began to look around for the hand that took the bread away. She saw a small, thin man standing next to a lamp post in front of her. He had on a cap which covered his messy hair and a good half of his face, and he stared hard at her with black eyes that seemed to be falling out.

That man, he did not run away, he just stood under the street lamp, rapidly stuffing bread into his mouth, and wolfing it down. The bread was so white, his eyes looked even blacker. Holding a small end of bread in his hand, the man stood under the street lamp, staring at her. (If you had come from south station, you would have known hunger.)

Another time there was a haggard man standing at a street corner. When she walked past him, alone, he said: Give me your purse. And Mother's hand that was holding onto the purse suddenly became empty. She asked: How am I to live then? The haggard man opened the purse and took all the money out. She looked at his face, which was like an old chopstick. It was a heavily lined face, his eyebrows and mouth looked liked straw baskets turned upside down.

How am I to live then? I'm hard up enough as it is, she said. He glanced at her, his sad face all wrinkled up. He took two of the banknotes, put the rest back into the purse, returned it to her, and left in a hurry. (If you had come from south station, you would have known poverty.)

If you had lived in Fisherman Harbour, you would have known violence. A young man, mouth full of chewing gum, said: Oh, so this miserable pittance is all you got? You'll get a taste of my knife then.

—did you see the temple
mother asked.

Mother had seen temples. There was this temple, she says, which had no beams. It was a strangely beautiful piece of architecture. The temple was made entirely of brick, from the ground to the roof. The roof was arched, like a bridge. There were no beams in the temple. When you looked up, you just saw the curves of the arches, one after another. If you stood in the middle of the main hall and looked up at the roof, you could see a skylight. It was just a hole.

There was a temple with a mountain cliff in front of it. A stream singing merrily in front of the mountain, and there were a large number of Buddha statues on the cliff. Some people said that this mountain had flown there from somewhere else. After just one night, there it was, with the statues of Buddha, and the stream at its foot. Those who came to see the mountain liked to go into the cave. They looked up at a small hole in the cave-roof where sunlight comes through from who knows where. They could see a bit of sky from the cave.

I saw the temple. When we woke up in the morning, it was still drizzling. We folded up our tents. We had some dry rations for breakfast. And then we went to see the temple. We saw smoke in the temple. Bunches of incense sticks were burning in the incense burner. There were many stalls around the temple, selling fragrant wood with healing powers, rosaries, and edible peas.

Silly said why don't we go and ask for a sign. He produced a bunch of incense sticks out of nowhere, stuck them into the incense burner, held onto the spill holder with both hands, and knelt down on a prayer mat. He shook the spill holder hard, *clack*, *clack*, and soon spills fell to the ground. The first time there were two. Silly picked them up, put them back into the holder, and shook again. This time he shook out one spill.

—what did you pray for
everyone asked.

—god bless my city
he said.

My Father Would Recall

Anna Swir

All his life my father
would recall the revolution
of Nineteen Five, how he carried
tracts with his comrades,
how he was on the Grzybow Square
when it all began, how the one
who stood to his right, pulled
from under his coat
a red banner and the one to his left
a revolver.

How he marched in a demonstration
in Marszalkowska Street and suddenly the charge
of Cossacks, above his head
horses' hooves, he was fleeing,
a Cossack cut off
his comrade's arm, it fell
on the pavement, another Cossack
cut off the head
of a woman, father was fleeing,
he had to flee
to America.

Father would sing till his death
songs from Nineteen Five.
Now
I sing them.

Child's Memory

Eleni Fourtouni

Every time I think of it
there's a peculiar trickle
on my throat
especially when I clean fish—
the fish my blond son brings me
proud of his catch—
and I must cut off the heads

my hand
holding the blade
hesitates
that peculiar trickle again
I set aside the knife
fleetingly I scratch my throat
I bring the knife
down
on the thick scaly neck—
not much of a neck really
just below the gills—
I hack at the slippery hulk of bass
my throat itches
my hands stink fish
they drip blood
my knife cuts through

the great head is off
I breathe

once again the old image comes
into focus

the proud, blond soldier
his shining black boots
his spotless green uniform

smiling
he lugs a sack
into the schoolyard

the children, curious, gather
he dips his ruddy hand inside the sack
the children hold their breath

what is it, what?
he must have been in our gardens again
looting the cabbage
the children think
their brown hands
fly to their eyes
No
we mustn't look
at it
it's too horrible

but we're full of curiosity
between our spread fingers
we see . . .

the soldier's laughter is gleefully loud
as he pulls out
the heads of two Greek partisans

quickly I rinse the blood off my knife

The Storm: A Poem in Five Parts

Meena Alexander

I. After the First House
Father's father tore it down
heaped rosewood in pits
as if it were a burial

bore bits of teak
and polished bronze
icons and ancient granary;

the rice grains clung
to each other
soldered in sorrow,

syllables
on grandmother's tongue
as she knelt.

She caught the stalks
in open palms
bleached ends
knotted in silk

cut from the walls
the stained
and whittled parts of fans

II. The Travellers
A child thrusts back a plastic seat
rubs her nose against glass,
stares hard as jets strike air,

the tiny men in their flying caps
with bright gold braid
invisible behind the silver nose.

Is there no almanac
for those who travel ceaselessly?
No map where the stars
inch on in their iron dance?

The gulls that swarm
on the sodden rocks
of the Red Sea, the Gulf of Aqaba
cry out to us in indecipherable tongues,
the rough music of their wings
torments us still.

Tears stream down the cheeks
of the child voyager,
from the hot tight eyes.
The mother combing out her hair
behind a bathroom door
tugging free a coiled hem,
cannot see her eldest daughter.

A mile or two away
in an ancient square
guns cough and stutter

Through acres of barbed wire
shutting off shops
and broken parlors
they bear the bodies of the dead

Pile them in lorries
and let the mothers
in their blackened veils approach.

Some collapse
on the steep slope of grief
crawl on hands and knees,
piteous supplication of the damned.

Others race to tear
the bloodstained cloth
gaze at the stiffened brow
and shattered jaw
parts without price
precious sediments of love.

In Baghdad's market places
in the side streets of Teheran,
in Beirut and Jerusalem
in Khartoum and Cairo,
in Colombo and New Delhi,
Jaffna, Ahmedabad and Meerut
on the highways of Haryana
in poorly lit cafes
to the blare of transistors
in shaded courtyards
where children lisp
we mourn our dead

Heaping leaves and flowers
that blossom only in memory
and the red earth
of this mother country
with its wells and watering places
onto countless graves.

* * * *

I sometimes think that in this generation
there is no more violence than there ever was,
no more cruelty, no greater damnation.

We have hung up white flags
in refugee camps, on clothes lines
strung through tenements,
on the terraces of high walled houses.

Peering through my window at dawn
I see the bleached exhausted faces,
men and women knee deep in mud in the paddy beds,
others squatting by the main road to the sea
break granite with blunt hammers

Sickles are stacked
by the growing pile of flint,
the hammers draw blood.

Children scrabble in the dirt
by the hovels of the poor.
In monsoon rain they scrawl
mud on their thighs,
their lips are filled with rain.

I see movie theaters built with black
money from the Gulf,
air-conditioned nightmares
bought for a rupee or two,
the sweaty faces of the rich
the unkempt faces of the struggling middle class.

Next door in a restaurant
food is served on white cloth
and the remnant flung to the crows.

Let me sing my song
even the crude parts of it,
the decrepit seethe of war,
cruelty inflicted in clear thought,
thought allied to brutal profiteering
the infant's eyes still filled with sores.

* * * *

Consider us crawling forward
in thunder and rain,
possessions strewn through airports
in dusty capitals,
small stoppages in unknown places
where the soul sleeps:

Bahrain, Dubai, London, New York,
names thicken and crack
as fate is cut and chopped
into boarding passes.

German shepherds sniff our clothes
for the blind hazard of bombs,
plastique knotted into bras,
grenades stuffed into a child's undershirt.

Our eyes dilate
in the grey light of cities
that hold no common speech for us,
no bread, no bowl, no leavening.

At day's close we cluster
amidst the nylon and acrylic
in a wilderness of canned goods,

aisles of piped music
where the soul sweats blood:

Migrant workers stripped
of mop and dirty bucket,
young mothers who scrub kitchen floors
in high windowed houses
with immaculate carpets,

Pharmaceutical salesmen in shiny suits
night nurses raising their dowry
dollar by slow dollar
tired chowkidars eking their pennies out
in a cold country

Students, aging scholars,
doctors wedded to insurance slips,
lawyers shoveling their guilt
behind satin wallpaper.

Who can spell out
the supreme ceremony
of tea tins
wedged
under the frozen food counter?

Racks of cheap magazines
at the line's end
packed with stars

Predict our common birth
yet leave us empty handed
shuffling damp bills.

* * * *

A child stirs in her seat
loosens her knees,
her sides shift
in the lap of sleep

the realm of dream
repairs

as if a woman
glimpsed through a doorway
whose name is never voiced

took green silk
in her palms

threaded it
to a sharp needle,
drew the pleats together:

a simple motion
filled with grace,
rhythmic repetition
in a time of torment.

In the child's dream
the mother seated
in her misty chair
high above water,
rocks her to sleep
then fades away.

The burning air
repeats her song,
gulls spin and thrash
against a stormy rock

rifts of water
picket light,
a fisherman stumbles
upright

in his catamaran.

The Break

May Opitz

The day I was born, a lot of stories of my life came into the world. Each one carries its truth and wisdom. Those who were around me through my experiences would probably offer an entirely different story of my childhood than I would. I can only tell my story as it made its impression on me, and if the negative events remain clearer in my memory than the positive ones, no apology is necessary. That's just the way it is. I'm going to expose some of myself here. Without accusation or pardon, without claim to reality, in experiencing truth. And in the certainty that everyone who reads my story will understand it differently.

When I was born I was neither black nor white. "Half-breed child" was the first name I got. It is hard to surround a child with love when her mother's grandparents say that the child is out of place. It is hard if the child doesn't fit into the mother's plans and when there's no money. And it all becomes even harder when her white mother doesn't want her child to be taken away to a Black world. The laws don't even allow the African father to take his little German daughter to an African mother.

It's not easy to put a child into an orphanage. She stays there a year and six months.

On the radio a couple somewhere heard about children like me: about those who can't find parents because they are "GI children," because they are handicapped or not blond enough or were born in prison. I became the dream child of a white German family and forgot the months in the orphanage. From that period only my foster parents' stories remain: "You couldn't even stand up. Because of the unbalanced diet you had rickets. Your upper body was fat and overfed, your little legs so crooked that every doctor thought you would never halfway straighten up."

There aren't any "adorable" baby pictures from that period. I'm always mindful of my foster parents' repeated warning: "Be careful! If you were fat as a baby you'll be fat later on, too. Always take care not to eat too much!" From that period I had a constant fear of getting old and fat, later emphasized by the stereotype of the "fat black mammy," that was pointed out to me in many TV films as a frightful warning.

Childhood is when a child wonders a lot, and the words a child speaks aren't understood. Childhood is when a child wets the bed and the parents react with beatings. Childishness is a child doing everything wrong, misbehaving, not understanding anything, being too slow, and making the same mistake over and over.

Childhood is when a child continues to wet the bed and no one understands that the child doesn't do it to punish its parents. Childhood is living in fear of beatings and not being able to get over it. Childhood is getting bronchitis every year and being sent repeatedly to a sanitarium. Years later a doctor says in response to my surprise over the sudden disappearance of my chronic bronchitis after I was fifteen: Didn't you know that that, like bedwetting, is a psychosomatic illness?

Fear that constricts the air passage? There certainly was enough fear. Probably fear of the outside world. Or fear of bursting open. Fear of breaking to pieces from beatings and scoldings and of not being able to find yourself again. Don't protest, swallow instead. Until it can't go any further and seeps out: in the bed or as a brutal coughing pain that drives any person with normal hearing to sleepless nights and fits of rage. That's how it is with oppression. As soon as you start swallowing it, you can be sure that the cup will fill up. When the limit is reached, the bottom will crack or some will overflow. Your own form of "self-defense" is unfortunately completely misunderstood or not understood at all. I can hear my mother complaining: "That darn coughing. It's enough to drive a person crazy!"

Childhood is laughing, too! Playing in the sandbox, roller skating, scooter riding, and learning to ride a bike. Snagging thousands of pairs of tights and taking the maternal anger as the price for a wonderful day. And love!

Love is when Mama cooks something delicious and when the child gets to go along downtown. When the child gets a lollipop at the church bazaar, Christmastime when everything's enchanted, and the child gets to go to the movies. Love is getting up very quietly in the morning and setting the table for Mama and Papa and thinking up nice presents. Love is when everybody goes on vacation in a happy mood.

Longing is the need to sense someone saying: "Hey, little one, are you feeling all right? You mean so much to us. Whether you're Black or white, fat or skinny, dumb or smart, I love you! Come let me hold you." Longing is know-ing what you want to hear and waiting in vain for it to be said. Sadness is when a child thinks she's too Black and too ugly. Horror, when Mama won't wash the child white. Why not? But everything would be much simpler. And the other children wouldn't shout "Negro" or "Negro Kiss." The child would no longer have to be ashamed or be especially proper or well-mannered. "Always behave nice and proper. What people think of you they think of all people of your color."

Life is too hard for me.

1. That damned fear of doing everything wrong. The crying all night if I lost something at school.

"Please, God, don't let Mama and Papa beat me when I tell them."

The constant trembling for fear of doing something wrong and then from such trembling breaking twice as many things as my other sisters and broth-ers. "No wonder nobody likes me."

2. The rotten grade school with the damn homework. Mama supervises everything with the kitchen spoon, especially the arithmetic homework. When the child doesn't figure fast enough she gets a smack on the head; when the problems aren't written neatly enough, the page gets ripped out. Except for recess and gym I don't especially like school. Why can't I ever invite or visit anyone? "Dear God, make Mama and Papa die and let us get other parents. Some that are only loving."

3. My parents say so often that I can't do anything, am nothing, and do everything too slowly. I secretly take one of my father's razor blades and hide it under my pillow. The fear and the longing for suicide—"The child plays with razor blades in bed! You must be out of your mind. Don't you know how dangerous that is? This child is driving me crazy!"

One time I decide to run away from home. I tell my little brother and say good-bye to him. I'm about nine and he is five. Recognizing the seriousness of the situation, he starts crying and tells my parents. They're a little nicer to me—"Dear God make me go to sleep and never wake up again."

4. Who destroyed my dream? The dream of "whiteness" ruined because of my parents' unwillingness and the weak cleaning power of soap. Even eating soap had no effect at all. The dream of "blackness" ruined because of the real-life appearance of my father. Before that, my secret: When I get big I'm going

to Africa. There everybody looks like me. When Mama, Papa, and my white sisters and brothers come to visit, people will point at them. I will console them and tell the people: "Don't do that!" And my parents will understand how it was for me in Germany.

Look! That's my father! He's really Black. "By comparison you're white."— "Does everybody in Africa look that black?"—"Well sure." You've all destroyed my dream.

One time when my father came to visit, all the kids ran away. But he had brought candy for all of us. Maybe we had played the game "Who's afraid of the Black man?" too often: "But what if he comes?"—"Then we run." Maybe the inoculations for black lies, black sins, and the black bogeyman had gone too deep. My brother and I would have liked to run away, but we knew we couldn't. Besides, there were nice presents.

My father was Uncle E. He was Uncle E because he was Uncle E for my white brother, and he was Uncle E because he was not my "father" to me. He remained Uncle E even in letters, when at some point I began writing, "Dear Father." My foster father wanted it like that. He thought that E would like that. Since I knew he was far away and would stay far away except for visits every few years, I did both of them the favor and wrote: "Dear Father." I wrote about my last vacation, my next vacation, my marks in school, and always about the weather. My foster father made sure that I did it right.

I never wondered whether I was supposed to be proud of him or hate him. From the few reports I got about him he seemed to be a positive, educated man, who for some reason had a child that he could not raise himself. I once asked for a story about the woman who brought me into the world. "A woman? She was a floozy." I never asked again.

In this feeling of exclusion I went around in circles. In particular, my foster parents' fear that I would end up on the "wrong track" kept me imprisoned. The fear that I would come home pregnant was the reason underlying every sanction against going out. Their worries and fears strangled me. Before I left home I spent one silent year in my family's home; that sealed the break.

In retrospect I know: my parents loved me. They took me into their care to sort of counteract the prejudice in this society. To give me the chance of a family life that I would never have had in the orphanage. Out of love, a sense of responsibility, and ignorance my parents reared me especially strictly, beat me, and imprisoned me. Cognizant of the prejudices that exist in white German society, they unintentionally adapted their rearing to those prejudices. I grew up with the feeling that they were committed to proving that a "half-breed," a "Negro," an "orphan child" is an equal person. Beside that, there was scarcely any time or space left to discover who I really was.

It took a long time until I became conscious of the fact that I have some value. When I reached the point where I could say "yes" to myself, without the secret wish to change, I was given the possibility to recognize the fissures in myself and my surroundings, to work through them and learn from them. I wasn't broken by my experiences; instead I gained strength and a certain kind of knowledge from them. The situation of not being able to be integrated forced me to the active struggle which I no longer regard as a burden, but rather as a special challenge for honesty. Always having to examine and explain my situation provided me with more clarity about myself and brought me to the recognition that I don't owe anyone an explanation. I hold no grudge against those people who subjected me to their power (and powerlessness) and who from time to time subordinated me or made me subordinate myself. Often I allowed others to make something out of me; now it's up to me to change that.

I've set out on the way.

I Won't Christen You

Elsa Spartioti

We hadn't met yet. I feared the mountains in darkness. I saw the same fear in everyone's face. Danger reddened my mother's eyes and blackened her clothes. There were also words that reached my ears, words bitten into as they were spoken. "Communists, bandits, butchers"

I asked around.

—you'll find out when you grow up,

instead I kept hearing . . . and hearing.

It was early in January 1949, at night, I was wakened by machine gun fire. My father was away.

I start up scared. Mother wraps her arms around me pressing her mouth into my hair and trying to soothe me.

—Don't be afraid, it will be daylight soon, the bandits strike in the dark to give themselves time to flee before airplanes can catch up with them.

Still, your artillery and your machine guns sounded nearer and nearer, and I coiled myself around her feet. When we had made it through, finally, she was telling everyone that if it were not for me she would now be dead which made me stick out my chest with pride. Up to that time I knew I owed her my life, and here she was owing me hers.

A stern woman, she concealed the softness of her heart. Often I pretended to be sick, and these were my happiest moments, she bent over my head, touched my forehead with her lips to see if I had a fever, that was her thermometer, which she did not trust much anyway, she sensed my trick, she let me hug her and that was luscious to me.

She said I saved her then because you all had not yet pulled out, rather you were firing mortars into houses and I hung, terrified, from her neck pulling her down to the floor at exactly the moment when the big window was blown in complete with its casement, heavy frame, glass panes and wall plaster. She wrapped herself around me as if she were the child and murmured, "if we were standing we would have been killed."

The whole house shook as you yelled to us to open so you could surprise the soldiers on the other side of the road, and she fooled you. She jumped out a rear window with me on her back, shells exploding on every side. Our sides touching, we crawled the distance to the hospital, the only safe place in town, turned into an army compound. We entered a large ward filled with people, she bundled me up in a bed sheet and hid me under a bed. There was a rumor you were approaching and you would gather the children and take them with you into the mountains.

She managed to find some bread for me, nothing for herself, and when she heard that the hospital would not hold out long, we left.

So this was the second night. We walked cautiously, down dark alleys, frightened by the sounds of our own footsteps. We had to find refuge in any house; yet, as the night got longer my mother feared even the sound of her hand on the wooden doors. We stopped, listened all around and then she made a cat-like scratch on the doors until, finally, someone heard us and let us in. She pulled me close to her as we were hurriedly taken in. After the first hugs they wanted to hear the latest news from us who were the new arrivals. The hours went by, and on the third morning nothing could be heard, no gun shots, no shouting, only a silence like sleep.

—What's happening? did they empty the town while we were hiding here?

—Give it time, we'll find out soon enough; give it time.

The silence dragged on when, around noon, someone stuck his head out to ask what was going on. Others from houses in the neighborhood did the same. All of a sudden everybody was repeating the same two sentences,

"retreated—they are gone, they have retreated—they are gone."

We ran out into the streets, we ran without stopping, we only stopped to search among the dead, to ask after friends, relatives, some were embracing and kissing, some screaming and throwing themselves on the bodies of the dead, houses burned, smoke covered the town like a cloud that brought a black rain, and I had clamped on the fingers of her left hand. She kept silence with me, and from time to time when her fingers loosened their grip I squeezed my head against her waist so she could feel me and so I wouldn't be lost. We went to our house, and although the sun was up it had gotten dark; it was burned out, gaping holes in it, three corpses dammed up the stream that ran through our garden, she stepped over them,

—wait right here, she said

and when she came out she was holding my father's engraved shell casing from a previous war, a water pot we always kept on the stove, and a tin cup,

"this is all we are left with," she stepped over the killed men once more and we went away.

We reached Thessaloniki by horse-drawn cart, in three days I forgot my terror, perched on her knees so she placed both her hands on my stomach.

My father and other people welcomed us with tears and with shouts, they had heard we had been killed and were mourning for us.

You I had not met yet, and Fanni, even though much older than me, was my friend. When she came back from the mountains we used to get together and talk for hours. It was shortly after the Christmas holidays that her troubles began. Rumor had it that about two thousand guerrillas were ready to capture Naoussa. She did not live in her house because it was too remote. On the night of the offensive she had gone together with other people to sleep at Lanara's mansion. Around nine P. M. they heard the first shots. They hid in the basement until the next day. Things got worse the following night. You had come very close to them and you were constantly firing artillery and mortar shells. You were within a hundred yards and you called out for them to surrender.

They escaped from you by sneaking out the back of the house and they barely got away just before you burned it down. They reached the Security police building where they found twice as many people hiding. But that was where all the gendarmes had gone and they were firing back at you from the roof. It was only a matter of time before they would be trapped in the rubble, and no sooner did the building catch fire than you captured them all. There were rumors that there were foreigners amongst you, Bulgarians, Albanians, but Fanni told me you were Greeks with the initial "D" (for Democratic Army) on your uniforms. You lined them up and trucked them to requisitioned homes. Naoussa looked like it had been entirely captured and nothing was heard except the single howitzer firing from the train station, in some fields about seven kilometers away.

You made straight for the mountains, Fanni had tried to escape in vain, the climb was hard, it was cold, and there were about two feet of snow on the ground. When you came to the first plateau, it was still dark, she could see Naoussa ablaze. You walked in the hours of darkness, and during the day hid under trees, in the snow, so the planes would not spot you.

You walked non-stop for days. You were used to it, but the exhaustion made the others talk crazy, one thought he was in a tavern and was ordering wine and a serving of sautéed chicken livers, someone else was lighting twigs and stuck them in the snow thinking they were wax candles, one woman kept laughing and saying over and over how many almond tarts her mother had baked and lots of similar blabber. Near Messovouni you heard the sound of planes and you had to walk even faster to find a place to hide before you were spotted and attacked. Their shoes were falling apart, they bandaged their feet in rags and head cloths, icicles formed on eyebrows and lashes, boils formed around their mouths, their feet bled. Eleven days later you were in the Florina region in a terrible state. You told them "you are now in Liberated Greece," you took care of them, you gave them meat, bread, marmalade and they recovered, rested for three days with those who suffered frostbite going to a sanitarium; in fact everybody's feet were swollen and purple.

On the fourth day you left for Platy of Prespa, you gave new clothing there, you armed them and began training and indoctrinating them. You treated them exceptionally and, in fact, Fanni told me that you were on good terms with each other also, you never quarreled. On their way to Mount Grammos you gave each an egg dyed red and so they realized it was Easter.

During the sweeping-up operations you kept retreating, getting ever closer to Albania and Fanni slipped away from you before you crossed the border. It was in the evening, she took refuge in the woods, and in the general confusion, rifle shots and mortar shells bursting everywhere, you did not notice her absence. Daylight came, by the grace of God, and she made her way back.

Stories like these nourished my days and nights before I came to meet you. Broken and broke we went to Athens. My father finally found work after many hardships and humiliations. Our name also changed. We now had two last names: "So-and-so—Guerrilla-victims."

Although our life was starting anew in Athens we went to back to Naoussa often. I was too old to feel and too young to understand. We used to stay with relatives and, after the destruction, we never went to our own house. I only sought it out once. I stood by the side of the yard facing the winter room and the library. The ground was gray, and neither snow nor rain could erase the traces of the three days and the three nights that so aged my twelve-year-old life.

That same day, around noon, I heard the grown ups say,

they brought her in, she tried to escape and they made dead meat out of her, they will display her under the big plane tree in the square.

I knew they were talking about you. I never learned your name. You were the "Hyena of Mount Vermion." In my thoughts you had a man's body and the head of an animal. I feared you and I hated you for the crack of the machine guns, the cinders smothering my yard, the stifling despair of my mother's black dresses, my father's bleary gaze. At night I often panicked, being sure you could go through doors and even walls in order to seize me.

I wanted to see you.

Indeed I did.

Without being seen I sneaked out. I mingled with groups of other people who had set out for the plane tree.

I could hear them: "finally, now that she too has been caught, we will be able to sleep in peace." There were those, too, who walked bowed, silent, sad.

When I got to the plane tree the bodies of the adults formed a solid wall in front of me blocking my view. Although I was a tall girl, I could not manage to see you, no matter how much I stretched on my tip toes. Whenever someone turned to the side, I elbowed my way toward the front. They had thrown you on your back under the tree of time. That is what we called it because that is where we counted our age, ten arms joined to embrace the trunk, then nine or eight; it meant we were growing up. Yet its lowest branches were still beyond my reach, its outspread shadow a second heaven.

Your eyes open, turned upward staring at the plane leaves, mouth half-closed and black, a good looking tanned face, the wind disheveling your thick, curly hair, blacker than night, jacket half unbuttoned to just reveal your breast, crossed bandolier tightly buckled on you separating and accentuating your breasts even more through the heavy material, your blood stiff on the khaki garments, your legs splayed where they had thrown you on the ground.

Young, beautiful, beside the roots of the plane tree.

I couldn't pull my eyes away from the bullet holes on your chest, the shadow of the plane tree lifted you above the heads of the people, above the heaven of the tree of time. I wanted to touch you, to button up your jacket, pull your legs together, untangle your hair, remove your bandolier so your breasts could spread. I was lost watching you until someone pushed me,

what are you doing here, this is no sight for a girl your age, go on to your mother.

I returned home. I was punished. They knew I had seen you. They did not ask. I did not say.

At first I preserved your image the way one stores and preserves important things. As I grew older, instead of fading, you have taken root and spread out to the point that I have not been able to distinguish if you were the woman of the plane tree, me, or both.

In all the forty-five years that have passed since the summer of 1950 I did not christen you. I want religion and myth to have no share in your name. You are pressing me against your belly and I can hear the sounds of the mountains, the silence of a cavern, the power of one morning. Your hair overspreads me, shelters me, it is love that persists.

I push it aside,	
I say to you	"teach me"
you say to me	"what"
I say to you	"yourself"
you say to me	"go to the hills"
I say to you	"I am losing my way"
you say to me	"touch my foot track"
I say to you	"it's rough"
you say to me	"put it on!"
I say to you	"I am scared, it smells like blood"

you shake me off your belly angrily, you run away in your stiff battle fatigues and your voice comes . . .

I run after you, naked, soft, salty

"you're alive" I shout at you "because I love you like a breast wounded by the milk I sucked."

My Father and My Mother Went Out to Hunt

Yona Wallach

My father and my mother went out to hunt
and I am alone.
My father and mother are in wonderful hunting fields
and what do I do.
My father and mother are hunting now
My father and mother hunt serious beasts
They never hunt funny beasts
like badgers or rabbits. Haa.
My father and mother are in glorious hunting fields
and I am bored and lazy.
My father and mother are eternal hunters
and I am at home. What is a home.
All the past of my father and mother
is of no matter to them when they hunt
and I too am stored as a memento
of which there will always be one lovelier.

All But My Life

Gerda Weissman Klein

(Chapter I)

There is a watch lying on the green carpet of the living room of my childhood.
The hands seem to stand motionless at 9:10, freezing time when it happened.
There would be a past only, the future uncertain, time had stopped for the
present. Morning—9:10. That is all I am able to grasp. The hands of the watch
are cruel. Slowly they blur into its face.

I lift my eyes to the window. Everything looks unfamiliar, as in a dream.
Several motorcycles roar down the street. The cyclists wear green-gray uniforms and I hear voices. First a few, and then many, shouting something that
is impossible and unreal. "Heil Hitler! Heil Hitler!" And the watch says 9:10.
I did not know then that an invisible curtain had parted and that I walked on
an unseen stage to play a part in a tragedy that was to last six years.

It was September 3, 1939, Sunday morning. We had spent a sleepless night
in the damp, chilly basement of our house while the shells and bombs fell. At
one point in the evening when Papa, Mama, my brother Arthur, then nineteen, were huddled in bewildered silence, my cat Schmutzi began to meow
outside in the garden and Arthur stepped outside to let her in. He had come
back with a bullet hole in his trousers.

"A bullet?"

"There is shooting from the roofs, the Germans are coming!"

Then, in the early gray of the morning we heard the loud rumbling of enemy tanks. Our troops were retreating from the border to Krakow, where they
would make their stand. Their faces were haggard, drawn, and unshaven, and
in their eyes there was panic and defeat. They had seen the enemy, had tried
and failed. It had all happened so fast. Two days before, on Friday morning, the
first of September, the drone of a great many German planes had brought most
of the people of our little town into the streets. The radio was blasting the
news that the Germans had crossed our frontier at Cieszyn and that we were
at war! Hastily, roadblocks had been erected. Hysteria swept over the people
and large numbers left town that day.

I had never seen Bielitz, my home town, frightened. It had always been so safe and secure. Nestled at the foot of the Beskide mountain range, the high peaks had seemed to shelter the gay, sparkling little town from intruders. Bielitz was charming and not without reason was it called "Little Vienna." Having been part of the Austro-Hungarian Empire before 1919, it still retained the flavor of that era. Almost all of Bielitz' inhabitants were bilingual; Polish as well as German was spoken in the stores. In the center of the city, among carefully tended flower beds, stood its small but excellent theater, and next to it the Schloss, the castle of the Sulkowskys, the nobility closely linked to the Imperial Hapsburgs.

Nothing in my lifetime had ever disturbed the tranquility of Bielitz. Only now, when I saw people deserting it, did I realize how close, dangerously close we were to the Czechoslovakian frontier; only twenty-odd miles separated us from Cieszyn.

There had been talk of war for many weeks, of course, but since mid-August our family had been preoccupied with Papa's illness. Mama and I had been away in Krynica, a summer resort, from early June until the middle of August. Papa and Arthur had been unable to accompany us, and we returned when we received a telegram from Papa, suggesting we come home because of the gravity of the international situation. It had been somewhat of a shock to see how ill Papa looked when he met us at the station. His right arm was bothering him and Mama, alarmed, had called the doctor. The doctor diagnosed the illness as a mild heart attack and Papa was put to bed immediately.

The following day two specialists were summoned to Papa's bedside. That same day we received a cable from Mama's brother Leo, who was in Turkey. It read: "Poland's last hour has come. Dangerous for Jews to remain. Your visas waiting at Warsaw embassy. Urge you to come immediately."

Mama stuck the cable in her apron pocket, saying, "Papa is ill, that is our prime concern."

Papa was to be spared excitement and worry at all costs, and visitors were cautioned not to mention the possibility of war to him. Mama little realized the fate we all might have been spared had she not concealed the truth from Papa. Yet on Friday morning, September 1, when German planes roared through the sky, Papa, who had been ill for two weeks, came face to face with reality. It was a tense day. I spent most of it in my parents' bedroom and instinctively stayed close to Papa.

As that first day drew to a close, nobody touched supper, no one seemed to want to go to sleep. Mama sat in a chair near Papa's bed, Arthur and I watched from the window. Horses and wagons loaded with refugees continued to roll toward the East. Here and there a rocket, like blood spouting from the wounded earth, shot into the evening sky, bathing the valley in a grotesque red. I looked at my parents. Papa appeared strange, almost lifeless. The yellow flowers on Mama's black housecoat seemed to be burning. Outside, the mountain tops were ablaze for a moment, then they resounded with a thunderous blast that made the glass in the windows rattle like teeth in a skeleton's head. Everything was burning now. I looked at Mama again. Her soft, wavy, blue-black hair clung to her face. Her large, dark eyes seemed bottomless against her pale skin. Her mobile mouth was still and alien. The red glow was reflected in each of our faces. It made hers seem strange and unfamiliar. There was Mama, burning with the strange fire of destruction, and in the street the horses and wagons, the carts and bicycles were rolling toward the unknown. There was a man carrying a goat on his back, apparently the only possession he had. On the corner several mothers were clutching their infants to their breasts, and near them an old peasant woman crossed herself. It was as if the world had come to an end in that strange red light. Then, all of a sudden, Papa spoke to me.

"Go, call the family and find out what they are doing."

I went downstairs. I sat down next to the phone with a long list of numbers. I started at the top and worked to the bottom, but there were no answers. The telephones kept ringing and ringing. I pictured the homes that I knew so well, and with each ring a familiar object or piece of furniture seemed to tumble to the floor.

I became panicky. It seemed as though we were alone in a world of the dead. I went back upstairs. My parents and Arthur apparently had been talking. They stopped abruptly.

"Nobody answered, isn't that right?" Papa asked. I could not speak. I nodded. There was no longer any pretense. Papa motioned me to sit down on his bed. He embraced me with his left arm.

"Children," he said, "the time has come when I have to say what I hoped I would never have to say. I remember as if it were yesterday the cries of the wounded and the pale faces of the dead from the last war. I didn't think it possible that the world would come to this again. You believed I could always find a solution for everything. Yet I have failed you. I feel you children should go. Mama just told me that Mr. and Mrs. Ebersohn have asked to take you with them to look for refuge in the interior of Poland. I am sick when you most need my strength. I want you to go, children. I command you to go!" His voice had assumed a tone of authority that I had never heard before. I saw Arthur look up startled at the mention of his girl friend's parents. More than ever he looked like Mama, but somehow he reminded me of Papa as he stood there tall, erect, and determined.

Almost without hesitation, he said, "No! We are going to stay together."

My parents' eyes met. I had a feeling there was relief and pride in their faces.

"I hoped you would say that," Papa said brokenly, "not for my sake, but because I hate to cast out my children to complete uncertainty. I believe that God will keep us together and under the roof of our house."

He dropped back exhausted on his pillows. The effort had been too much for him, and sudden stillness fell over the room. Strangely, all sound ceased outside as well and we noted that the sky was no longer red.

When I awoke the next morning everything was as peaceful as ever. The sun shone so brightly in my room. The fall flowers in our garden were in full bloom. The trees were laden with fruit. In my room everything was as it had always been, and what's more, even Papa was out of bed. His arm was in a sling, but he was up, and it seemed so wonderful I was sure the night before had all been a nightmare. No, not quite, because in my parents' faces I could read something that hadn't been there yesterday.

When we met downstairs for breakfast everybody seemed cheerful. Papa was joking. Mama joined in this seemingly carefree banter. The maid had left to be with her relatives. Papa jokingly asked me whether I wanted the job. Nobody mentioned the war. I walked to the radio and turned it on. There was a sharp click, but no sound. I tried the phone, the lights, but all electricity was off. In a way that was good. There was no contact with the outside world. It was a wonderful, peaceful Saturday. But evening brought fury to the end of that last peaceful day. Sporadic shooting started from the rooftops, an attempt at delaying the enemy while our army retreated to Krakow. We looked for shelter in our cellar and sat there through the night. Toward morning the shooting stopped altogether and the vehicles of the Polish army ceased to roll. We came up from the cellar for a cup of tea in the living room. At I sat down on the couch near the window I could see the people outside in an obviously gay and festive mood, talking and laughing, carrying flowers, and everywhere the clicking of cameras.

"Mama, look," Arthur said. "Do you suppose—?" and he broke in the middle of the sentence, not daring to say what seemed impossible.

"No," Mama answered, and then Arthur pulled his watch out of his pocket, the roar of a motorcycle broke the stillness of our home, and his watch fell to the floor. It was 9:10 A.M.

I looked out again. A swastika was flying from the house across the street. My God! They seemed prepared. All but us, they knew.

A big truck filled with German soldiers was parked across the street. Our neighbors were serving them wine and cake, and screaming as though drunk with joy, "Heil Hitler! Long live the Führer! We thank thee for our liberation!"

I couldn't understand it. I didn't seem to be able to grasp the reality of what had happened. What are those people doing? The same people I had known all my life. They have betrayed us.

The breakfast tea turned cold on the table. Papa and Mama looked down at the floor. Their faces were blank. Papa seemed so old, so gray. He had changed so much.

I smelled something burning. A hot coal from the big green tile oven had fallen through the grill onto the carpet. I remembered a similar accident a year or two before and Mama had been terribly upset. Afterward she had turned the carpet so that the burned spot was under the couch. This time I wanted to shout a warning, but my throat froze when I saw my parents staring at that coal. They saw the carpet burn slowly, but they didn't seem to care. Finally, Papa got up and with his shoe carelessly shoved the coal back to the grill. Nobody spoke.

I looked out the window and there was Trude, a girl I had known since childhood. She and her grandmother lived rent-free in a two-room apartment in our basement in return for laundry service. Now I saw her carrying flowers from our garden, white roses of which we had been so proud because they bloomed out of season. She handed them to a soldier, breaking her tongue with the unfamiliar German, "Heil Hitler!" The soldier reached for the flowers, but somebody offered him some schnapps. He took the glass instead, the flowers tumbled to the dusty road, the boots of the soldiers trampled on them.

I started sobbing, crying, releasing all my emotions and anxieties in that outburst. Arthur jumped over to me, put his hand over my mouth. "Are you crazy? Do you want to give us away?" But I did not hear him. The tears felt so good. He finally slapped me. "Think of Papa's life. If they hear you crying—" I couldn't stop. He pulled me down from the couch, dragged me over the carpet, and up the stairs with Mama holding my mouth. They put me to bed, where I cried into the pillow until, exhausted, I fell asleep.

Early in the afternoon the drunken, jubilant mob was still celebrating its "liberation" and hoarsely shouting "Heil Hitler." Papa and Mama smiled. Their smiles seemed more painful to me than my screams and tears, and I learned at that moment that I must not always cry when I wanted. I realized that we were outsiders, strangers in our own home, at the mercy of those who until then had been our friends. Although I was only fifteen I had a strong feeling, more instinct than reason, that our lives were no longer our own, but lay in the hands of a deadly enemy.

The Child of the Enemy

Ursula Duba

my Greek friend comforted me
when she heard
that my father died
she knows how it feels
to be five thousand miles away
and not have anybody to cry with

she rushes to my house
with homemade bread
a chicken dish
flavored with rosemary and thyme
she puts her arms around me
and I cry into her shoulder

my Greek friend remembers
the occupation of her land
by my people
she remembers wounds and scars
of her people tortured by Nazis
men taken away
never to return
mass executions
in her native village
in the mountains of Greece

when Iraq is bombed
and I tell her
how enraged I am
at attacks at civilians
no matter what the reasons

because I remember how it feels
to be a child of six
and live in a city
hit by carpet bombing
surrounded by adults
half crazed with terror and hunger
and when I tell her
how it feels
to crawl out from under
after an air raid
to look down the street
and see whose house was hit
and how I cannot forget
adults whispering in horror
that phosphor bombs
missed the railroad station
and hit the slums instead
and people running through the streets
like living torches
screaming
until they jumped
into the river
to drown themselves

my voice chokes
and tears run down my face
my Greek friend does not comfort me
when she sees my tears of rage
at more suffering of civilians—
my Greek friend leans back
and I see in her eyes
that I am the child of her enemies
she remembers the atrocities
committed by my people
in her native village
in the mountains of Greece

A Little Arab Girl's First Day at School

Assia Djebar

A little Arab girl going to school for the first time one autumn morning, walking hand in hand with her father. A tall erect figure in a fez and a European suit carrying a bag of school books. He is a teacher at the French primary school. A little Arab girl in a village in the Algerian Sahel.

Towns or villages of narrow white alleyways and windowless houses. From the very first day that a little girl leaves her home to learn the ABC the neighbours adopt that knowing look of those who in ten or fifteen years' time will be able to say "I told you so!" while commiserating with the foolhardy father, the irresponsible brother. For misfortune will inevitably befall them. Any girl who has had some schooling will have learned to write and will without a doubt write that fatal letter. For her the time will come when there will be more danger in love that is committed to paper than love that languishes behind enclosing walls.

So wrap the nubile girl in veils. Make her invisible. Make her more unseeing than the sightless, destroy in her every memory of the world without. And what if she has learned to write? The jailer who guards a body that has no words—and written words can travel—may sleep in peace: it will suffice to brick up the windows, padlock the sole entrance door, and erect a blank wall rising up to heaven.

And what if the maiden does write? Her voice, albeit silenced, will circulate. A scrap of paper. A crumpled cloth. A servant-girl's hand in the dark. A child, let into the secret. The jailer must keep watch day and night. The written word will take flight from the patio, will be tossed from a terrace. The blue of heaven is suddenly limitless. The precautions have all been in vain.

At seventeen I am introduced to my first experience of love through a letter written by a boy, a stranger. Whether acting thoughtlessly or out of bravado, he writes quite openly. My father, in a fit of silent fury, tears up the letter before my eyes and throws it into the waste-paper basket without letting me read it.

As soon as term ends at my boarding school, I now spend the summer holidays back in the village, shut up in the flat overlooking the school playground. During the siesta hour, I piece together the letter which has aroused my father's fury. The mysterious correspondent says he remembers seeing me go up on to the platform during the prize-giving ceremony which took place two or three days previously, in the neighbouring town. I recall staring at him rather defiantly as I passed him in the corridors of the boys' high school. He writes very formally suggesting that we exchange friendly letters. In my father's eyes, such a request is not merely completely indecent, but this invitation is tantamount to setting the stage for rape.

Simply because my father wanted to destroy the letter, I interpreted the conventional French wording used by this student on holiday as the cryptic expression of some sudden, desperate passion.

During the months and years that followed, I became absorbed by this business of love, or rather by the prohibition laid on love; my father's condemnation only served to encourage the intrigue. In these early stages of my sentimental education, our secret correspondence is carried on in French: thus the language that my father had been at pains for me to learn, serves as a go-between, and from now a double, contradictory sign reigns over my initiation . . .

As with the heroine of a Western romance, youthful defiance helped me break out of the circle that whispering elders traced around me and within me . . . Then love came to be transformed in the tunnel of pleasure, soft clay to be moulded by matrimony.

Memory purges and purifies the sounds of childhood; we are cocooned by childhood until the discovery of sensuality, which washes over us and gradually bedazzles us . . . Voiceless, cut off from my mother's words by some trick of memory, I managed to pass through the dark waters of the corridor, miraculously inviolate, not even guessing at the enclosing walls. The shock of the first words blurted out: the truth emerging from a break in my stammering voice. From what nocturnal reef of pleasure did I manage to wrest this truth?

I blew the space within me to pieces, a space filled with desperate voiceless cries, frozen long ago in a prehistory of love. Once I had discovered the meaning of the words—those same words that are revealed to the unveiled body—I cut myself adrift.

I set off at dawn, with my little girl's hand in mine.

Dotty Noona

Salwa Bakr

Apart from her father and the officer, his wife and son, almost no one, when the question was asked at the office of the public attorney, knew Noona. The only exceptions were: Hasanein the seller of bread; Futeih the grocer; Salim the man who did the ironing; and the garbage man. The latter, on being questioned, said he had no idea at all about her features, because he was always concerned with looking at the rubbish bin when she used to hand it over to him for emptying into his basket each morning.

Everyone's statements conflicted on the question of her features, for while the officer was certain she was snub-nosed and that her upper jaw protruded slightly, his wife answered at the office of the public attorney, "Did she have any features?" then added, "She was a very dotty girl, very weird." As for her father, he contented himself by saying, as he dried his tears, "She would have been a lovely bride, a girl in a million"—and to prove to the government the truth of his statement, he produced from the inner pocket of his *galabia* a small golden earring with a blue bead, which was the total bridal gift presented by the future husband, whom she had never seen.

Even Noona herself didn't know her own features well. The most she knew was that the officer's son had beautiful black hair like his mother and a vast nose like that of his father, except that the latter's nose had small black specks scattered around on it. She had noticed them any number of times when he got excited and wrinkled it up as he exclaimed "Check" in a voice hoarse and strangled with laughter to his opponent at chess.

In any case, the girl Noona was not concerned about her looks, which she often saw reflected on the surface of mirrors, either in the bedroom of the officer and his wife, or in their son's room, when she would enter to clean and tidy—quickly lest time flew and the school hours came to an end. She would snatch hurried moments in which to search yet again for "the pupil of the eye," that being she never believed existed although the teacher had confirmed it over and over again. Each time, standing on tiptoe, she would crane forward with her short body and get as near as she could to the mirror, then would pull down her lower lids with her swollen fingers, which were covered with burn marks and small cuts, and in bewildered astonishment, get her eyes to bulge out, two black circles, while she peered around in search of two arms or two feet, or a nose or a neck, or any of the human parts of the body of that person, "the pupil of the eye." When, bored, tired and feeling that the tips of her feet had begun to ache because of her stance, she would lower herself, screw up her lips in rage, fill up her mouth with air, or put out her tongue and move it around in continuous circular movements, then go back quickly and start making the beds, hanging up the clothes and putting things in their proper places.

It is impossible to deny that the girl Noona had a secret desire to be pretty and charming, not like the officer's wife, who owned all sorts and kinds of clothes, something short and something long, and something with sleeves and something without sleeves, but pretty, like the teacher whom she used to imagine in the likeness of the fairy-tale princess whenever there came to her from beyond the window, while Noona stood in the kitchen, her beautiful voice asking the girls to repeat after her the hemistich, "Flanks of antelope, legs of ostrich."

"Flanks" used to puzzle Noona greatly, so when she began to repeat it with the girls and listen to the effect of her high-pitched solo voice declaiming "flanks of antelope," she would stop for a while scouring the dish she was washing in the sink, or stirring what was cooking in its saucepan on the stove, and would rest her right leg against her left for a time and start sucking her thumb with relish as she thought about the real meaning of this "flanks" and asking herself, Is it clover? Or candy with chick-peas? Or a young donkey?

The images burst forth in her imagination as she searched for the truth. When the questions defeated her and she discovered that water was beginning a trickle over the top of the sink, or that the cooking had boiled enough, she would apply herself again to her work, while rage and perplexity built up, a huge force within her body, and she would rub and scour the dishes till they were sparkling, or rearrange the spoons and forks in their places more neatly, while muttering the words "legs of ostrich" and looking out of the window enclosed by the iron bars through which she could see the school building opposite, and the open blue sky sheltering it. There travelled up to her the voices of the girls in one strong harmonious sound, and she would feel that she was on the brink of madness, and she would shout, along with them, with all the strength of her throat, "He lopes like a wolf, leaps like a fox."

She yearned to know the secrets of many other things, things she had heard from this magical world hidden from her behind the window, just as she longed to know the true meaning of "flanks," that word on which, through the girls' school, she had made raids from time to time, and which had made her learn by heart strange words she didn't understand and made her wish she would find someone to assuage her heart's fire and explain their meanings to her. She had in fact attempted to get to know the meaning of these words by asking Hasanein the bread-seller about "flanks," but he had just winked at her and raised his eyebrows obscenely and made a movement with his thumb that reminded her of the village women. Though she cursed him and reviled his father and his scoundrelly ancestors, she was frightened after that to make another attempt with Futeih the grocer. She would have made the decision to ask the officer's son, if it hadn't been for what occurred on the day of the square root, which caused her never to think of it again. Surprised one day by her mistress when stirring the onions and scrutinizing them in her search for hydrogen sulphate, which the teacher had said was to be found in them, Noona adamantly refused to tell her the truth of the matter when she asked her in surprise what she was doing. She contented herself by saying that she was looking for something strange in the onions, which caused the officer's wife to say in reference to this occasion—and numerous other occasions—that Noona was dotty and weird and that her behaviour wasn't natural, particularly when she saw her jumping around in the kitchen, raising her legs up high and extending them forwards, in exactly the same way she had seen the girls do when they wore their long black trousers in the spacious school courtyard.

The lady used to say this about Noona and would add, whenever she sat among her women friends of an evening in the gilt reception room the like of which Noona reckoned the headman of her village himself couldn't possibly have seen, that the girl was a real work-horse and had the strength to demolish a mountain, despite the fact she wasn't more than thirteen years of age. She said she'd never throw her out of the house, despite her being mad, specially as maids were very few and far between these days and hard to come by.

Although this opinion didn't please Noona at all, and although the lady once slapped her on the face because of her having sworn at her young son and called him an idiot, she didn't dislike the officer's wife, for she knew that the slap had been a spontaneous reaction, just as Noona's swearing had been.

The boy had been sitting in the living room with the teacher, with his mother seated opposite them knitting and making cracking noises with her chewing-gum, when Noona came in carrying the tea-tray just as the teacher was asking the boy about the square root of twenty-five and the good-for-nothing was picking his nose and looking at his mother stupidly and giving no answer. As Noona had heard a lot from the schoolmistress about square roots, she couldn't help herself, when suddenly the boy brazenly answered four, from shouting in excitement, just as the schoolmistress used to do, "Five, you idiot," which almost caused the tray to fall from her hands. The teacher guffawed in amazement, and the boy ran towards her trying to hit her. The mother, however, got there first, for she had been concerned about the crystal glasses breaking, and had slapped Noona: the one and only slap she had given her during the three years she had been in the house. And whereas the lady didn't lie when she said to the teacher that Noona had no doubt heard that from the schoolmistress, one window looking right on to the other, Noona learnt never to talk about such things with anyone in the house lest the lady might think of dismissing her, for she wished to remain forever where the schoolmistress and the girls were, that beautiful world whose sounds she heard every day through the kitchen window, a world she never saw.

Despite all this there was a fire of longing that burned night and day in her breast for her mother and her brothers and sisters, and a desire to run about with the children in the fields, to breathe in the odour of greenness and the dewy morning, to see the blazing sun when she went out each morning, to hear the voice of her mother calling to her, when she was angry and out of sorts, "Na'ima, Na'ouma, come along and eat, my darling, light of your mother's eyes."

She used to love her real name Na'ima, also her pet name Na'ouma, but found nothing nice about the name Noona which had been given to her by the lady and by which everyone called her from the time of her arrival at the house from the country up until the time she left it for ever on that day after which nothing more was known of Noona. Before that her life had been going along in its usual routine: she had woken as was her habit, had brought the bread, had made breakfast for the officer, his wife and son, had handed over the tin container to the garbage man and had entered the kitchen after they had all gone out. It wasn't until about four o'clock that her life began to change when there was a knock at the door and Abu Sarie, her father, put in an appearance in order to drop his bombshell. After saying hello and having lunch and tea, and assuring her about her mother, and about her brothers and sisters one by one, and chewing the cud with her for a while, her father had said, as he eyed her breasts and body and smiled happily so that his black teeth showed, that he had come to take her back because she was going to be married. He showed her the gold earring that had been bought for her by the husband-to-be, who had returned from the land of the Prophet bearing with him enough money to furnish the whole of a room in his mother's house, and more besides. At that moment Noona's heart had sunk down to her heels and she had been on the point of bursting into tears. Smiling as he saw the blood drain out of her face and her colour become like that of a white turnip, Abu Sarie told her not to be frightened, for this was something that happened to all girls and that there was no harm in it. He asked her to make herself ready because they would be going off together next morning. Then he decided to make her happy with the same news that had made him happy, so he informed her that the lady would give her an additional month's wages as a bonus, also two pieces of cloth untouched by scissors, and that her younger sister would take her place in the job, if God so willed it.

"And everything was normal that night"—so said the officer's wife at the public attorney's office. Her husband and son both agreed with her, and even Abu Sarie himself. Noona had prepared supper, had washed up the dishes, had given the boy tea while he was studying in his room—"and there was nothing about her to arouse one's suspicions," she added—and this was in fact so. What happened was that Noona spent the night in her bed in the kitchen without having a wink of sleep, staring up at the dark ceiling and from time gazing to-wards the window behind which stood towering the school building, with above it a piece of pure sky in which stars danced. She was in utter misery, for she did not want to return to the village and to live amidst dirt and fleas and mosqui-toes; she also did not want to marry, to become—like her sisters—rooted in suffering. The tears flowed that night from her eyes in rivers, and she remained sleepless till dawn broke. She saw with her two eyes the white colour of the sky and the black iron of the window, but by the time the lady called out to her to get up and go to the market to buy the bread, sleep had overcome her. She dreamed of the schoolmistress and the girls, and of the officer's son who, in her dream, she was slapping hard because he didn't know the square root of twenty-five. She also saw "flanks," and it was something of extreme beauty; she didn't know whether it was a human or a *djinn*, for it seemed to be of a white colour, the white of teased cotton, with two wings in the beautiful colours of a rainbow. Noona seized hold of them and "flanks" flew with her far away, far from the kitchen and from the village and from people, until she was in the sky and she saw the golden stars close to, in fact she almost touched them.

Those who had seen Noona on the morning of that day mentioned that her face had borne a strange expression. Both the officer and his wife said so, confirming that the look in her eyes was not at all normal when she had handed her master his packet of cigarettes as he was about to go out and when her mistress had asked her to straighten her kerchief before going to buy the bread.

The officer's wife was heard to say, with many laughs, to her women friends, after having told them the story of Noona, as she sat with them in the large living room, "Didn't I tell you—she was crazy and altogether dotty? But as for her sister, I can't as yet make her out."

Diaspora

Diana Der-Hovanessian

"Children of massacre,
children of destruction,
children of dispersion,
oh, my diaspora . . ."
someone was calling
in my dream.
Someone was explaining
why Armenian children
are raised with so much
wonder, as if they
might disappear
at any moment.
"Tsak. Tsakoug."
Someone was explaining
why Armenian sons love
their mothers to excess,
why daughters-in-law are
cherished, why mothers-
in-law are treasured,
why everything
is slightly different
in an Armenian home,
stared at,
as if it might melt.
Someone was telling me
why Armenians love
earth and gardening so much
and why there is a hidden rage
in that love.
Someone was explaining

why I surround
myself with green plants
that do not flourish
in spite of great care.
"The slant of the sun is wrong."
Someone was gently chiding
for the strange angle of
my outside plants.
Someone was saying
I spoke English with a slight accent
even after three generations.
Someone was calling
in a forgotten language.

four

Exiles and
Refugees

Song

Muriel Rukeyser

The world is full of loss; bring, wind, my love,
My home is where we make our meeting-place,
And love whatever I shall touch and read
Within that face.

Lift, wind, my exile from my eyes;
Peace to look, life to listen and confess,
Freedom to find to find to find
That nakedness.

The Aftermath

Agate Nesaule

My mother was taken away by the soldiers again, this time because a meal she had been ordered to supervise was unsatisfactory. The hungry women in the kitchen had eaten most of the meat, and the soldiers held my mother responsible. We were all taken outside again to be shot, but a different officer ordered us to be taken back inside. The violence and chaos in the basement continued.

But the story grows repetitious.

Gradually things changed. Fewer soldiers entered the basement, fewer stayed. There was nothing more for them to find. Finally one morning, about ten days after the soldiers had first arrived, only women and children remained. We had been taken outside earlier that morning to watch as three soldiers were shot for violating the order against killing civilians. They were evidently the same who had shot Heidi's mother, though they looked like all the rest. It was the last execution we were forced to witness.

Afterwards the soldiers drifted away. It took us a while to realize that no one was standing watch over us so that we would not leave the basement. No one was cursing or threatening us. We sat still in the desolate space for several hours before we surmised that evidently we were free to go.

We walked down the lake path in the direction of the village, then crossed the fields to an abandoned farm. The soldiers were probably still in the village, so that going there was dangerous. One of the women in the basement had come from the woods, where she had seen a strange signaling station, about a day's walk from Lobethal. She wished she could have stayed there forever. Behind the huge mirrors and searchlights were buildings full of food and supplies. She had eaten canned meat and thick sweetened milk and had carried some with her.

My mother and Aunt Hermine speculated about trying to find this place, but finally decided against it. It was too far away for us to walk. Ōmite was exhausted, Astrida was flushed and feverish, her skin gray from the ashes and dust with which she had tried to disguise herself, and I felt weak because of the pain in my chest. Even if we did get there, the station might be occupied or looted by the soldiers, or both. And my father and uncle and cousin would never find us if we went too far. If they were still alive and if they were released, they would look for us in Lobethal. If they could not find us, they might return to Latvia, and we would never see them again.

For several days we walked furtively from one abandoned farm to another. We made makeshift beds out of any old clothes we could find, so that we could all huddle together in the same space in the corner of a room furthest away from the doors and windows. We looked for food, but except for a few raw potatoes and beets, we did not find much.

Sleeping was hardest in these early days and for months afterwards. I would stretch out, close my eyes, count to a hundred and back, as my mother had told me to do, but I would still be awake when I finished. I could feel soldiers creeping toward us. When she asked me if I had said "Our Father," I nodded and counted to a hundred a second time instead. As I felt myself drifting off to sleep, I would jerk myself awake because I thought that with my eyes closed I would not hear the approaching soldiers. Or I would doze off, only to be startled wide awake, my heart pounding because I felt soldiers' hands fastening around my throat. Everyone else was usually awake too, listening in silence, praying that the far-distant trucks would continue on their way, past us. I would give up trying to sleep and watch the moonlight shining into uncurtained windows and over the bare floors, over my sister and mother and grandmother. Each was lying very still, pretending to sleep, in order not to disturb the others.

Finally there did not seem to be much point in wandering about the countryside like this, and we decided to go back to Lobethal. Food had been stored there, and my father and the others might be there, or at least we might get news of them. The soldiers might still be there too, but we had nowhere else to go.

The road from the gate was empty, but the ditches were littered with bleached and misshapen photographs, empty gasoline cans, ripped clothing, single shoes. The windows of the main building were smashed, the doors off their hinges, the locks broken. The sun was very bright; flies and insects buzzed on the littered veranda. It was all very familiar, unsurprising, even right somehow.

We moved slowly through the rooms, afraid of what we might see next.

Everything that could be smashed had been, but we found no corpses. The kitchen was empty, the floor littered with broken cups and bowls. Flour had been scattered in a fine film over everything. No one was there, but someone had wiped clean the top of one of the huge institutional stoves and lined up a few pots.

We made our way to the basement. We were anticipating the jellied meat and the sweet preserves, we were ravenously hungry. But when we opened the door to the main storage room, we saw that everything there had been smashed. The stench of rotting food mixed with excrement rose to meet us. We held our breaths, covering our nostrils and mouths with our hands. Shards of glass were embedded in the foul slippery mess, and we tried to avoid stepping into the deepest parts.

Except for the sauerkraut, the drunken soldiers had destroyed everything. The wooden barrels where the sauerkraut had been stored were licked clean. Nothing was left for us to eat.

The stairs creaked behind us and we froze in terror. It should not have made much difference when we were killed, but we were constantly afraid anyway. We stood still, looking guiltily at each other, breathing the foul air, our hearts pounding. The steps came closer.

When the door was pushed aside, it was only Frau Braun, the dead director's wife. Her face was haggard, her eyes red, her clothes hung loosely about her. She was wearing what looked like one of Pastor Braun's jackets over a shapeless summer dress. Her hair was limp, her dark eyes were enormous. She bore little resemblance to the fashionable woman she had been just a few weeks ago. Then, wearing strings of pearls and a smart suit with padded shoulders, an alligator bag held firmly in her hand, she had sat confidently next to her husband when they set off to see the officials in Berlin.

She shook her head, anticipating our questions. "There's nothing to eat here. But they have carrots, over behind the barns. They are boiling them now."

I turned to go, I was halfway up the stairs, running past Frau Braun.

"Would we be welcome?" my mother asked, and I stopped, afraid of what Frau Braun would say. She had always been cool towards my mother, perhaps because she disliked Pastor Braun's evident attraction to her.

Frau Braun hesitated, then said kindly, "Everyone is welcome. This is Lobethal, we welcome the homeless here."

Then she looked directly at my mother. "I am glad you have come back," she said, "it's much safer for you here."

"Thank you," my mother said, her voice trembling, "thank you for your great kindness."

"And we also need you here. You can help us clean all this up." Frau Braun gestured at the layer of rotting food and filth. It did not seem possible this basement could ever be immaculate and orderly again, let alone filled with food and supplies.

"Carrots," I said. I was worried that there would be none left if we waited. I also hoped that Frau Braun would come with us, so we would not be driven away by the people who had them. I knew they were not ours and we had no right to them.

"Come," Frau Braun said, "I'll show you where." She brushed past me, then took my hand. "It isn't very far."

Later that afternoon we walked what seemed like endless miles to the village hall. Here too the windows were shattered and most had been boarded up, but a few unshaven, tired men stared out through the cracks. More men looked out between the bars in the second-floor windows. A Russian soldier sat tilted back in a chair in the entrance, his gun resting on his knees. He stretched lazily and squinted at us in the afternoon sun, but he made no attempt to drive my mother and sister away.

My mother talked to a few of the men closest, then called up to those staring out of the second-story windows. After a commotion, a wait and another commotion, my father appeared in the window above us. My Uncle Gustavs and Cousin Guks were behind him. Thinner, with blue circles under their eyes, they looked tired past the point of exhaustion.

"Are you alive? Are you all right?" my mother called.

"It's been terrible," said my father.

"I'm sorry. Have you had anything to eat?" my mother asked.

"We are all right, Valda. We are still alive." My mother's brother interrupted whatever else my father was going to say. "Are you all right yourself? Where is Hermine? Is Astrida all right?"

My mother cupped her hands again. "Yes, we are all right. Hermine and Astrida too." Her voice was lifeless.

We stood silent, looking at each other, too far away to talk or to touch.

"They took my wedding ring." My father raised his hand and pointed to the bare finger where the ring had been. He seemed to have forgotten that we had all seen him struggling to remove the ring while the soldier laughed.

"Later a soldier ordered me outside, away from the others. I thought he was going to shoot me. But he only made me take off all my clothes in the lavatory and he took them. He took my boots too, I am barefoot." He gestured toward his feet, as if we could see them.

My mother reached her arms towards him to comfort him. I could see the white indentations on my mother's fingers and wrist. She did not say anything about her own missing gold wedding band and other rings, and he did not ask. Something much greater than possessions had been taken from them both.

"We will be released soon," said Uncle Gustavs, "maybe tomorrow. All they are waiting for is another list of Nazi officers to check us against, and there isn't anyone like that here." The men crowding around the windows were either old or they were very young boys who had somehow escaped the final conscriptions at the end of the war.

"Will you be all right?" my mother asked my father.

"Yes." His voice shook a little, and I was afraid he was going to cry, but he did not. "They wanted to shoot me earlier, but Pastor Braun intervened. He saved me. I am grateful to God and to Pastor Braun."

"Yes," my mother said, listlessly.

We stood about for a while longer, gazing up. There wasn't much else to say, and we were afraid to make the soldier angry by staying too long. We waved goodbye and started back to Lobethal.

I had been longing to see my father again, and when he came to the window, my heart leapt wildly with joy. Now, walking back to the Institution, nobody said anything. My mother's face was sad, and I did not ask her to smile. Rather than being happy as I had expected to be, I felt sad. A permanent gray film spread over everything.

My parents were reunited. We all worked very hard to clean up the chaos and filth. We carried buckets of foul-smelling garbage to the back of the house, swept up broken glass and picked up the litter that lined the roadsides. We watched the adults board up windows, boil whatever soiled clothing still looked usable, scald the surfaces in the kitchen and scour the few unbroken dishes. A huge fire blazed outside on which we piled everything that could not be salvaged. A few of the inmates were already sick with dysentery and typhoid, so the cleaning must have been part of a futile attempt to check the spread of the disease as well as a way to reestablish order.

One by one the rooms were cleared. Our family shared a single room, by choice rather than by necessity, since many rooms on either side stood bare and empty. Later, when Ōmite got sick with dysentery, she moved into one of these rooms because she feared infecting us. When we heard trucks or tanks at night, we listened together.

Everyone slept badly. People went about exhausted, ashen-faced, their eyes rimmed with red. But during the day, we worked. The only hope lay in trying to restore order.

Maybe my parents talked to my sister and me, maybe they talked to each other about what had happened, but I cannot remember them saying anything at all. I see them now, silent, working instead of speaking, my mother in a coarse gray dress, down on her hands and knees, scouring the floors with sharp sand in the absence of soap, my father dragging broken furniture and stained mattresses towards the pyre in the backyard. I stayed where I could watch my mother. But I was afraid to get too close to her.

I remember others talking, though; in fact, only the stories remain vivid from this period. People told them as we stood leaning on brooms and rakes around the pile of broken, excrement-smeared furniture and watched it burn. Or we sat in the sun on rough gray blankets or burlap, the ruins of the church and a wing of the bombed orphanage in the distance behind us. The stories seemed inordinately funny. Women lifted their aprons and wiped tears that had gathered from laughing too hard, the few men repeated the punchlines and burst into raucous laughter.

One story was about high-ranking Russian officers, including generals, giving a formal ball in one of the mansions they had commandeered in Berlin. Common soldiers and prostitutes—that is, the starving German women who followed them—were not even allowed into the ballroom; the dance was going to be much too elegant for them. The orchestra struck up a polonaise, the lights strung on trees glistened in the garden, the tables groaned with food. At first some beautiful German women arrived. They too were camp followers, but they were friends of the officers, not of the common soldiers. These women were well dressed and well fed. They wore evening gowns and light summer wraps, flowers and jewels adorned their hair, they talked charmingly of music and art. Only German women knew what real elegance was, only they had taste.

Next came the fat Russian women, wives of the officers. The Russian women were coarsely painted, their hair was tightly curled, but they were wearing satin and silk nightgowns—yes, nightgowns. They had been allowed to choose whatever they wanted from the warehouses full of finery that had been taken away from civilians and this is what they had chosen, nightgowns. No self-respecting German woman would be seen outside her bedroom in one of those. Weren't the Russian women stupid, fat, uneducated, inferior, dumb? "Charming, charming," a Russian general had murmured. In spite of his power and privilege, he was an ignorant bumpkin too. "Charming, charming," we squealed hysterically.

Another story was about a Russian soldier who had stopped an old woman on the street and had made her give up the man's overcoat she was wearing. Soldiers did this all the time; we had all seen them point to boots, coats, shoes, anything they wanted, now that no one had any jewelry left. The old woman cried that she was cold, she begged to be allowed to keep her coat, she would freeze to death without it. But the soldier was unmoved. The old woman got down on her knees and kissed the soldier's hand, then his foot. She begged him to remember his mother and at least to exchange coats. The soldier, drunk and impatient, took the old woman's coat, but in a sentimental gesture he flung his stinking, tattered army jacket on the ground for the old woman.

And guess what? The old woman was really very clever, she knew what she was doing. The sleeves and pockets of the filthy jacket were lined with hundred and hundreds of gold watches. The greedy soldier had been too drunk to remember his treasure. The watch would keep the woman well fed and warmly clothed; she could trade them one by one. She could eat whatever she wanted for the rest of her life, she could stay warm and snug in her house forever. But the cruel soldier would wake up with a terrible hangover the following morning and would he be sorry! He would search for the old woman but would never find her. Finally the soldier would have to report for duty, but he would have no army coat, so he would be punished. He would be shot, as he deserved. As he was waiting for the bullets to tear him apart, he would cry aloud and beg forgiveness for looting and robbing and raping and beating and killing.

The pleasure of this story was further enhanced by an incident that took place a few weeks later. The soldiers ordered us all into the dining hall at the

Institute to watch a film about the victory of the Russians over the Germans. A sheet was tacked onto a wall, and we sat on benches facing it, while my mother translated as an officer spoke about Russians liberating many countries, for which we should all be grateful. He told us that the Russians had been minimally assisted by the Allies in their great victory as we would see, but that we should get down and kiss the earth because we were now in Russian hands.

Finally they turned out the lights and the screen lit up. Tanks and trucks filled with American soldiers rolled down the streets, women and children offered flowers and waved flags. I had never seen a movie before, I thought it was magic. This was better than the tiny people who I had once believed lived inside radios. It was possible to sit here and see something that had happened earlier somewhere far away. I was entranced. The cameras shifted to a square filled with soldiers expecting the historic meeting of General Eisenhower and General Zhukov in Berlin. A stern voice spoke of the significance of this moment, the victorious Allied forces coming together in Berlin. Eisenhower walked towards Zhukov with a determined step; the military band played. Zhukov came towards him eagerly, his arms extended in welcome.

"*Ubri, Ubri*,"—watches, watches—someone shouted from the back of the dining room. The timing was exactly right, the mocking imitation of the Russian accent perfect. Zhukov was after Eisenhower's watch. The audience exploded with laughter.

The projectionist turned off the film and turned on the lights. Soldiers with guns pushed between the tables and benches looking for the culprit. In front of the blank screen, the officer stood scolding. We managed to stifle our laughter.

Finally the lights were turned off again and the film was shown from the beginning. The soldiers were lined up in the square again, flags waved, the band played the welcoming march. Zhukov stretched out his arms expectantly.

"*Ubri, Ubri*," came a shout from a different part of the room.

"*Ubri, Ubri*," a voice like the one that had spoken earlier replied.

We laughed and could not stop when the soldiers turned on the lights again. They dragged a few inmates to their feet. By slapping one of them, the soldiers finally succeeded in getting everyone in the audience to sit straight-faced.

They turned off the lights again. Shouts of "*Ubri, Ubri*" erupted as soon as the first Russian soldier appeared on the screen. This time they turned on the lights and did not try to show the film again. Over the shouts of the soldiers, we filed out, snickering. The common laughter almost made up for not see-ing the rest of the movie. For several days afterwards all anyone had to say was "*Ubri, Ubri,*" and we would collapse with laughter.

Other stories had to do with food, especially with the difficulties and de-ceptions in finding it. A man secretly traded his wife's wedding ring for two cans of butter on the black market. He had been offered a taste of it from a can he had been allowed to select himself. The butter was indescribably deli-cious—creamy, fresh, cool, sweet, glistening. But when he got home and opened the can, it held gritty mashed potatoes. He opened the second can and that too was filled with the same inedible mess. And for this he had given his wife's wedding ring.

Another man was offered a pork roast, so he dug up all his family treasure that he had buried earlier and took it to the railroad station where he was to meet his contact, a man with dark skin and darker eyes. They exchanged suit-cases surreptitiously, and the man started for home happy, his mouth watering for the pork roast he would have for dinner. But when he set his suitcase down on the next platform, a thin trickle of blood seeped out, as he had feared it would. A Russian soldier noticed it and ordered him to open the suitcase. The man begged and tried to bribe the Russian to split whatever the suitcase con-tained, and the soldier finally agreed. But when they opened it, no roast or ham greeted their eyes. Inside was the corpse of a small child, carved into chunks, and the severed head, with the eyes wide open, staring at them.

I spent a lot of time thinking about these stories, inventing variants and new endings. I would somehow get to Latvia and dig up the silver samovar and spoons my father had buried next to the day lilies and irises at the Parsonage. I would only stop to pick up another pair of boots for my father, which looked like the ones I imagined my mother's Uncle Žanis wearing in the dark forests of Russia. These boots would bring my father power and happiness. I would hurry back to Germany and successfully trade all the treasure because I would know not to accept anything sight unseen. Or I would walk into the woods and find the signaling station filled with cans of meat and sweetened milk. I would somehow convince a soldier to give back my mother's and father's wed-ding rings, and my parents would be happy again. All the uncles and aunts would gather once more for a huge meal. Or I would meet the old woman who had the soldier's coat, and if I was very good, she would give me some of the watches and jewels. My mother would be overjoyed, she would kiss me and say, "Thank you, precious." Everything would be the way it was in Latvia, only better.

These stories and my daydreams underlined what was happening in Lobethal and elsewhere. As the supply of carrots dwindled, people told fewer stories, they grew grimmer, we laughed less at our conquerors. Starvation began in earnest.

Hilda wandered around muttering, her already slender body now thin to transparency. She was pregnant. The fetus clamped onto her frame, his cruel Mongolian eyes narrowed even further, seemed visible under her clothes, sucking nourishment out of her, pulling her downwards, strangling her. Ōmite had tried to keep an eye on her, and my mother and Frau Braun took over when my grandmother got sick. But one night Hilda drowned herself in the lake, just as she had threatened to do.

I used to dream about her during the years I was married. I would see her thrashing about in the dark water, struggling not to be pulled under by the monstrous fetus that would not let her go. She tried to speak, to call for help, to explain herself, to scream, but no words would come. No one could hear her. I woke in terror at four each morning during those long years, but I tried to forget about it during the day. The war had not been so bad, no one in my family had been killed, as others had. I was a failure because I could not forget about it. During the long gray years I stayed married, I kept dreaming about Hilda because there was no one who had the courage to hear, no one I trusted enough to tell. There was no one with whom I could talk in bed.

Exile

Eva Hoffman

The worst losses come at night. As I lie down in a strange bed in a strange house—my mother is a sort of housekeeper here, to the aging Jewish man who had taken us in in return for her services—I wait for that spontaneous flow of inner language which used to be my nighttime talk with myself, my way of informing the ego where the id had been. Nothing comes. Polish, in a short time, has atrophied, shriveled from sheer uselessness. Its words don't apply to my new experiences; they're not coeval with any of the objects, or faces, or the very air I breathe in the daytime. In English, words have not penetrated to those layers of my psyche from which a private conversation could proceed. This interval before sleep used to be the time when my mind became both receptive and alert, when images and words rose up to consciousness, reiterating what had happened during the day, adding the day's experiences to those already stored there, spinning out the thread of my personal story.

Now, this picture-and-word show is gone; the thread has been snapped. I have no interior language, and without it, interior images—those images through which we assimilate the external world, through which we take it in, love it, make it our own—become blurred too. My mother and I met a Canadian family who live down the block today. They were working in their garden and engaged us in a conversation of the "Nice weather we're having, isn't it?" variety, which culminated in their inviting us into their house. They sat stiffly on their couch, smiled in the long pauses between the conversation, and seemed at a loss for what to ask. Now my mind gropes for some description of them, but nothing fits. They're a different species from anyone I've met in Poland, and Polish words slip off of them without sticking. English words don't hook on to anything. I try, deliberately, to come up with a few. Are these people pleasant or dull? Kindly or silly? The words float in an uncertain space. They come up from a part of my brain in which labels may be manufactured but which has no connection to my instincts, quick reactions, knowledge. Even the simplest adjectives sow confusion in my mind; English kindliness has a whole system of morality behind it, a system that makes "kindness" an entirely positive virtue. Polish kindness has the tiniest element of irony. Besides, I'm beginning to feel the tug of prohibition, in English, against uncharitable words. In Polish, you can call someone an idiot without particularly harsh feelings and with the zest of a strong judgment. Yes, in Polish these people might tend toward "silly" and "dull"—but I force myself toward "kindly" and "pleasant." The cultural unconscious is beginning to exercise its subliminal influence.

The verbal blur covers these people's faces, their gestures with a sort of fog. I can't translate them into my mind's eye. The small event, instead of being added to the mosaic of consciousness and memory, falls through some black hole, and I fall with it. What has happened to me in this new world? I don't know. I don't see what I've seen, don't comprehend what's in front of me. I'm not filled with language anymore, and I have only a memory of fullness to anguish me with the knowledge that, in this dark and empty state, I don't really exist.

Mrs. Lieberman, in the bathroom of her house, is shaving my armpits. She had taken me there at the end of her dinner party, and now, with a kind of decisiveness, she lifts my arms and performs this foreign ablution on the tufts of hair that have never been objectionable to anyone before. She hasn't asked me whether I would like her to do it; she has simply taken it upon herself to teach me how things are done here.

Mrs. Lieberman is among several Polish ladies who have been in Canada long enough to consider themselves well versed in native ways, and who seem to find me deficient in some quite fundamental respects. Since in Poland I was considered a pretty young girl, this requires a basic revision of my self-image. But there's no doubt about it; after the passage across the Atlantic, I've emerged as less attractive, less graceful, less desirable. In fact, I can see in these women's eyes that I'm somewhat of a pitiful specimen—pale, with thick eyebrows, and without any bounce in my hair, dressed in clothes that have nothing to do with the current fashion. And so they energetically set out to rectify these flaws. One of them spends a day with me, plucking my eyebrows and trying various shades of lipstick on my face. "If you were my daughter, you'd soon look like a princess," she says, thus implying an added deficiency in my mother. Another counselor takes me into her house for an evening, to initiate me into the mysteries of using shampoos and hair lotions, and putting my hair up in curlers; yet another outfits me with a crinoline and tells me that actually, I have a perfectly good figure—I just need to bring it out in the right ways. And several of them look at my breasts meaningfully, suggesting to my mother in an undertone that really, it's time I started wearing a bra. My mother obeys.

I obey too, passively, mulishly, but I feel less agile and self-confident with every transformation. I hold my head rigidly, so that my precarious bouffant doesn't fall down, and I smile often, the way I see other girls do, though I'm careful not to open my lips too wide or bite them, so my lipstick won't get smudged. I don't know how to move easily in the high-heeled shoes somebody gave me.

Inside its elaborate packaging, my body is stiff, sulky, wary. When I'm with my peers, who come by crinolines, lipstick, cars, and self-confidence naturally, my gestures show that I'm here provisionally, by their grace, that I don't rightfully belong. My shoulders stoop, I nod frantically to indicate my agreement with others, I smile sweetly at people to show I mean well, and my chest recedes inward so that I don't take up too much space—mannerisms of a marginal, off-centered person who wants both to be taken in and to fend off the threatening others.

About a year after our arrival in Vancouver, someone takes a photograph of my family in their backyard, and looking at it, I reject the image it gives of myself categorically. This clumsy looking creature, with legs oddly turned in their high-heeled pumps, shoulders bent with the strain of resentment and ingratiation, is not myself. Alienation is beginning to be inscribed in my flesh and face.

I'm sitting at the Steiners' kitchen table, surrounded by sounds of family jokes and laughter. I laugh along gamely, though half the time I don't understand what's going on.

Mrs. Steiner, who is Polish, has semiadopted me, and I spend whole days and weekends in her house, where I'm half exiled princess, half Cinderella. Half princess, because I'm musically talented and, who knows, I may become a famous pianist one day. Mrs. Steiner was an aspiring pianist herself in her youth, and she takes pleasure in supervising my musical progress: she has found a piano teacher for me, and often listens to me play. However, the Steiners are fabulously rich, and I am, at this point in my life, quite fabulously poor—and those basic facts condition everything; they are as palpable as a tilted beam that indicates the incline between us, never letting me forget the basic asymmetry of the relationship.

The Steiners' wealth is quite beyond the Rosenbergs', and quite beyond my conception of actual human lives. It exists on some step of the social ladder that jumps clear out of my head, and I can't domesticate its owners to ordinary personhood. Surely, the rich must be different. If I feel like a fairy-tale character near them, it's because they live in the realm of fable. Rosa Steiner is a stepmother with the power to change my destiny for good or evil. Mr. Steiner simply rules over his dominion, quietly, calmly, and remotely. I wouldn't dream of revealing myself to him, of making an imposition on his attention.

This is, of course, only one part of the story, though it is the part of which I am painfully conscious. Stefan Steiner accepts my presence in his domestic life graciously. And as for Rosa, she is, aside from everything else, a friend who understands where I come from—metaphorically and literally—better than anyone else I know in Vancouver. In turn, there is something in her I recognize and trust. She is a vivacious, energetic woman in her forties, beautiful in a high-cheekboned, Eastern European way, with a deep, hoarse voice and with a great certainty of her own opinions, judgments, and preferences. She reminds me of the authoritative women I knew in Poland, who did not seem as inhibited, as insistently "feminine" as the women I meet here. Her views are utterly commonsensical: she believes that people should try to get as much pleasure, approval, money, achievement, and good looks as they can. She has no use for eccentricity, ambivalence, or self-doubt. Her own task and destiny is carrying on the tradition of ordinary life—and she goes about it with great vigor and style. Except for the all-important disparate income, her inner world is not so different, after all, from my parents'. The disparity means that she's the fulfilled bourgeoise, while they've been relegated to aspiration and failure. It is her fulfillment, I suppose—yes, our feelings can be cruel—that reassures me. When I'm near her, I feel that satisfaction and contentment are surely possible—more, that they're everyone's inalienable right—possibly even mine.

Mrs. Steiner's snobberies are as resolute as everything else about her. She too believes there are "better people"—people who are successful, smart, and, most of all, cultured. She envisions her house as a kind of salon, to which she invites groups of Vancouver's elect; sometimes, on these occasions, I'm re-

cruited to raise the tone of the proceedings and perhaps advance my own for-
tunes by playing some Beethoven or Chopin. The Steiners' house, which over-
looks both the sea and the mountains of Vancouver's harbor, is surrounded by
large expanses of grounds and garden; inside, there are contemporary paint-
ings, grand pianos, and enormous pieces of Eskimo sculpture. I don't know
whether I like any of this unfamiliar art, but I know that's quite beside the
point.

Mrs. Steiner takes me to her house often, and I'm happiest there when I'm
with her alone. Then we talk for hours on end, mostly about my problems and
my life. I'm a little ashamed to reveal how hard things are for my family—how
bitterly my parents quarrel, how much my mother cries, how frightened I am
by our helplessness, and by the burden of feeling that it is my duty to take
charge, to get us out of this quagmire. But I can't help myself, it's too much of
a relief to talk to somebody who is curious and sensitive to my concerns. Although her sensitivity has its limits: she cannot always make the leap of empathy
across our differences. My mother's voice on the telephone ("She always sounds
as if there's something wrong. Sometimes she speaks so softly I have to tell her
to speak up.") bothers her. And when my father quits his job at a lumber mill,
Rosa is full of disapproval; he has a family to support, she tells me; isn't this a
bit irresponsible? Suddenly, I feel the full bitterness of our situation. My father
is no longer very young, I tell her; the job was the hardest at the mill. He had
to lift heavy logs all day—and he has a bad back, the legacy of the war. He was
in pain every day. Rosa is abashed by my sudden eruption, and she retreats.
She didn't know all this, she says; of course, I may be right. But there is added
irony in this exchange, which isn't lost on either of us: the Steiners own a lumber mill. In the Steiner kitchen, I've heard mention of the problems they've
sometimes had with their workers.

Still, I can speak to Rosa frankly; we can hash this sort of thing out. But
some of the ease of our exchange vanishes when other members of the family
enter the scene. Mrs. Steiner is fiercely devoted to her daughters, and in her
eyes they are princesses pure and simple. I believe her; what else can I do? I'm
both too shy and too removed from their lives to check out what I think of
them for myself. Elisabeth, the older one, has just started going to a small, elite
college—a place of which I can only gather that there are extremely interesting young people there, most of them near geniuses, and that Elisabeth has
occasionally taken to wearing odd garments, like Mexican skirts and black

stockings. Elisabeth talks without fully opening her mouth and swallows the endings of her words—so that I can understand her even less than most people, and I find myself saying "I beg your pardon" so often, that finally it becomes more polite to pretend I know what she's saying than to keep repeating the question.

Laurie is only two years older than myself, and she tries to befriend me. She often comes to our house—I invariably fight embarrassment at its stripped-down bareness—to drive me to the Steiners', and on the way there she talks about herself. Much of the time, it takes an enormous effort on my part to follow her fast chatter and to keep saying yes and no in the right places, to attempt to respond. I try to cover up this virtual idiocy by looking as intelligent as I can. But I do gather from these conversations that Laurie has just been at some international camp in Austria, that she will travel in Europe the following summer, that her parents differ from others in giving her affection and care—she has many friends whose parents try to compensate with money for their basic indifference. Isn't that terrible? I try, at this point, to look properly sympathetic, but the scale of problems she describes is so vastly different from what I know, and our mutual incapacity to penetrate each other's experience is so evident to me, that I harden myself against her. If I were really to enter her world, if I were really to imagine its difficulties, I would be condemned to an envy so burning that it would turn to hate. My only defense against the indignity of such emotion is to avoid rigorously the thought of wanting what she has—to keep her at a long, safe distance.

In the evening, we sit down to a family dinner and its jokey banter—an American ritual meant to sharpen the young women's edges for their encounters with the world and to affirm their superiority in that world. The Steiners, led by Laurie, who is clever and quick, are teasing each other, each bit of witty attack a verbal glove challenging the others to up the ante. I feel miserably out of it, laughing too loud, but knowing that I can't enter the teasing circle. After all, Cinderella can't get snarky with her half sisters, can she? I can only approve; I can't even implicitly criticize—and this seems almost as basic a definition of my position as the lack of money. Razzing can only happen between equals or else it's a deliberate presumption, which brings attention to inferior status. But I'm too proud to engage in this latter kind.

I've had a nice day in the Steiner household; Rosa and I took a long, brisk walk, we ate an excellent lunch, I played the piano for her and she made some comments, and now I'm sitting at their kitchen table, to all appearances almost a family member. When I get home, I'm terribly depressed. There's a yellow light in the downstairs room where my mother is waiting for me; my father, I know, will have fallen asleep in a stupor of disorientation and fatigue. But when my mother asks me about my day with a curiosity that pains me—she almost never gets invited to the Steiners'—I only tell her what a wonderful time I had.

In later years, I'll come to sit at the Steiners' table often, and look back on the polite and rankled girl I was then and flinch a little at the narrowing sympathies I felt in my narrow straits. I'll come to know that Laurie might have been jealous of me, might have feared, even, that I would displace her in her mother's affections—but I could not imagine then that I could rouse jealousy in anyone. I'll see how much time and attention and goodwill the Steiners lavished on me, more than in our busy and overfilled lives people can give to each other nowadays. Really, they thought about me more seriously than I thought about myself. Who was I, after all? Eva's ghost, perhaps, a specter that tried not to occupy too much space. They were more generous toward me than I was toward them; but then, a sense of disadvantage and inferiority is not a position from which one can feel the largeheartedness of true generosity.

Packing My Bags

Claribel Alegría

"The barbarians are arriving today."
—*C. Cavafi*

It's time to think
about my baggage
the suitcase is tiny
my perfumes won't fit
nor my necklaces
much less my books.
What will I take with me
to the other side?
Naturally the first
lightning bolt
that kindled our love
I'll also take
the razor glance
of that child
it wasn't for me
nor for anyone
blindly it grazed me
and opened this wound
that will not close.
I must be selective
in my memories
carefully compressing
those I pack
and out of self-compassion
abandoning the rest.
I will take with me
of course

the afternoon in Cahill's Tavern.
I told you about Sandino
and Farabundo
and you didn't understand
but wanted to learn
and little by little
we wandered into
the Halls of Los
and you were William Walker
and I Rafaela Herrera
and what was I doing
amongst the barbarians of the north
who invaded us
invade us now
and will invade again?
What was I doing
far from Izalco
far from my homeland?
And the night kept falling
quietly
and we were there inside
penetrating ever more deeply
trapped by our pasts
by our futures
and your tongue is foreign
I barely understand you
what am I doing here?
But I look at you and know
that you will be my man
and you still don't know it
and I stifle a laugh
and don't say anything
I choke down words.
It's impossible, I think,
what am I doing here
so far from my country?

and a tremor seized me
when I crossed the threshold:
my first earthquake
erupting in my Jurassic strata
and I encountered the mother
the children
the brother
Persephone
and Kali
and Tlaloc
and the night kept falling
quietly
on the empty bottles
and the glasses
and the waiter told us
it was closing time
and I walked out squeezing your hand
it was the first tremor
the first tidal wave
of the blind throbbing
that never abandons me.
You were the fish
slapping the water
with your tail
engendering these concentric circles
that open
expand
disperse:
waves that break
on my farther shore.

Beauty Contest

Janice Mirikitani

After the war, the camps;
when we moved to Chicago

all I remember was the cold.

When they called me Jap and slant eyed girl,
laughed and disappeared.

Momma took in ironing for extra money.
Daddy left for his red lipped honey.

I'm glad we split from Chicago.

All I remember was the cold . . .

A Woman in Exile

Mahnaz Afkhami

I am an exile. I have been in exile for twenty years. I have been forced to stay out of my own country, Iran, because of my work for women's rights. I recognized no limits, ends, or framework in this work outside those set by women themselves in their capacity as independent human beings. The charges against me are "corruption on earth" and "warring with God." Being charged in the Islamic Republic of Iran is being convicted. There is no defense or appeal, although I would not have known how to defend myself against such a grand accusation as warring with God anyway. There has not been a trial, not even in absentia, and no formal conviction. Nevertheless, my home in Tehran has been ransacked and confiscated, my books, pictures, and mementos taken, my passport invalidated, and my life threatened repeatedly.

My life in exile began at dawn on November 27, 1978. I was awakened by the ringing of the telephone. My husband's voice sounded very near. It took me a while to remember he was calling from Tehran. He had just spoken with Queen Farah who had suggested I cancel my return trip from New York scheduled for the following day. The government was trying to appease the opposition by making scapegoats of its own high-ranking officials. Feminists were primary targets for the fundamentalist revolutionaries. I had recently lost my cabinet post as minister of state for women's affairs as the regime's gesture of appeasement to the mullahs. It was very likely, my husband was saying, that as the most visible feminist in the country I would be arrested on arrival at the airport.

I searched for my glasses on the table by the bed and turned on the light, still clutching the receiver. I looked out the window at the black asphalt, glistening under the street lights. It must have rained earlier, I thought as I listened to my husband's voice, tinged with despair, yet somehow aloof and impersonal, as if this had little to do with him. Two months later when I would call to discuss the deteriorating situation and the need for him to get away, I would sound the same to him. The ties between a person and her home are such that even those nearest fear to intervene directly.

When I said good-bye I was wide awake but not clear-headed. What will I do here, I wondered. During the past few weeks my days had been spent negotiating with the United Nations' lawyers the terms of an agreement between the government of Iran and the UN, setting up the International Research and Training Institute for the Advancement of Women (INSTRAW) in Tehran. Evenings had been spent in meetings with groups and individuals trying desperately to affect the outcome of events in Iran.

Now it was suddenly all over for me. I could not go back home. I was left with a temporary visa, less than $1,000 in cash, and no plans whatsoever. I crossed the small room and automatically turned on the television to the Reuter news channel. The moving lines of the news tape were a familiar sight. In the last few weeks I had spent many hours staring at the screen, following the latest news, waiting for the inevitable items on Iran. When I looked up, the sun was streaming through the room.

Where would I go, I wondered as I dressed. I remembered I had planned to buy a coat that day. "What sort of a coat?" I asked myself. What sort of life will I be leading and what kind of a coat will that life require? Who am I going to be now that I am no longer who I was a few hours ago? I smiled at my reflection in the mirror. Need there be such existential probing connected to the buying of a winter coat? Even though I was far from the realization of the dimensions and the meaning of what had happened to me, my identity was already becoming blurred. The "I" of me no longer had clear outlines, no longer cast a definite shadow.

For a decade I had defined myself by my place within the Iranian women's movement. The question "Who am I?" was answered not by indicating gender, religion, nationality, or family ties but by my position as the secretary general of the Women's Organization of Iran, a title that described my profession, indicated my cause, and defined the philosophic framework for my essence. On that November morning in 1978, I realized that an immediate and formal severance of my connection to WOI was absolutely necessary. In those days of turmoil, when the movement's very existence was threatened, WOI did not need a secretary general who had become persona non grata to the system and its opposition. I sat at the desk in my hotel room and began to write a letter of resignation.

During the next days I lived a refusal to believe, a denial of the event, an inability to mourn—a state of mind which for me continued for years to come.

A flurry of activity related to making arrangements concerning the death of a loved one is the surest means of keeping full realization of the fact of it at bay. So I plunged myself into a series of actions aimed at ensuring survival in the new setting. The first priority was obtaining permission to stay in the United States. You need this to get a job although sometimes you can't get it without having a job—one of the many vicious circles encountered in the life of exiles. Those who enter the country as exiles discover that what had been their natural birthright at home will now depend on the decision of an official who may, for any reason at all or none, deny permission. A process from which there is no recourse.

As soon as possible, I was told, one must get the necessary cards—a driver's license, social security, credit card. These are to help one to assure the community that one exists and will continue to exist for the foreseeable future and can be trusted to handle a car and pay a bill. There is a certain excitement involved in all this. Finding a place to live, learning new routines, looking for a job, establishing new relationships—all within a separate reality, outside the framework of one's customary existence. It is possible to once again ask, "What do I want to be?" I contemplated whole new careers, from real estate to law, from teaching to opening a small business. They all seemed equally possible yet uniformly improbable.

All of this activity buys one time to assimilate the fact of loss and time to prepare to face it. You are told often that you must distance yourself from the past, that you must start a new life. But as in the case of death of kin you don't want to move away, close his room, give away his clothes. You want to talk about him, look at pictures, exchange memories. You shun contact with all those healthy, normal natives who are going about their business as if the world is a safe, secure, and permanent place a piece of which belongs to them by birthright. You work frantically to retain the memory and to reconstruct the past.

When you mourn a loved one, you wish more than anything to be either alone or with others who share your sense of loss. I sought mostly the company of other exiled Iranians. Together we listened to Persian music, exchanged memories, recalled oft-repeated stories and anecdotes, and allowed ourselves inordinate sentimentality. We remembered tastes, smells, sounds. We knew that no fruit would ever have the pungent aroma and the luscious sweetness of the fruit in Iran, that the sun would never shine so bright, nor the moon shed such light as we experienced under the desert sky in Kerman. The green of the vegetation on the road to the Caspian has no equal, the jasmine elsewhere does not smell as sweet.

Like children who need to hear a story endless times, we repeated for each other scenes from our collective childhood experiences. We recalled the young street vendors sitting in front of round trays on which they had built a mosaic of quartets of fresh walnuts positioned neatly at one inch intervals. We recalled the crunchy, salty taste of the walnuts we carried with us in a small brown bag as we walked around Tajrish Square, taking in the sounds and sights of an early evening in summer. We recalled the smell of corn sizzling on makeshift grills on the sidewalk. We remembered our attempts to convince the ice cream vendor, a young boy not much older then ourselves, to give us five one-rial portions of the creamy stuff smelling of rose water, each of which he carefully placed between two thin wafers. We knew that any combination of sizes would get us more than the largest—the five-rial portion. But the vendor, in possession of the facts and in command of the situation, sometimes refused to serve more than one portion to each child. We remembered walking past families who were picnicking, sitting on small rugs spread by the narrow waterways at the edge of the avenue, laughing and clapping to the music which blared from their radios, oblivious to the traffic a few feet away. We laughed about our grandmothers or aunts who sat in front of the television enjoying images from faraway places, around which they constructed their own stories, independently of the original creator's intention.

During the early years I kept myself frantically busy with phone calls, lectures, and meetings. Slowly, the life I had fashioned for myself in the new surroundings began to take shape. I now had a home in a suburb of Washington, D.C. Artist friends helped me collect a small selection of the works of Iranian women painters. A growing library of my old favorite books of poetry and fiction found a place in my room. The Foundation for Iranian Studies, a cultural institution that I helped create and managed with the aid of former colleagues, began to expand its activities. My family survived the travails and threats against them and all gathered near each other around Washington. Iran as a physical entity grew dimmer in our memory and more distant. But we remained obsessed with the events and processes that had led to our exile. All conversations, social occasions, and readings centered around what happened to us and more often than not ended in assigning blame.

As I went about building a life for myself in America, I learned through many encounters to simplify the spelling of my name, to mispronounce it to make it more easily comprehensible for my new contacts. I made small changes in my walk, posture, way of dressing to approach the new environment's expectations. In the process I drifted farther away from my self. The woman exclaiming about the weather to the sales girl at Macy's, calling herself Menaaz was not me. The original word, *Mahnaz*, had a meaning—Mah, moon, Naz, grace. Translating myself into the new culture made me incomprehensible to myself. I barely recognized this altered version of my personality. Frost once said "poetry is what is lost in translation." I realized that whatever poetry exists in the nuances which give subtlety to one's personality is lost in the new culture. What remains is dull prose—a rougher version, sometimes a caricature of one's real self. This smiling, mushy person was not me. It was my interpretation of the simplicity and friendliness of American social conduct. I embarrassed myself with it.

In public places I acted as if I were alone. In Iran, even in places where I was unlikely to meet someone I knew, I always acted "socially"—as if the people I met were potentially people I might come to know, people I might see again. I conducted myself with a consciousness of this assumption of possible further acquaintance, of a reasonable continuity of events. In America I acted totally isolated and separate, as if there were no chance that someone on the street might ever relate to me in any other way than as a total stranger. I caught glimpses of my American friends in a neighborhood restaurant chatting with the owner, greeting friends at other tables, talking about their plans, their homes, their professions, discussing the variations in the menu with the waiter, amazed that life went on as if nothing much had happened. I longed for this elemental sense of connection with my environment.

I kept on searching for the effects of dislocation on my feelings and reactions and spent much of my time studying my own mental state. The preoccupation had come close to neurotic proportions. Fortunately, in my work with the Sisterhood Is Global Institute, an international feminist think tank, I had become acquainted with a number of women from various countries who, like myself, were in exile. Gradually, through our conversations, I began to see that the only way to understand myself was to stand back from my own experiences and focus on someone else, that the best way to see inside my mind was to concentrate on another as she looked inside hers. It was in talking with them that I began to reappropriate myself.

My conversations with twelve of these women led to the publications of

Women In Exile, a project that became a cathartic and healing experience for me. I learned through writing their stories that although my past was mine in the specifics of my experiences, I shared so much of its deeper meaning with other women in exile. Working with them I began to see the fine thread that wove through all our varied lives and backgrounds. The narratives all followed the same pattern.

Our stories begin with descriptions of a society's disingenuous ways of shaping the woman's personality to fit the patriarchal mold. Even those who are active participants in political movements are often outsiders without the power to influence the decision-making process in their society. Political events beyond our control lead to upheaval. We are vulnerable and as caretakers of families our lives are most affected by disruptive and cataclysmic events. There comes a time when our own safety or that of our children requires us to take charge of our lives and make the decision to escape. Many of us are forced to undertake journeys of turbulence and danger. Once in the United States we realize that the physical dangers we have endured are only the preliminary stages to a life of exile. Slowly we begin to absorb the full impact of what has happened to us. A period of bereavement is followed by attempts to adjust to the new environment. Along with the loss of our culture and home comes the loss of the traditional patriarchal structures that flouted our lives in our own land. Exile in its disruptiveness resembles a rebirth. The pain of breaking out of our cultural cocoon brings with it the possibility of an expanded universe and a freer, more independent self. Reevaluation and reinvention of our lives leads to a new self that combines traits evolved in the old society and characteristics acquired in the new environment. Our lives are enriched by what we have known and surpassed. We are all "damaged," but we repair ourselves into larger, deeper, more humane personalities. Indeed, the similarities between our lives as women and as women in exile supersede every other experience we have encountered as members of different countries, classes, cultures, professions, and religions.

We appreciate the United States as a safe haven, a place which welcomes us and allows us to find ourselves. We appreciate the relative freedom of women in this society. We are, however, conscious that the country is hospitable for the young and the strong. We fear the loneliness and fragility of the old and the weak in this country. We regret that we have lost the closer ties and more committed interpersonal relationships with the extended family we enjoyed at home. Yet we know that for women part of the price of having those close ties is loss of independence and freedom of action.

In the years since exile began, for some of us, conditions in our home countries have changed, allowing them to return. Those who returned home discovered the irreversible nature of the exile experience even when it became possible to return. They realized not only that their country had changed but that they themselves are no longer who they were before they left. They learned that once one looks at one's home from the outside, as a stranger, the past, whether in the self or in the land, cannot be recaptured.

We are aware that we have lost part of ourselves through the loss of our homeland. We find substitutes for our loss; for some work acts as a replacement, for others, language. We echo each other when we say the world is our home and repeat wistfully that it means we have no home. We talk of having gained identification with a more universal cause.

We have learned first hand that nothing is worth the suffering, death, and destruction brought about by ideologies that in their fervor uproot so much and destroy so many and then fade away, blow up, or self-destruct. We learned in looking back over our lives that nothing is worth the breach of the sanctity of an individual's body and spirit. The sharing of our narratives of exile made us conclude simply that we wish to seek a mildness of manner, a kindness of heart, and a softness of demeanor. When has a war, a revolution, an act of aggression brought something better for the people on whose behalf it was undertaken? we asked ourselves and each other. We have paid with the days of our lives for the knowledge that nothing good or beautiful can come from harshness and ugliness.

Mother Tongue

Demetria Martínez

His nation chewed him up and spat him out like a piñon shell, and when he emerged from an airplane one late afternoon, I knew I would one day make love with him. He had arrived in Albuquerque to start life over, or at least sidestep death, on this husk of red earth, this Nuevo Méjico. His was a face I'd seen in a dream. A face with no borders: Tibetan eyelids, Spanish hazel irises, Mayan cheekbones dovetailing delicately as matchsticks. I don't know why I had expected Olmec: African features and a warrior's helmet as in those sculpted basalt heads, big as boulders, strewn on their cheeks in Mesoamerican jungles. No, he had no warrior's face. Because the war was still inside him. Time had not yet leached its poisons to his surfaces And I was one of those women whose fate is to take a war out of a man, or at least imagine she is doing so, like prostitutes once upon a time who gave themselves in temples to returning soldiers. Before he appeared at the airport gate, I had no clue such a place existed inside of me. But then it opened up like an unexpected courtyard that teases dreamers with sunlight, bougainvillea, terra-cotta pots blooming marigolds.

It was Independence Day, 1982. Last off the plane, he wore jeans, shirt, and tie, the first of many disguises The church people in Mexico must have told him to look for a woman with a bracelet made of turquoise stones because he walked toward me. And as we shook hands, I saw everything—all that was meant to be or never meant to be, but that I would make happen by taking reality in my hands and bending it like a willow branch. I saw myself whispering his false name by the flame of my Guadalupe candle, the two of us in a whorl of India bedspread, Salvation Army mattresses heaped on floorboards, adobe walls painted Juárez blue. Before his arrival the chaos of my life had no axis about which to spin. Now I had a center. A center so far away from God that I asked forgiveness in advance, remembering words I'd read somewhere, words from the mouth of Ishtar: *A prostitute compassionate am I.*

July 3, 1982

Dear Mary,

I've got a lot to pack, so I have to type quickly. My El Paso contact arranged for our guest to fly out on AmeriAir. He should be arriving around 4 p.m. tomorrow. As I told you last week, don't to forget to take the Yale sweatshirt I gave you just in case his clothing is too suspicious looking. Send him to the nearest bathroom if this is the case. The Border Patrol looks for "un-American" clothing. I remember the time they even checked out a woman's blouse tag right there in the airport—"Hecho en El Salvador." It took us another year and the grace of God to get her back up after she was deported.

Anyhow, when he comes off the plane, speak to him in English. Tell him all about how "the relatives" are doing. When you're safely out of earshot of anyone remind him that if anyone asks, he should say he's from Juárez. If he should be deported, we want immigration to have no question he is from Mexico. It'll be easier to fetch him from there than from a Salvadorian graveyard. Later on it might be helpful to show him a map of Mexico. Make him memorize the capital and the names of states. And I have a tape of the national anthem. These are the kinds of crazy things la migra asks about when they think they have a Central American. (Oh yes, and if his hair is too long, get him to Sandoval's on Second Street. The barber won't charge or ask questions.) El Paso called last night and said he should change his first name again, something different from what's on the plane ticket. Tend to this when you get home.

I've left the keys between the bottom pods of the red chile ristra near my side door. Make yourselves at home (and water my plants, please). I've lined up volunteers to get our guest to a doctor, lawyers, and so forth for as long as I'm here in Arizona. God willing, the affidavit from the San Salvador archdiocese doctor will be dropped off at the house by a member of the Guadalupe parish delegation that was just there. That is, assuming the doctor is not among those mowed down last week in La Cruz.

As I told you earlier, our guest is a classic political asylum case, assuming he decides to apply. Complete with proof of torture. Although even then he has only a two percent chance of being accepted by the United States. El Salvador's leaders may be butchers, but they're butchering on behalf of democracy so our government refuses to admit anything might be wrong. Now I know St. Paul says we're supposed to pray for our leaders and I do, but not without first fantasizing about lining them up and shooting them.

Now see, you got me going again. Anyway, we used to marry off the worst cases, for the piece of paper, so they could apply for residency and a work permit. But nowadays, you can't apply for anything unless you've been married for several years and immigration is satisfied that the marriage is for real. Years ago, when Carlos applied, immigration interrogated us in separate rooms about the color of our bathroom tile, the dog food brand we bought, when we last did you-know-what. To see if our answers matched. Those years I was "married" I even managed to fool you. That is, until we got the divorce, the day after he got his citizenship papers. But you were too

Bosnia, or What Europe Means to Us

Slavenka Drakulic

It was the best *sarma* I had ever tasted: small, tightly wrapped in sauerkraut and compact. The *sarma* is made of minced meat mixed with chopped onions, some garlic, salt, a whole egg and spices. The Bosnian *sarma* comes without sauce and is served with sour cream instead, which gives it that special, delicious taste. I used to make it myself from time to time, but I would mix rice into the meat and make a sauce of sweet red paprika and tomato puree, the variation of the recipe on the Adriatic coast, where I come from.

As well as the *sarma*, the Sunday lunch table was laid with filled onions called *dolma*; *burek*, a pie of a thin home-made pastry stuffed with meat, and *zeljanica*, another with spinach and cheese; and a plate of tasty grilled meat, *čevapčići*. In the middle there was a beautiful round loaf of bread, twisted into a plait. You don't cut this with a knife, you just break off pieces and stuff yourself with it until you can hardly breathe. And, of course, to end it all, there was *baklava*, a traditional sweet made with nuts without which no festive Bosnian meal would be complete. Considering the fact that we were in Stockholm, this lunch was even more special, because the Bosnian family who had invited us had had to put a lot of effort into finding all the right ingredients. But they must have known exactly where to get them, because everything was just perfect, as if you were eating in the middle of Sarajevo.

I asked Fatima, the mother who prepared the meal with the help of her twenty-year-old daughter, Amira, what kind of meat she used for the *sarma*. Was it half beef, half pork, as I used? "Oh, no," she said, "I use only beef. It gives the *sarma* a much better taste." It occurred to me then that the reason she didn't use pork was probably that they were religious Muslims, but I immediately regretted making that assumption. A couple of years ago such a thought would not even have entered my head, but now, after four years of war, even a question about a recipe was no longer innocent. Since then, we have all gradually learned how to think differently, how to divide people into Muslims, Croats and Serbs, even in terms of food. This is what war did to us. It brought us to extreme awareness, extreme sensitivity, because belonging to one nation or another could make the difference between life and death. I was ashamed of having automatically categorised the family. And in any case, I was wrong. Zijo, the father, was drinking brandy—*rakija*—along with the rest of us and there was whisky and wine offered at the table, too. Evidently they were non-religious, though brought up with the influence of the Muslim culture, as are the majority of Bosnian Muslims.

The family—Zijo, Fatima and Amira—had come to Sweden in 1992, soon after the war in Bosnia had started. The Swedish authorities found them a sunny, two-bedroomed apartment in a working-class suburb of Stockholm. They were also given money with which to furnish it. They had spent some of this on a television set, which was clearly the most important feature of their pleasant living room, if not the centre of their lives. During lunch, the set remained switched on, even if the volume was turned down. The father glanced at it frequently, waiting for the satellite news programme. He watches both the Serbian and Croatian broadcasts. There was a video, too. One of Zijo's activities—and he has little else to do—is to visit his friends, Bosnian refugees in other parts of the city, and exchange or borrow tapes from the "homeland," whatever that word means to these people nowadays. It doesn't matter if it is a movie, a musical, a show or a news programme, anything will do. They watch them all. They can't live without them; or at least, Zijo can't.

Zijo was a civil servant in his former life. Now, in his mid-fifties, he no longer has a job and cannot provide for his family. Too young to retire, he just doesn't know what to do with himself. In the middle of a conversation he falls silent because he spots something on the television which takes him back into his old world. Or he just drifts away into his own thoughts, sitting there, listening, but not really participating. His body is idle; there is no wood to cut, no way to be useful. It's easier for women, they always have something to do, he says with a shy smile, as if he is at the same time apologising for his patriarchal mentality in this very "politically correct" country. But he speaks a simple truth. Fatima runs the household, just as she used to do in Bosnia. In fact for her, things are a bit easier now, because she used to work full time and do all the housework. She misses her job a lot, but she has not lost the meaning of her life. She still has to keep her family together, to cook, to take care of the house. She also goes to a Swedish-language class provided free by the state for refugees.

For their daughter, the problems of adapting to a new country are less severe. In four years she has learned the language all by herself and is now working for her high-school degree. Like any person of her age, Amira has plans. She wants to study in Stockholm. In the meantime, she takes on temporary jobs; she goes out with her new friends to a disco, perhaps, and generally doesn't miss Bosnia all that much, except for her old friends. But most of them are no longer there anyway.

Perhaps because of the nature of her daily work, Fatima is more focused on the present. She thinks that the family should stay in Sweden and see what happens after the Dayton Agreement, whether peace in Bosnia will hold. She knows that their daughter has better opportunities for education and getting a good job in Sweden than she would have in insecure Bosnia, and she is prepared to stay until Amira gets her university degree. Zijo does not directly oppose his wife—how could he, when she has valid, rational arguments on her side? But you can tell that he would leave this cosy apartment in an instant to find himself among his own people again. It doesn't mean that he has any illusions about them, that he doesn't ask himself how much they will have changed because of the war. But he would still give up the comfort and security for what he is missing the most, his country, if only he could. You would probably have to start your life from scratch there, I say. He nods. He knows that in order to regain the life he once had back home, he would need to work hard for many years all over again. In Sweden, everything was just given to them. And just like that, says Zijo. He is appreciative, but he can't help asking himself how any society can be affluent enough to afford all that. I sense that he feels he is a burden, and that this cannot be a nice feeling.

The family has a brand-new washing machine in the bathroom, something you don't often see in Swedish households. People usually share two or three washing machines between a whole apartment building. This system works well, except that you have to put yourself on a list about a week in advance to do your laundry, but not knowing about it, the family bought their own machine. It is difficult to be forced to live in another country, to be obliged to change your habits, so they try to stick to what they know when they can. They wash their clothes in their own machine, and they travel about forty-five minutes or more to the market in the centre of town to get all the right ingredients for *dolma* or *zeljanica* or *baklava*. Surrounded by a tidy park, silent neighbours and a strange language, their life is divided between two realities— one here, in Sweden, in Europe; the other back home, in Bosnia.

Zijo shows interest in only a couple of topics: the latest news and the possibilities for peace (which for him equates to when he might be able to go home), and the past, or how did it all happen to us? He has no doubt that it was the political elite, not ordinary people like himself, who started the war. First people were talked into it, next they found it forced upon them, and then it was too late, he says. "Now I feel like the country I've left—cut into pieces. Some parts of me are still there, some parts are here, but certain parts are lost forever."

When I ask him what he thinks of Europe he waves his hand dismissively, as if one should not waste too many words on the subject. Only when I insist that he describe his attitude towards Europe does he start by telling me a story about a wooden house. He saw it recently nearby, a wooden house built in the typical Swedish style. "I was admiring its simplicity," he tells me, "and then I thought that I should take a photograph of that house and send it to my relatives back home. But I did not do it. I changed my mind. Having lived here for some time now, I understand that the house is beautiful to me because I am able to understand its beauty. In Bosnia they would think it was poor. Who, in my part of the world, but very poor people would build a wooden house? People there are proud when they build a two-storey ugly cement block, the bigger the better, so that the neighbours can see that you've made it. There are certain differences between us and Europe, but there are many misunderstandings, too." Zijo, like many other Bosnians, has seen both faces of Europe, the nice one and the ugly one.

The Bosnians were so painfully naïve. I remember them saying, even when the war had already started, "Europe will not let us be divided." Even after the heavy shelling of Sarajevo, and the deaths of tens of thousands of people, the Bosnians still looked towards Europe with hope. "Europe must do something to stop the killing," they would say. If you did not know what "Europe" was, you might well conclude that it was not a continent, but a single entity, a powerful, Godlike being. It took the Bosnians years to realise that Europe was not what they had imagined it to be, and only then after they were let down in the most shameful way. Europe is just a bunch of states with different interests, and the Bosnians had to discover this through their hesitation, indifference and cynicism. Paradoxically, hundreds of thousands of them ended up in European countries as refugees, and it was only then that they were helped.

If peace should have been imposed in the Balkans, the European countries should have imposed it in the first place, not left it to the Americans. They know the Balkans better. For decades Yugos used to clean their streets and build their cities as *Gastarbeiter*. With a minimum of effort Europeans can distinguish Zagreb from Belgrade or Sarajevo, and Banja Luka from Skopje, and there is a fair chance that some of them might once have even visited Dubrovnik. Yet, the European countries had trouble regarding the Balkans as a part of Europe. At the beginning of the war, for a long time the European states behaved as if it was a problem of semantics.

Zijo, lost in Stockholm, eating *sarma* and watching a television programme from back home, is suffering the consequence of this semantic problem. But the consequence of this problem is tens of thousands of wounded and disabled in Bosnia as well. This should and could have been prevented in the first place. If the war in Bosnia could not have been prevented, it could at least have been stopped long before Dayton and on many occasions. Every time the Serbs were really threatened and became afraid of being bombed, they would withdraw and agree to negotiate. Lives could have been saved, and the exodus of more than 2 million people prevented. Providing that the Dayton Agreement is the end of the ordeal, the results of the war in the Balkans will be borders changed by force (according to a European precedent after the Second World War), the acknowledgement of ethnic cleansing and the pushing of the Bosnian Muslims into the hands of fundamentalist Muslims from the Middle East—perhaps an irreversible European mistake.

Nobody should be killed because of his "wrong" national affiliation or the "wrong" colour of his eyes. But it is an even bigger tragedy if people are killed because of what they are not. This terrible fate is exactly what has befallen the Bosnians. They were "ethnically cleansed" at the beginning of the war on the pretext that they were religious Muslims, even fundamentalists. Of course, this was not true, merely a justification for what both the Serbs and the Croats wanted to do: to scare people away from "their" territory. It is astonishing, however, that the European states, too, behaved as if the Muslims in Bosnia were religious. It should not have been too difficult to look at a few simple facts about the Bosnian Muslims in order to understand the problem. For example, they are not Arabs, but are of Slavic origin; they were given Muslim nationality in the mid-seventies by Tito, in order to maintain the balance between Serbs and Croats in Bosnia. Although their culture, as a result of the Turkish occupation, is Muslim-influenced, the majority do not practice the

Muslim religion. For some reason, however—was it fear of the rise of Muslim fundamentalism in Europe, combined with the very convenient theory of the "ancient hatred" of the peoples in the Balkans?—it was taken as read that the Bosnian Muslims were about to establish a Muslim fundamentalist republic in the heart of Europe. For this purpose, the Balkans suddenly became part of Europe, and this could not be permitted. So the Bosnian Muslims were not helped by the European states, but instead by countries like Iran.

What was their alternative? If you were being killed as Muslim fundamentalists in spite of being a European, non-religious, Slavic people of Muslim nationality, and the only source of help were Muslim countries you would finally be forced to turn Muslim in order to survive. Bosnians made a pact with the Devil, but there was nobody else to make a pact with. After that, Bosnia was probably lost to Europe, as Europe was lost to the Bosnians a long time before.

It seems to me that a part of the tragedy of the Bosnians lies in their belief that Europe is what it is not. Europe did not intervene, it did not save them, because there was no Europe to intervene. They saw a ghost. It was us, the Eastern Europeans, who invented "Europe," constructed it, dreamed about it, called upon it. This Europe is a myth created by us, not only Bosnians, but other Eastern Europeans, too—unfortunate outsiders, poor relatives, the infantile nations of our continent. Europe was built by those of us living on the edges, because it is only from there that you would have the need to imagine something like "Europe" to save you from your complexes, insecurities and fears. Because for us, the people from the Balkans, the biggest fear is to be left alone with each other. We have learned better than others what you do to your own brother.

Sitting there at the Sunday lunch with Zijo, Fatima, Amira and their friends, I felt the absurdity of their situation. Why were these people in Stockholm? Was the food they were eating—*sarma, dolma, pita, čevapčići*—the reason why they had been driven from their own country? The idea seems crazy, I know, but what else is the reason? They didn't look different from me, or from those who had scared them away from their home. We even share the language, the education and history of the last fifty years. Our culture and habits might be slightly different, as are our names. Then, there is the food—delicious, tasty and spicy—that somehow seems to have been declared "wrong." But if what you eat decides what side you are on, then I should be on the "wrong" side, too.

It was a sad lunch, because we understand that everything Zijo politely calls "misunderstandings"—on both the Bosnian and the European sides—could perhaps have been avoided. Ever since that day in Stockholm, Europe has had another meaning for me. Every time I mention that word, I see the Bosnian family in front of me, living far away from whatever they call home and eating their own wonderful food because that's all that is left for them. The fact remains that, after fifty years, it was possible after all to have another war in Europe; that it was possible to change borders; that genocide is still possible even today. This should be enough to scare us all. This, and the fact that "Europeans"—that is, people in France, Great Britain, Germany, Italy, Austria or Spain—watched all this, paralysed. It was all there, on the television screens in their living rooms, shells, bombs, slaughter, rape, blood, destruction—the entire war unfolded in front of their eyes. Everybody knew what was going on and this, in a way, is the curse of the war in Bosnia, in the Balkans, and in—well, in what is called Europe.

Should we not, must we not ask, then, what is Europe after Bosnia?

The Moon, the Wind, the Year, the Day

Ana Pizarro

After so many years, and in spite of appearances, nothing fundamental seems to have changed. This recent concession, the government giving permission for you and a few others to go home, is only a gesture, forced on them by a deteriorating image abroad, by pressure from those who can't openly support a military dictatorship which presents such a face to the world, by the protests of the international organizations. They can allow people who present no evident risk to go back, secure in the knowledge that they have the situation under control. You sip the canned juice. Suddenly the stewardess's voice rings in your ears again, making you tremble: only two hours. To be honest, after twenty years it's not long enough.

For a moment you are shaken by how close you are. But it's hard to get a hold on this imminent future of brown grimacing faces, uniforms and helmets, suits and ties; everything grey, gloomy, indistinct. You try to place the images in the foreground but they won't come into focus, they fade into the background and disappear. The future doesn't exist, not even the immediate future, because the only images possible bleed into the clichés of printed news pictures, and your memory gets lost in the vague outline of the airport you left, that you'd rarely been to before, that you're approaching now. Your memory jumps from place to place, unable to fix on to a concrete present which, if it exists at all, is only the cabin of the plane, and travels through formless space, until it finally manages to touch down.

"People don't understand the affairs of the heart," Pepa says as she applies her lipstick, moving her lips in the mirror.

You think of the magazines, *For You* and *Margarita*, tidily stacked on the bureau in her room. You know about affairs of the heart from the illustrations on the covers and at the beginning of each story. A lady like Pepa, grown up, but sad and very slender, reclining on a couch, one arm hanging down, the other covering her face. Or another lady, a mirror in one hand, arranging the feathers of her headdress with the other. Usually they wear dresses covered in little flowers, and hats that come down to their big, highly made-up eyes. The

gentlemen have shirts with collars and ties and wide-brimmed hats and sometimes they hold the ladies in their arms, or it looks as if they're on the way to
the door, about to leave. You don't know where they're going because you can't
read such tiny letters, only the school reading book. Then Pepa says something about "moral prejudices" as she presses her lips together to make sure the
lipstick is even. "The rules of society are wrong, all wrong." The lipstick must
be just right because she stands back from the mirror and examines the effect.
You ask her what the rules are and she says, "You'll know soon enough, when
you're older," as she buffs the high-heeled shoes you like because they make
her look like the ladies in *For You*. And you think that that's when you'll understand why they cry so much in the radio serial, what birthright* means and
all that sort of thing.

She slings her bag over her shoulder and murmurs something about the
wickedness of some people. You ask who, and she says, "That Isadora in the
three o'clock comedy." She says goodbye and goes to the door. You think *she's*
the one who's wicked because she won't take you with her, so you burst into
tears at the door and look up at her miserably, but she won't give in. She tells
you she's got a lot to do and it'll be very boring, kisses you and takes off fast
along the still unpaved road towards the centre, crossing the avenue in her
high-heeled shoes.

It doesn't matter that a picture of Grandma, with her apron printed with
white flowers, her small round glasses on her snub nose and her face that's
never known make-up, doesn't spring instantly to mind. Your memory is vague
at this point, hesitant, and you have to reconstruct the occasion from the feeling, the fragments you can latch on to. She'll be at the back, sitting on her
straw mat, inviting you to husk corn cobs. Now the picture is clear, easy to remember. You're laying the leaves in a line, in pairs, one inside the other, ready
for her to put in the corndough, to wrap them up and tie them in little parcels,
separating the sweet ones for you and Pepa from the salty ones for herself, and
you're calming down again. She'll talk to you about the hens, tell you what
they do, what time of day each one lays its daily egg, why some of them have
bald necks, what they are all called and why she gave them those particular
names, which always have something to do with their looks or behaviour. It's
lovely to go and find the eggs just after you hear the hens clucking, some beige,
others a pale green, almost grey. You look for them in the nesting boxes or under the plants and, picking them up, hold them close, still warm against the

skin of your face. You have to be careful because sometimes the hens get mad, and then you back away, frightened, and wait for them to leave their nests. But from then on that warmth, which you'll come across later in all sorts of different ways, will be the ultimate expression of contact with life.

Grandma Luisa's life is a slow silent walk through the house. She never talks about her past, her background, her family. She sometimes repeats José's words of advice, but that's all: José her life-partner who taught her everything she knows, who brought her to this town and built her this house where she has been comfortable and secure. José who gave her her daughters and who slipped away into the other world one day, as unnoticed as when he arrived. Being with him was her life: sewing his buttons, making sure his shirts were clean and white and well-ironed, being there whenever he came in, making him a cup of tea or *mate* with lemon verbena at night, providing him with a good meal, which she'd put on to heat up when she heard the sound of the truck dropping him off from work at the door. He would arrive in the starry night and describe the crops at dawn or the springy straw in the wheatfields, with his stubbly chin and his great body which seemed to open all the doors and fill the house with his voice of lightning or the condor. His vicuña poncho kept out the cold when he was working out in the fields; he'd come in with a firm tread and the dog would give him a good welcome, hoping for a stroke from those rough country hands of his. She never spoke of how or when they met. Nor did she ever say that she loved him, because she never considered the possibility of not loving him. José worked away from home for weeks at a time and she awaited his return calmly, giving no sign of worry, getting on with her daily chores and keeping his clothes in order. In the evening she would take out a wicker chair and sit in the doorway watching the world go by. Her acquaintances would stop, ask after her health and Don José's, and pass on the town gossip: who had died, who was getting married, who was ill; the boys' pranks, the price of greens, the latest outrage from the butcher who sold his meat for whatever price came into his head and had even stopped giving away scraps for the cat.

One night José came home even more tired than usual. She was worried because she'd never seen him so low. They sat down together in front of the fire. When she was brewing his *mate* she looked up from the stove to ask if he wanted his sugar toasted or would he be happy with white, and thought she saw tears in his eyes. She bent her head so as not to look at him and toasted it anyway. José sighed deeply and asked if she knew about Adriana. She had some idea, because women had tried more than once to tell her of an evening in the doorway; but she'd never listened, replying only with a comment on the quality of vegetables, the high cost of living or the dog's illness. José told her that Adriana had just died and that he had had two daughters with her. She didn't look at him but she heard a hoarse sob and then there was silence. She kept staring at the fire for a long time, hands folded in her lap; then she coughed and said she'd go and fetch the girls.

That was how she gave birth, she who never carried a child inside, and from this pain was born the quiet, steady affection she always had for the girls, who no one ever would have doubted were her own daughters.

Luisa was born in the mountains, up there where carob trees, thorny and woody from lack of moisture, are the only vegetation. She didn't tell you, you guessed when you went on a long bus journey once. The engine got louder and louder as it climbed and there were moments when it looked as if it was going to stop, or roll back over the cliff. People traveled in silence and, apart from the engine, the only sound was the squawk of a hen or a cat miaowing at being shut up so long in a basket. The rest of the baggage had been put on top of the bus and you kept thinking that the road was so steep it might fall off at any moment, and that if the bus stopped it would never be able to get going again, so it would be difficult to collect it. But it didn't happen. After a few hours the bus reached its destination and everyone set off on foot with their bundles. You found it hard going. But Grandma walked at an incredible pace, finding exactly the right spot to put each foot as she picked her way between the stones. Eventually you arrived. It was a peculiar place. There was no vegetation, only a few buildings made of stones placed one on top of the other and fields separated by walls of the same sort—*pircas*, dry-stone walls, Grandma said. One day, when you were older, you would see somewhere similar in a movie—Greek, Turkish or Armenian—and you'd recognize in the people who lived in those stone houses the same frugality, the dependability your grandmother had. Only then would you realize that Luisa was born of the stones, that she inherited from them her strength of character.

You couldn't see who lived in this place. In your memory there are only shadows, moving inside the dark houses. You've stayed outside in the sun which beats down on your head. You're having fun chasing the young goats. They leap from rock to rock and run off up the mountain with their mothers.

Border Country

Alicia Nitecki

On a map, the forests of the Upper Palatinate (Oberpfalz) appear to huddle along the lower leg of the triangle the Czech Republic makes as it pushes into Germany dividing the lands of the former East from those of the West. An unnamed, unnumbered country road roughly outlines the national border for a stretch, now through dark forests, now through green and yellow open lands in order to connect the tiny villages and farms on the southeastern limits of Germany. Not much traffic passes along this road; tourists tend to stick to the broader, better "Ostmarkstrasse" some ten kilometers west, which goes from Passau in the south, through the crystal and china manufacturing towns of Weiden and Neustadt an der Waldnaab, to Bayreuth in the north.

The isolation of the Upper Palatinate could lead one to imagine it as sleepy, but the fields here are sharply defined; the corn dark green and stocky and upright; the house fronts bright and freshly painted; industriousness and prosperity are evident even in the most far-flung hamlet.

I had intended that we should stay at Neustadt, but we came there right after a rainstorm; the leaden sky had emptied the streets, turned the façades of the town's famous baroque houses livid, violent colors, and the man who passed me as I stood on the blue-and-white tiled floor at the foot of the dim stairs in the labyrinthine hotel seemed threatening. We found, instead, accommodations a short way out of town at a local inn facing a former station house, a disused railroad track, a litter of granites; at an inn where, in that quintessentially Bavarian way, a group of men sat talking and drinking beer at a round table beneath a crucifix; where a drunk with bad teeth and a pedigreed long-haired dachshund pressed on us his incomprehensible "pfälzische" dialect together with a miniature bottle of plum brandy; where a bride in an off-the-shoulder formal wedding dress and her husband in a short-sleeved cotton shirt drank bottle after bottle of champagne, and the little bridesmaids with silver lace at their necks tripped and tumbled on the linoleum floor going down again and again in tears and waves of satin; where, outside, my daughter could run, turn somersaults, leap off walls with screaming, laughing, bigger kids, and marvel at the flecks of crystal in the granites.

I had come to the Upper Palatinate because it was here, in a village five or so miles due east of this inn, a terminal German village on that unnumbered road along the border, a village of some two thousand inhabitants of farmers and laborers and quarriers, that in May 1938, Heinrich Himmler, supreme commander of the SS, established Flossenbürg concentration camp.

In this camp, my fifty-eight-year-old grandfather, a retired major from the prewar Polish army, had been imprisoned between sometime in 1944 and April 1945, not because of who he was—not because by accident of birth he had been a member of the Polish intelligentsia and by dint of that targeted for extermination as thousands of others like him had been—but because, when Poland had been part of the Government General of Germany, he had, in the city of Warsaw, deliberately and intentionally and in full knowledge of the consequences of his action, committed the crime of sheltering Jews.

Flossenbürg was an area in my family's life identified but not explored. My grandfather never spoke about it in my presence, and chose to present it to his wife and daughter and son in a mediated way, reading to them one evening in his attic bedroom (whose caches of paper, paint brushes, pencil, pens, and canvases I used to rifle through when he was out) his memoir of the months he had spent there.

When my conversations with my mother led her, at first, to use the generic term "concentration camp" ("What did Grandad do during the war, Mom?" "You know. He was in a concentration camp") or, later, to the specific, "Flossenbürg," there would be the slightest momentary pause, and then she would pick up along another route.

In the sturdy white chocolate box in which my mother kept photographs from those semi-fictional war years—years I remembered only in faded mental snapshots of my own—photos of the pebbly beach in Nice on which my father stood peering tensely beyond the camera; photos of bedraggled people against a background of firs in Lauterbach; photos of my mother and grandmother looking young and pretty in Warsaw—photos I peered into as into a dream, aide-mémoire which aided little, there was a small photo of my grandfather. A bleached-out mug shot of him in a pale striped shirt buttoned high at the throat, his head shaved to white stubble, his face expressing little, his eyes bulging slightly. The background blank. The picture belonged to those lost years, as did the later one of him in army uniform, three-quarters face, the corners of his mouth pulled down, the eyes looking at nothing. He was as removed in these photographs as his war years were from family conversations. I would stare at them intently, trying to find in them the slightly portly, kindly, funny man I knew. ("Mrs. Korenkiewicz," he had said one day to the friendly local Mrs. Malaprop, "You look like Venus today." "Oh, Major," he reported her as replying, "I'm not in the least venereal.")

The bleached-out picture, in particular, puzzled me. Had he been ill? Was he in hospital? I never asked. Once, when I was back from the States visiting her, my mother found me staring at the photo when she came into the room to put something away. She snatched it out of my hand, saying, "Oh, that's a dreadful photograph. Let's throw the thing out!" My mother's uncharacteristic violence had startled me into silence, and I sat mutely as she left the room ripping the photo. It was only then that it dawned on me that in it my grandfather was wearing concentration camp clothes.

Our house was washed by the fast moving waters, now murky now iridescent, of my grandmother's tales. I splashed about willingly in that river in which names stuck out like rock, bathed again and again by the fresh flows of her narrative. My grandfather's past was locked deep in some mountain on a bank I lacked the courage to reach, and though, occasionally, some piece of story would blow my way, I never looked for the source.

Once, I learned that he had grabbed and hit two Polish gentile boys for picking on a Jewish kid. "He would have been shot dead on the spot if the Germans had seen him," my mother said.

Another time, I heard that his apartment had been a temporary safe-house for a series of Jews. The last of them had been young, still a child really. He stayed for three months. When the people from the Home Army were transferring him somewhere else, the Germans caught them and he was killed. The next day they came to arrest my grandfather.

Yet another time, I learned how he had managed to survive. At the end of the war, they had marched the prisoners to another camp. They took a rest and my grandfather fell asleep. He woke to find himself alone, the SS men must have miscounted, but he was so befuddled that he followed in the direction they had gone. He even passed two German soldiers and asked them the way. They must have been very tired, too, because they waved him on. Normally, they would have shot him.

Little narratives rich in verbs, paradigms. "He grabbed, he hit, he hid. They killed, they came, they took, they shot." Footholds to a language I never learned to speak.

The last summer I visited my mother in England, when she already knew, but I didn't, that she was dying, she asked me whether I would be interested, perhaps, in reading my grandfather's Flossenbürg memoir. We were, I remember, sitting next to each other in her living room, and she was looking down at her needlepoint. I could not respond to her question, although I had somehow anticipated it, and I muttered something under my breath.

"It's better you don't read it; it's filled with horrors. He cried when he read it out to us. Not for himself," she added quickly, "but for other people, for what they did to them."

"Like what?" I asked.

She hesitated for a moment, and again looking down at her work said, "For the girl they beat so badly that she could neither sit nor lie down. Such things. Better you don't read it."

After my mother had died, her dying breath closing the door to my childhood, I searched for the memoir but did not find it, and I regretted our inarticulateness: what my mother, in her desire not to force an obligation on me, had not said, which was that she wanted her father's memories preserved; what I had never been able to say to her, which was that I was afraid to read them and reluctant to reveal an interest in the horrors he had lived, because such an interest seemed perverse.

Exile

Tatyana Mamonova

My future was running from me
                    like a horse
just when I thought things couldn't
                    get worse
I was exiled from my country
and the sign said "no entry"
I lay awake in a cold sweat
judged by people I never met
I couldn't make myself settle down
I couldn't pack my night gown
I couldn't answer the phone calls
It was like I'd run into a wall
Then I was watching the whole world
going by and getting old
my city below looked like a dime—
It froze in time

five

Domestic and Political Violence

War Pictures

Carol Dine

In the snapshot taken in Virginia,
my father is an army captain
dressed in his khaki shirt and trousers.
I'm wearing overalls, and he has scooped me up,
cushioned me between his hands.
Our dark hair is slicked back,
the slopes of our foreheads match.

Needles on the low branch
of a palm tree tickle my bare feet.
If I wanted to, I could hide beneath its skirt.
I am right up against my father's heart.
He has bowed his head to kiss me goodbye,
but they tell him he doesn't have to fight—
the war is over.

In another photograph,
I'm standing in my playpen;
shadows of wooden slats
spill across the floor.
I have dropped my stuffed donkey.
I am squeezing my eyes shut
as if my father were marching
into the frame
looking for the enemy.

Against the Pleasure Principle

Saida Hagi-Dirie Herzi

Rahma was all excitement. Her husband had been awarded a scholarship to one of the Ivy-League universities in the United States, and she was going with him. This meant that she was going to have her baby—the first—in the US. She would have the best medical care in the world.

But there was the problem of her mother. Her mother did not want her to go to the US. Rahma was not sure just what it was that her mother objected to but partly, no doubt, she was afraid she'd lose Rahama if she let her go. She had seen it happen with other girls who went abroad: most of them did not come back at all and those who did came only to visit, not to stay. And they let it be known that they had thrown overboard the ways of their people and adopted the ways of the outside world—they painted their lips and their faces; they wore western dress; they went about the city laughing and singing outlandish songs; they spoke in foreign languages or threw in foreign words when they spoke the local language; and they generally acted as though they were superior to all those who stayed behind.

Her mother also seemed worried about Rahma having her baby in the US. Rahma had tried and tried again to reassure her that there was nothing to worry about: she would have the best medical attention. Problems, if any, would be more likely to arise at home than there. But it had made no difference. Her mother kept bombarding her with horror stories she had heard from Somali women coming back from the US—the dreadful things that happened to them when they went to US hospitals, above all when they had their babies there.

Like all women in her native setting, Rahma was circumcised, and, according to her mother, that would mean trouble for her when she was going to have a baby unless there was a midwife from her country to help her. Her mother was convinced that US doctors, who had no experience with circumcised women, would not know what to do.

Rahma had never given much thought to the fact that she had been only four years old when it happened, and nineteen years had passed since then. But she did remember.

It had not been her own feast of circumcision but that of her sister, who was nine then. She remembered the feeling of excitement that enveloped the whole house that morning. Lots of women were there; relatives were bringing gifts— sweets, cakes, various kinds of delicious drinks, trinkets. And her sister was the centre of attention. Rahma remembered feeling jealous, left out. Whatever it was they were going to do to her sister, she wanted to have it done too. She cried to have it done, cried and cried till the women around her mother relented and agreed to do it to her too. There was no room for fear in her mind: all she could think of was that she wanted to have done to her what they were going to do to her sister so that she too would get gifts, she too would be fussed over.

She remembered the preliminaries, being in the midst of a cluster of women, all relatives of hers. They laid her on her back on a small table. Two of the women, one to the left of her and the other to the right, gently but firmly held her down with one hand and with the other took hold of her legs and spread them wide. A third standing behind her held down her shoulders. Another washed her genitals with a mixture of *melmel* and *hildeed*, a traditional medicine. It felt pleasantly cool. Off to one side several women were playing tin drums. Rahma did not know that the intent of the drums was to drown the screams that would be coming from her throat in a moment.

The last thing she remembered was one of the women, a little knife in one hand, bending over her. The next instant there was an explosion of pain in her crotch, hot searing pain that made her scream like the rabbit when the steel trap snapped its legs. But the din of the drums, rising to a deafening crescendo, drowned her screams, and the women who held her expertly subdued her young strength coiling into a spring to get away. Then she must have passed out, for she remembered nothing further of the operation in which all the outer parts of her small genitals were cut off, lips, clitoris and all, and the mutilated opening stitched up with a thorn, leaving a passage the size of a grain of sorghum.

When she regained consciousness, she was lying on her mat in her sleeping corner, hot pain between her legs. The slightest movement so aggravated the pain that tears would well up in her eyes. She remembered trying to lie perfectly still so as not to make the pain worse.

For some time after the operation she walked like a cripple: her thighs had been tied together so that she could move her legs only from the knees down, which meant taking only the tiniest of steps. People could tell what had happened to her by the way she walked.

And she remembered how she dreaded passing water. She had to do it sitting because she could not squat, and she had to do it with her thighs closed tightly because of the bindings. To ease the pain of urine pushing through the raw wound of the narrow opening, warm water was poured over it while she urinated. Even so, it brought tears to her eyes. In time the pain abated, but urinating had been associated with discomfort for her ever since.

She remembered being told that she had needed only three thorn stitches. Had she been older, it would have taken four, perhaps five, stitches to sew her up properly. There are accepted standards for the size of a girl's opening: an opening the size of a grain of rice is considered ideal; one as big as a grain of sorghum is acceptable. However, should it turn out as big as a grain of maize, the poor girl would have to go through the ordeal a second time. That's what had happened to her sister; she herself had been luckier. When the women who inspected her opening broke out into the high-pitched *mash-harad* with which women in her society signalled joy, or approval, Rahma knew that it had turned out all right the first time.

Rahma's culture justified circumcision as a measure of hygiene, but the real purpose of it, Rahma was sure, was to safeguard the woman's virginity. Why else the insistence on an opening no larger than a grain of sorghum, one barely big enough to permit the passing of urine and of the menstrual blood? An opening as small as that was, if anything, anti-hygienic. No, if the kind of circumcision that was practised in her area had any purpose, it was to ensure that the hymen remained intact. Her society made so much of virginity that no girl who lost it could hope to achieve a decent marriage. There was no greater blow to a man's ego than to find out that the girl he married was not a virgin.

Rahma knew that, except for the first time, it was customary for women to deliver by themselves, standing up and holding on to a hanging rope. But the first time they needed assistance—someone to cut a passage large enough for the baby's passage. That was what so worried Rahma's mother. She did not think a US doctor could be trusted to make the right cut. Not having had any experience with circumcised women he would not know that the only way to cut was upward from the small opening left after circumcision. He might, especially if the baby's head was unusually big, cut upward *and* downward. How was he to know that a cut towards the rectum could, and probably would, mean trouble for all future deliveries? Nor would he know that it was best for the woman to be stitched up again right after the baby was born. It was, Rahma's mother insisted, dangerous for a circumcision passage to be left open.

When it became obvious that her words of warning did not have the desired effect on Rahma, her mother decided to play her last trump card—the *Kur*, a ritual feast put on, usually in the ninth month of a pregnancy, to ask God's blessing for the mother and the baby about to be born. Friends and relatives came to the feast to offer their good-luck wishes. It was her mother's intention to invite to the *Kur* two women who had had bad experiences with doctors in the US. They would talk about their experiences in the hope that Rahma would be swayed by them and not go away.

The *Kur* feast was held at her mother's place. When the ritual part of it was over and the well-wishers had offered their congratulations, some of the older women, who had obviously been put up to it by her mother, descended on Rahma trying to accomplish what her mother had failed to do—persuade her to put off going away at least until after the baby's birth.

It did not work. From the expression on Rahma's face that was only too obvious. So her mother signalled for the two special guests to do their part. The first, whose name was Hawa, had spent two years in the US as a student. She talked about the problems of a circumcised woman in a society that did not circumcise its women. "When people found out where I was from," she told her audience in a whisper, "they pestered me with questions about female circumcision. To avoid their questions, I told them that I had not been circumcised myself and therefore could not tell them anything about it. But that did not stop them from bugging me with more questions." The topic of circumcision, she told them, continued to be a source of embarrassment for as long as she was there.

Hawa then talked about her experience at the gynaecologist's office. She had put off seeing a gynaecologist as long as possible, but when she could not put it off any longer, she looked for, and found, a woman doctor, thinking that she would feel comfortable with a woman. When the doctor started to examine her, Hawa had heard a gasp. The gasp was followed by a few stammering sounds that turned into a question. The doctor wanted to know whether she had got burned or scalded. When Hawa signalled by a shake of her head that she had done neither, the doctor asked her whether she had had an operation for cancer or something, in which the outer parts of her genitals had been amputated. Again Hawa denied anything, and to avoid further questions quickly added that the disfigurement which the doctor found so puzzling was the result of circumcision.

At that, Hawa's doctor went on with the examination without further questions. When she was finished, she turned to Hawa once more. "You had me
confused there," she muttered, more to herself than to Hawa. "Don't hold my
ignorance against me. I have heard and read about circumcision, but you are
the first circumcised woman I have seen in my career. I neither knew that it was
still practised nor did I have any idea it went so far.

"You know," she continued after a moment's pause, "I cannot for the world
of me understand why your people have to do this to their women. Intercourse
cannot be much fun for someone mutilated like that. Perhaps that's why they
do it, to make sure the women won't get any pleasure out of sex. And what
misery it must be for a woman sewn up like that to have a baby."

Hawa said she went away from the doctor's office thinking how right the
doctor was about sex not being fun for circumcised women. She remembered
the first time her husband made love to her, how horribly painful it had been.
And it had continued to be painful for her even after she got used to it. She
knew that for most of the women in her society sex was something to be endured not enjoyed. With all the sensitive parts of womanhood cut away, it was
all but impossible for them to be sexually aroused and quite impossible for
them to experience any of the pleasurable sensations that would redeem the act.

Hawa said she walked home feeling like a freak: what was left of her genitals must look pretty grim if the sight of it could make a doctor gasp. Why did
her people do this to their women? Hundreds of millions of women the world
over went through life the way God had created them, whole and unmutilated.
Why could her people not leave well enough alone? It seemed to her, at least
in this case, that man's attempts to improve on nature were a disaster.

The second woman, Dahabo, seemed to believe in circumcision as such.
However, when a circumcised woman moved to a part of the world that did not
practise circumcision problems were bound to arise. She too had lived in the
US. She too had had her encounters with US doctors. She talked at length
about her first such encounter. Like Hawa's doctor, hers was a woman; unlike
Hawa's hers was familiar with the idea of female circumcision. Nevertheless,
Dahabo was her first case of a circumcised woman. Dahabo told her audience
about the questioning she was subjected to by her doctor after the examination:

Doctor: Did you have any sort of anaesthesia when they circumcised you?

Dahabo: No, I did not, but I did not really feel any pain because I fainted and remained unconscious during the whole operation.

Doctor: Is circumcision still practised in your culture?

Dababo: Yes, it is. I had it done to my five-year-old daughter before coming here.

Doctor: Any difference between your way and your daughter's way?

Dahabo: None whatsoever: the same women who circumcised me circumcised her.

At that point, Dahabo told her listeners, something happened that puzzled her: her doctor, eyes full of tears, broke into loud sobs, and she continued to sob while she opened the door to usher her patient out into the corridor. Dahabo said she had never understood what had made her doctor cry.

Rahma had no trouble understanding what it was that had moved the doctor to tears. She was close to tears herself as she left her mother's house to walk home. How much longer, she wondered, would the women of her culture have to endure this senseless mutilation? She knew that, though her people made believe circumcision was a religious obligation, it was really just an ugly custom that had been borrowed from the ancient Egyptians and had nothing to do with Islam. Islam recommends circumcision only for men.

The *Kur* did not achieve what her mother had hoped. Rahma was more determined than ever to accompany her husband to the US. True, there was still the problem of her mother; no doubt her mother meant well, no doubt she wanted the best for her, but Rahma had different ideas about that. She was, for instance, convinced that having her baby in the US was in the best interest of her and of the baby. She would like to have her mother's blessing for the move, but if that was not possible she would go without it. She had always hated circumcision. Now she hated it more than ever. No daughter of hers would ever be subjected to it.

Nada

Judith Ortíz Cofer

Almost as soon as Doña Ernestina got the telegram about her son's having been killed in Vietnam, she started giving her possessions away. At first we didn't realize what she was doing. By the time we did, it was too late.

The army people had comforted Doña Ernestina with the news that her son's "remains" would have to be "collected and shipped" back to New Jersey at some later date, since other "personnel" had also been lost on the same day. In other words, she would have to wait until Tony's body could be processed.

Processed. Doña Ernestina spoke that word like a curse when she told us. We were all down in El Basement—that's what we called the cellar of our apartment building: no windows for light, boilers making such a racket that you could scream and almost no one would hear you. Some of us had started meeting here on Saturday mornings—as much to talk as to wash our clothes—and over the years it became a sort of women's club where we could catch up on a week's worth of gossip. That Saturday, however, I had dreaded going down the cement steps. All of us had just heard the news about Tony the night before.

I should have known the minute I saw her, holding court in her widow's costume, that something had cracked inside Doña Ernestina. She was in full luto—black from head to toe, including a mantilla. In contrast, Lydia and Isabelita were both in rollers and bathrobes: our customary uniform for these Saturday morning gatherings—maybe our way of saying "No Men Allowed." As I approached them, Lydia stared at me with a scared-rabbit look in her eyes.

Doña Ernestina simply waited for me to join the other two leaning against the machines before she continued explaining what had happened when the news of Tony had arrived at her door the day before. She spoke calmly, a haughty expression on her face, looking like an offended duchess in her beautiful black dress. She was pale, pale, but she had a wild look in her eyes. The officer had told her that—when the time came—they would bury Tony with "full military honors"; for now they were sending her the medal and a flag. But she had said, "No, *gracias*," to the funeral, and she sent the flag and medals back marked *Ya no vive aquí*: Does not live here anymore. "Tell the Mr. President of the United States what I say: No, gracias."

Then she waited for our response.

Lydia shook her head, indicating that she was speechless. And Elenita looked pointedly at me, forcing me to be the one to speak the words of sympathy for all of us, to reassure Doña Ernestina that she had done exactly what any of us would have done in her place: yes, we would have all said *No, gracias*, to any president who had actually tried to pay for a son's life with a few trinkets and a folded flag.

Doña Ernestina nodded gravely. Then she picked up the stack of neatly folded men's shirts from the sofa (a discard we had salvaged from the sidewalk) and walked regally out of El Basement.

Lydia, who had gone to high school with Tony, burst into tears as soon as Doña Ernestina was out of sight. Elenita and I sat her down between us on the sofa and held her until she had let most of it out. Lydia is still young—a woman who has not yet been visited too often by *la muerte*. Her husband of six months had just gotten his draft notice, and they have been trying for a baby—trying very hard. The walls of El Building are thin enough so that it has become a secret joke (kept only from Lydia and Roberto) that he is far more likely to escape the draft due to acute exhaustion than by becoming a father.

"Doesn't Doña Ernestina feel *anything*?" Lydia asked in between sobs. "Did you see her, dressed up like an actress in a play—and not one tear for her son?"

"We all have different ways of grieving," I said, though I couldn't help thinking that there *was* a strangeness to Doña Ernestina and that Lydia was right when she said that the woman seemed to be acting out a part. "I think we should wait and see what she is going to do."

"Maybe," said Elenita. "Did you get a visit from *el padre* yesterday?"

We nodded, not surprised to learn that all of us had gotten personal calls from Padre Álvaro, our painfully shy priest, after Doña Ernestina had frightened him away. Apparently el padre had come to her apartment immediately after hearing about Tony, expecting to comfort the woman as he had when Don Antonio died suddenly a year ago. Her grief then had been understandable in its immensity, for she had been burying not only her husband but also the dream shared by many of the barrio women her age—that of returning with her man to the Island after retirement, of buying a *casita* in the old pueblo, and of being buried on native ground alongside *la familia*. People *my* age—

those of us born or raised here—have had our mothers dutifully drill this fantasy into our brains all of our lives. So when Don Antonio dropped his head on the domino table, scattering the ivory pieces of the best game of the year, and when he was laid out in his best black suit at Ramírez's Funeral Home, all of us knew how to talk to the grieving widow.

That was the last time we saw both her men. Tony was there, too—home on a two-day pass from basic training—and he cried like a little boy over his father's handsome face, calling him Papi, Papi. Doña Ernestina had had a full mother's duty then, taking care of the hysterical boy. It was a normal chain of grief, the strongest taking care of the weakest. We buried Don Antonio at Garden State Memorial Park, where there are probably more Puerto Ricans than on the Island. Padre Álvaro said his sermon in a soft, trembling voice that was barely audible over the cries of the boy being supported on one side by his mother, impressive in her quiet strength and dignity, and on the other by Cheo, owner of the bodega where Don Antonio had played dominoes with the other barrio men of his age for over twenty years.

Just about everyone from El Building had attended the funeral, and it had been done right. Doña Ernestina had sent her son off to fight for America and then had started collecting her widow's pension. Some of us asked Doña Iris (who knew how to read cards) about Doña Ernestina's future, and Doña Iris had said: "A long journey within a year"—which fit with what we thought would happen next: Doña Ernestina would move back to the Island and wait with her relatives for Tony to come home from the war. Some older women actually went home when they started collecting social security or pensions, but that was rare. Usually, it seemed to me, somebody had to die before the island dream would come true for women like Doña Ernestina. As for my friends and me, we talked about "vacations" in the Caribbean. But we knew that if life was hard for us in this barrio, it would be worse in a pueblo where no one knew us (and had maybe heard of our parents before they came to *Los Estados Unidos de América*, where most of us had been brought as children).

When Padre Álvaro had knocked softly on my door, I had yanked it open, thinking it was that ex-husband of mine asking for a second chance again. (That's just the way Miguel knocks when he's sorry for leaving me—about once a week—when he wants a loan.) So I was wearing my go-to-hell face when I threw open the door, and the poor priest nearly jumped out of his skin. I saw him take a couple of deep breaths before he asked me in his slow way—he tries to hide his stutter by dragging out his words—if I knew whether or not Doña Ernestina was ill. After I said, "No, not that I know," Padre Álvaro just stood there, looking pitiful, until I asked him if he cared to come in. I had been sleeping on the sofa and watching TV all afternoon, and I really didn't want him to see the mess, but I had nothing to fear. The poor man actually took one step back at my invitation. No, he was in a hurry, he had a few other parishioners to visit, etc. These were difficult times, he said, so-so-so many young people lost to drugs or dying in the wa-wa-war. I asked him if *he* thought Doña Ernestina was sick, but he just shook his head. The man looked like an orphan at my door with those sad, brown eyes. He was actually appealing in a homely way: that long nose nearly touched the tip of his chin when he smiled, and his big crooked teeth broke my heart.

"She does not want to speak to me," Padre Álvaro said as he caressed a large silver crucifix that hung on a thick chain around his neck. He seemed to be dragged down by its weight, stoop-shouldered and skinny as he was.

I felt a strong impulse to feed him some of my chicken soup, still warm on the stove from my supper. Contrary to what Lydia says about me behind my back, I like living by myself. And I could not have been happier to have that mama's boy Miguel back where he belonged—with his mother, who thought that he was still her baby. But this scraggly thing at my door needed home cooking and maybe even something more than a hot meal to bring a little spark into his life. (I mentally asked God to forgive me for having thoughts like these about one of his priests. *Ay bendito*, but they too are made of flesh and blood.)

"Maybe she just needs a little more time, Padre," I said in as comforting a voice as I could manage. Unlike the other women in El Building, I am not convinced that priests are truly necessary—or even much help—in times of crisis.

"Sí, Hija, perhaps you're right," he muttered sadly—calling me "daughter" even though I'm pretty sure I'm five or six years older. (Padre Álvaro seems so "untouched" that it's hard to tell his age. I mean, when you live, it shows. He looks hungry for love, starving himself by choice.) I promised him that I would look in on Doña Ernestina. Without another word, he made the sign of the cross in the air between us and turned away. As I heard his slow steps descending the creaky stairs, I asked myself: what do priests dream about?

When el padre's name came up again during that Saturday meeting in El Basement, I asked my friends what *they* thought a priest dreamed about. It was a fertile subject, so much so that we spent the rest of our laundry time coming up with scenarios. Before the last dryer stopped, we all agreed that we could not receive communion the next day at mass unless we went to confession that afternoon and told another priest, not Álvaro, about our "unclean thoughts."

As for Doña Ernestina's situation, we agreed that we should be there for her if she called, but the decent thing to do, we decided, was give her a little more time alone. Lydia kept repeating, in that childish way of hers, "Something is wrong with the woman," but she didn't volunteer to go see what it was that was making Doña Ernestina act so strangely. Instead she complained that she and Roberto had heard pots and pans banging and things being moved around for hours in 4-D last night—they had hardly been able to sleep. Isabelita winked at me behind Lydia's back. Lydia and Roberto still had not caught on: if they could hear what was going on in 4-D, the rest of us could also get an earful of what went on in 4-A. They were just kids who thought they had invented sex: I tell you, a telenovela could be made from the stories in El Building.

On Sunday Doña Ernestina was not at the Spanish mass and I avoided Padre Álvaro so he would not ask me about her. But I was worried. Doña Ernestina was a church cucaracha—a devout Catholic who, like many of us, did not always do what the priests and the Pope ordered but who knew where God lived. Only a serious illness or tragedy could keep her from attending mass, so afterward I went straight to her apartment and knocked on her door. There was no answer, although I had heard scraping and dragging noises, like furniture being moved around. At least she was on her feet and active. Maybe housework was what she needed to snap out of her shock. I decided to try again the next day.

As I went by Lydia's apartment, the young woman opened her door—I knew she had been watching me through the peephole—to tell me about more noises from across the hall during the night. Lydia was in her baby-doll pajamas. Although she stuck only her nose out, I could see Roberto in his jockey underwear doing something in the kitchen. I couldn't help thinking about Miguel and me when we had first gotten together. We were an explosive combination. After a night of passionate lovemaking, I would walk around thinking: Do not light cigarettes around me. No open flames. Highly combustible materials being transported. But when his mama showed up at our door, the man of fire turned into a heap of ashes at her feet.

"Let's wait and see what happens," I told Lydia again.

We did not have to wait long. On Monday Doña Ernestina called to invite us to a wake for Tony, a *velorio*, in her apartment. The word spread fast. Everyone wanted to do something for her. Cheo donated fresh chickens and island produce of all kinds. Several of us got together and made arroz con pollo, also flan for dessert. And Doña Iris made two dozen *pasteles* and wrapped the meat pies in banana leaves that she had been saving in her freezer for her famous Christmas parties. We women carried in our steaming plates, while the men brought in their bottles of Palo Viejo rum for themselves and candy-sweet Manischewitz wine for us. We came ready to spend the night saying our rosaries and praying for Tony's soul.

Doña Ernestina met us at the door and led us into her living room, where the lights were off. A photograph of Tony and one of her deceased husband Don Antonio were sitting on top of a table, surrounded by at least a dozen candles. It was a spooky sight that caused several of the older women to cross themselves. Doña Ernestina had arranged folding chairs in front of this table and told us to sit down. She did not ask us to take our food and drinks to the kitchen. She just looked at each of us individually, as if she were taking attendance in class, and then said: "I have asked you here to say good-bye to my husband Antonio and my son Tony. You have been my friends and neighbors for twenty years, but they were my life. Now that they are gone, I have nada. Nada. Nada."

I tell you, that word is like a drain that sucks everything down. Hearing her say *nada* over and over made me feel as if I were being yanked into a dark pit. I could feel the others getting nervous around me too, but here was a woman deep into her pain: we had to give her a little space. She looked around the room, then walked out without saying another word.

As we sat there in silence, stealing looks at each other, we began to hear the sounds of things being moved around in other rooms. One of the older women took charge then, and soon the drinks were poured, the food served—all this while strange sounds kept coming from different rooms in the apartment. Nobody said much, except once when we heard something like a dish fall and break. Doña Iris pointed her index finger at her ear and made a couple of circles—and out of nervousness, I guess, some of us giggled like schoolchildren.

It was a long while before Doña Ernestina came back out to us. By then we were gathering our dishes and purses, having come to the conclusion that it was time to leave. Holding two huge Sears shopping bags, one in each hand, Doña

Ernestina took her place at the front door as if she were a society hostess in a receiving line. Some of us women hung back to see what was going on. But Tito, the building's super, had had enough and tried to steal past her. She took his hand, putting in it a small ceramic poodle with a gold chain around its neck. Tito gave the poodle a funny look, then glanced at Doña Ernestina as though he were scared and hurried away with the dog in his hand.

We were let out of her place one by one but not until she had forced one of her possessions on each of us. She grabbed without looking from her bags. Out came her prized *miniaturas*, knickknacks that take a woman a lifetime to collect. Out came ceramic and porcelain items of all kinds, including vases and ashtrays; out came kitchen utensils, dishes, forks, spoons; out came old calendars and every small item that she had touched or been touched by in the last twenty years. Out came a bronzed baby shoe—and I got that.

As we left the apartment, Doña Iris said "Psst" to some of us, so we followed her down the hallway. "Doña Ernestina's faculties are temporarily out of order," she said very seriously. "It is due to the shock of her son's death."

We all said "Sí" and nodded our heads.

"But what can we do?" Lydia said, her voice cracking a little. "What should I do with this?" She was holding one of Tony's baseball trophies in her hand: 1968 Most Valuable Player, for the Pocos Locos, our barrio's team.

Doña Iris said, "Let us keep her things safe for her until she recovers her senses. And let her mourn in peace. These things take time. If she needs us, she will call us." Doña Iris shrugged her shoulders. "*Así es la vida, hijas*: that's the way life is."

As I passed Tito on the stairs, he shook his head while looking up at Doña Ernestina's door: "I say she needs a shrink. I think somebody should call the social worker." He did not look at me when he mumbled these things. By "somebody" he meant one of us women. He didn't want trouble in his building, and he expected one of us to get rid of the problems. I just ignored him.

In my bed I prayed to the Holy Mother that she would find peace for Doña Ernestina's troubled spirit, but things got worse. All that week Lydia saw strange things happening through the peephole on her door. Every time people came to Doña Ernestina's apartment—to deliver flowers, or telegrams from the Island, or anything—the woman would force something on them. She pleaded with them to take this or that; if they hesitated, she commanded them with those tragic eyes to accept a token of her life.

And they did, walking out of our apartment building, carrying cushions, lamps, doilies, clothing, shoes, umbrellas, wastebaskets, schoolbooks, and note-books: things of value and things of no worth at all to anyone but the person who had owned them. Eventually winos and street people got the news of the great giveaway in 4-D, and soon there was a line down the stairs and out the door. Nobody went home empty-handed; it was like a soup kitchen. Lydia was afraid to step out of her place because of all the dangerous-looking characters hanging out on that floor. And the smell! Entering our building was like com-ing into a cheap bar and public urinal combined.

Isabelita, living alone with her two children and fearing for their safety, was the one who finally called a meeting of the residents. Only the women at-tended, since the men were truly afraid of Doña Ernestina. It isn't unusual for men to be frightened when they see a woman go crazy. If they are not the cause of her madness, then they act as if they don't understand it and usually leave us alone to deal with our "woman's problems." This is just as well.

Maybe I *am* just bitter because of Miguel—I know what is said behind my back. But this is a fact: when a woman is in trouble, a man calls in her mama, her sisters, or her friends, and then he makes himself scarce until it's over. This happens again and again. At how many bedsides of women have I sat? How many times have I made the doctor's appointment, taken care of the children, and fed the husbands of my friends in the barrio? It is not that the men can't do these things; it's just that they know how much women help each other. Maybe the men even suspect that we know one another better than they know their own wives. As I said, it is just as well that they stay out of the way when there is trouble. It makes things simpler for us.

At the meeting, Isabelita said right away that we should go up to 4-D and try to reason with *la pobre* Doña Ernestina. Maybe we could get her to give us a relative's address in Puerto Rico—the woman obviously needed to be taken care of. What she was doing was putting us all in a very difficult situation. There were no dissenters this time. We voted to go as a group to talk to Doña Ernestina the next morning.

But that night we were all awakened by crashing noises on the street. In the light of the full moon, I could see that the air was raining household goods: kitchen chairs, stools, a small TV, a nightstand, pieces of a bed frame. Every-thing was splintering as it landed on the pavement. People were running for cover and yelling up at our building. The problem, I knew instantly, was in apartment 4-D.

Putting on my bathrobe and slippers, I stepped out into the hallway. Lydia and Roberto were rushing down the stairs, but on the flight above my landing, I caught up with Doña Iris and Isabelita, heading toward 4-D. Out of breath, we stood in the fourth-floor hallway, listening to police sirens approaching our building in front. We could hear the slamming of car doors and yelling—in both Spanish and English. Then we tried the door to 4-D. It was unlocked.

We came into a room virtually empty. Even the pictures had been taken down from the walls; all that was left were the nail holes and the lighter places on the paint where the framed photographs had been for years. We took a few seconds to spot Doña Ernestina: she was curled up in the farthest corner of the living room, naked.

"Cómo salió a este mundo," said Doña Iris, crossing herself.

Just as she had come into the world. Wearing nothing. Nothing around her except a clean, empty room. Nada. She had left nothing behind—except the bottles of pills, the ones the doctors give to ease the pain, to numb you, to make you feel nothing when someone dies.

The bottles were empty too, and the policemen took them. But we didn't let them take Doña Ernestina until we had each brought up some of our best clothes and dressed her like the decent woman that she was. *La decencia*. Nothing can ever change that—not even la muerte. This is the way life is. *Así es la vida*.

My Harem Frontiers

Fatima Mernissi

I was born in a harem in 1949 in Fez, a ninth-century Moroccan city some five thousand kilometers west of Mecca, and one thousand kilometers south of Madrid, one of the dangerous capitals of the Christians. The problems with the Christians start, said Father, as with women, when the *hudud*, or sacred frontier, is not respected. I was born in the midst of chaos, since neither Christians nor women accepted the frontiers. Right on our threshold, you could see women of the harem contesting and fighting with Ahmed the doorkeeper as the foreign armies from the North kept arriving all over the city. In fact, foreigners were standing right at the end of our street, which lay just between the old city and the Ville Nouvelle, a new city that they were building for themselves. When Allah created the earth, said Father, he separated men from women, and put a sea between Muslims and Christians for a reason. Harmony exists when each group respects the prescribed limits of the other; trespassing leads only to sorrow and unhappiness. But women dreamed of trespassing all the time. The world beyond the gate was their obsession. They fantasized all day long about parading in unfamiliar streets, while the Christians kept crossing the sea, bringing death and chaos.

Trouble and cold winds come from the North, and we turn to the East to pray. Mecca is far. Your prayers might reach it if you know how to concentrate. I was taught how to concentrate when the time was appropriate. Madrid's soldiers had camped north of Fez, and even Uncle 'Ali and Father, who were so powerful in the city and ordered around everyone in the house, had to ask permission from Madrid to attend Moulay Abdesalam's religious festival near Tangier, three hundred kilometers away. But the soldiers who stood outside our door were French, and of another tribe. They were Christians like the Spaniards, but they spoke another language and lived farther north. Paris was their capital. Cousin Samir said that Paris was probably two thousand kilometers away, twice as far away from us as Madrid, and twice as ferocious. Christians, just like Muslims, fight each other all the time, and the Spanish and the French almost killed one another when they crossed our frontier. Then, when neither was able to exterminate the other, they decided to cut Morocco in half. They put soldiers near 'Arbaoua and said from now on, to go north, you needed a pass because you were crossing into Spanish Morocco. To go south, you needed another pass, because you were crossing into French Morocco. If you did not go along with what they said, you got stuck at 'Arbaoua, an arbitrary spot where they had built a huge gate and said that it was a frontier. But Morocco, said Father, had existed undivided for centuries, even before Islam came along fourteen hundred years ago. No one ever had heard of a frontier splitting the land in two before. The frontier was an invisible line in the mind of warriors.

Cousin Samir, who sometimes accompanied Uncle and Father on their trips, said that to create a frontier, all you need is soldiers to force others to believe in it. In the landscape itself, nothing changes. The frontier is in the mind of the powerful. I could not go and see this for myself because Uncle and Father said that a girl does not travel. Travel is dangerous and women can't defend themselves. Aunt Habiba, who had been cast off and sent away suddenly for no reason by a husband she loved dearly, said that Allah had sent the Northern armies to Morocco to punish the men for violating the *hudud* protecting women. When you hurt a woman, you are violating Allah's sacred frontier. It is unlawful to hurt the weak. She cried for years.

Education is to know the *hudud*, the sacred frontiers, said Lalla Tam, the headmistress at the Koranic school where I was sent at age three to join my ten cousins. My teacher had a long, menacing whip, and I totally agreed with her about everything: the frontier, Christians, education. To be a Muslim was to respect the *hudud*. And for a child, to respect the *hudud* was to obey. I wanted badly to please Lalla Tam, but once out of her earshot, I asked Cousin Malika, who was two years older than I, if she could show me where the *hudud* actually was located. She answered that all she knew for sure was that everything would work out fine if I obeyed the teacher. The *hudud* was whatever the teacher forbade. My cousin's words helped me relax and start enjoying school.

But since then, looking for the frontier has become my life's occupation. Anxiety eats at me whenever I cannot situate the geometric line organizing my powerlessness.

Musée des Faux Arts

Rose Styron

"About suffering they were never wrong,
the Old Masters," mused Auden
gazing at Brueghel gazing at Icarus
falling into the sea.   The farmer plowing,
the shepherd dreaming, he fell into the sea.
Across the gallery the sun kept shining
for other lads skating their icy pond
on balanced blades, while the one
determined to meet the sun, to play
the sun on his lucent homemade wings
by afternoon was gone without a trace.

How often I've thought of Brueghel's
intricate scenes.   Once, through a gate
I watched our neighbor's son
go off at dawn to his daily job
at the torture house, pale stucco
on our very elm-lined street
in last year's Santiago.   Thought:
someday will he watch a boy he's known
whose wings of conscience made him dare
the local laws of gravity
suddenly reappear, be left, drowning?

Toward home one gilded nightfall,
the sky's gong melting into the sea,
he stopped at the soccer stadium.   There
Victor Jara light-long played guitar,
sang a wild song.   Brave fingers

crushed by compatriots, and severed tongue
were not the business of our neighbor's son.

A different time, poised on brocade divans
and sampling chocolates in an Asian palace
we were audience for the Prince.   Thought:
an hour ago at Phnom Penh's ruined school
too near the killing fields we stood,
staring at beds museumed in the classroom,
manacles clamped to their leather slats
that sagged in body-shapes, electric
wires still tuned to cure the young

under their immortality—the blown-up
photographs secured against each blackboard—
cross-eyed violinist, startled soccer champ,
chaste poet I had talked about
halfway across the world and then forgot.

Now close, Kosinski: artist of the underworld,
curator of his lives' exhibits, exile's clown.
Some dread whim (I have made myself believe),
led him to sink his last invention, drown
in the tub.   Thought: how could a flimsy
plastic bag snuff out his eyes' Inferno,
become the mask wrought wet and tight
to frighten or seduce a tardy lover?

"Play hide and seek with me," he used to cry.
Even then we were too old for games.
But in his secret room we'd play, Jerzy
afraid of Poles and Jews, hiding from history's
judgment and perhaps from grown-up instincts
just to disappear.   Thin as a Chinese kite,
folding his hollow bones as he had learned to do
from painted birds who floated when they

could not fly, he lay flat between the stove
and wall, shimmering.   Sideways on imaginary water.

It took me—then the angry others—hours
to find him, he and I gleeful by the end
at our long our dazzled puzzlement, his rescue.
I had not thought I'd tire of games so soon.

After a decade of abandonment, scant
reason and scant days before the drowning,
he called.   "Come play!" the voice implored.
Outside my country window the late sun
rose and rose and fell, green flash into a white
antarctic sea.   Shackleton, Amundsen, Cook exploring
one more childhood summoned.
Although I must have said "Why not?"
surely I meant: "Never."

About accidents we are often wrong. . . .

Female Goods

Taslima Nassrin

Woman, you'd like a woman?
All kinds of women,
fair-skinned women, tall women, hair down to their knees,
slim waist, firm and shapely figure.
She's got no fat, no salt, you won't find
     any wrinkles in her skin.

Pierced nose, pierced ears, pierced digestive tract,
check with your fingers that nothing else is pierced.
No hand has touched her virgin limbs, her liquids
have not spilled, a woman not yet enjoyed.
Woman, you'd like a woman?

Feed her three square meals a day,
give her *saris*, ornaments, and good soap
to smooth on her body.
She won't raise her eyes, she won't raise her voice,
she's a shy and modest woman,
she can cook seven dishes for one midday meal.

This female item can be used any way you like!
If you wish, chain her feet, chain her hands,
put her mind in chains.
If you wish, divorce her, say divorce,
and you've divorced her.

Child of the Dark

Carolina María de Jesus

December 25 Xmas Day [1958]

João came in saying he had a stomach ache. I knew what it was for he had eaten a rotten melon. Today they threw a truckload of melons near the river.

I don't know why it is that these senseless businessmen come to throw their rotted products here near the favela,[1] for the children to see and eat.

In my opinion the merchants of São Paulo are playing with the people just like Caesar when he tortured the Christians. But the Caesars of today are worse than the Caesar of the past. The others were punished for their faith. And we, for our hunger!

In that era those who didn't want to die had to stop loving Christ.

But we cannot stop loving eating.

December 26

That woman who lives on Paulino Guimarães Street, number 308, gave a doll to Vera. We were passing when she called Vera and told her to wait. Vera said to me:

"I think I'm going to get a doll."

I replied:

"And I think we are going to get bread."

I sensed her anxiety and curiosity to see what it was going to be. The woman came out of the house with the doll.

Vera said to me:

"Didn't I tell you! I was right!"

She ran to get the doll. She grabbed it and ran back to show me. She thanked the woman and told her that the other girls in the favela would be jealous. And that she would pray every day that the woman should be happy and that she was going to teach the doll how to pray. I'm going to take her to Mass so she can pray for the woman to go to Heaven and not to have any painful illnesses.

December 27

I tired of writing, and slept. I woke up with a voice calling Dona Maria. I remained quiet because I am not Maria. The voice said:

"She said that she lives in number 9."

I got up, out of sorts, and went to answer. It was Senhor Dorio. A man that I got to know during the elections. I asked Senhor Dorio to come in. But I was ashamed. The chamber pot was full.

Senhor Dorio was shocked with the primitive way I live. He looked at everything surprisedly. But he must learn that a favela is the garbage dump of São Paulo and that I am just a piece of garbage.

December 28

I lit a fire, put water on to boil, and started to wash the dishes and examine the walls. I found a dead rat. I'd been after him for days and set a rat trap. But what killed him was a black cat. She belongs to Senhor Antonio Sapateiro.

The cat is a wise one. She doesn't have any deep loves and doesn't let anyone make a slave of her. And when she goes away she never comes back, proving that she has a mind of her own.

If I talk about a cat it is because I am happy that she has killed the rat that was ruining my books.

December 29

I went out with João and Vera and José Carlos. João took the radio to be fixed. When I was on Pedro Vicente Street, the watchman at the junk yard called me and said that I was to go and look for some bags of paper that were near the river.

I thanked him and went to find the sacks. They were bags of rice that had rotted in a warehouse and were thrown away. I was shocked seeing that wasted rice. I stared at the bugs that were there, and the cockroaches and rats that ran from one side to another.

I thought: Why is the white man so perverse? He has money, buys and stores rice away in the warehouse. He keeps playing with the people just like a cat with a rat.

December 30

When I went to wash the clothes I met some women who were discussing the courage of Maria, the "companion" of a *Baiano*.[2]

They had separated and she went to live with another *Baiano*, that was their neighbor.

A woman's tongue is a candlewick. Always burning.

December 31

I spent the afternoon writing. My boys were bouncing a ball near the shacks. The neighbors started to complain. When their kids play I don't say anything.

I don't fight with the children because I don't have glass in the windows and a ball can't hurt a board wall.

José Carlos and João were throwing a ball. The ball fell in Victor's yard and Victor's wife punched a hole in it. The boys started to curse her. She grabbed a revolver and ran after them.

If the revolver had fired!

I'm not going to sleep. I want to listen to the São Silvestre race.[3] I went to the house of a gypsy who lives here. It bothers me to see his children sleeping on the ground. I told him to come to my shack at night and I would give him two beds. If he came during the day the women would transmit the news, because everything here in the favela is news.

When the night came, he came. He said he wants to settle here and put his children in school. That he is a widower and likes me very much. And asked me if I want to live with or marry him.

He hugged me and kissed me. I stared into his mouth adorned with gold and silver. We exchanged presents. I gave him some candy and clothes for his children and he gave me pepper and perfume. Our discussion was on art and music.

He told me that if I married him he would take me out of the favela. I told him that I'd never get used to riding in a caravan. He told me that a traveler's life was poetic.

He told me that the love of a gypsy is as deep as the ocean and as hot as the sun.

That was all I needed. When I get old I'm going to become a gypsy. Between this gypsy and me there exists a spiritual attraction. He did not want to leave my shack. And if I could have I would not have let him leave.

I invited him to come over any time and listen to the radio. He asked me if I was alone. I told him that my life was as confusing as a jigsaw puzzle. He likes to read so I gave him some books.

I went to see the appearance of the shack. It was pleasanter after he set up the beds. João came looking for me, saying that I was lingering too long.

The favela is excited. The *favelados* are celebrating because it is the end of a year of life.

Today a *nortista* woman went to the hospital to have a baby and the child was born dead. She is taking transfusions. Her mother is crying because she is the only daughter.

There is a dance in Victor's shack.

January 1, 1959

I got out of bed at 4 A.M. and went to carry water, then went to wash clothes. I didn't make lunch. There is no rice. This afternoon I'm going to cook beans with macaroni. The boys didn't eat anything. I'm going to lie down because I'm sleepy. It was 9 o'clock. João woke me up to open the door. Today I'm sad.

January 4

In the old days I sang. Now I've stopped singing, because the happiness has given way to a sadness that ages the heart. Every day another poor creature shows up here in the favela. Ireno is a poor creature with anemia. He is looking for his wife. His wife doesn't want him. He told me that his mother-in-law provoked his wife against him. Now he is in his brother's house. He spent a few days in his sister's house, but came back. He said they were throwing hints at him because of the food.

Ireno says that he is unhappy with life. Because even with health life is bitter.

January 5

It's raining. I am almost crazy with the dripping on the beds because the roof is covered with cardboard and the cardboard is rotten. The water is rising and invading the yards of the *favelados*.

January 6

I got out of bed at 4 A.M., turned on the radio, and went for water. What torture it is to walk in water in the morning. And I catch cold so easily! But life is like that. Men are leaving for work. They are carrying their shoes and socks in their hands. Mothers keep the children inside the house. They get restless because they want to go out and play in the water. People with a sense of humor say that the favela is a sailors' city. Others say it is the São Paulo Venice.

I was writing when the son of the gypsy came to tell me that his father was calling me. I went to see what he wanted. He started to complain about the difficulties of living here in São Paulo. He went out to get a job and didn't find one.

He said he was going back to Rio, because there it is easier to live. I told him that here he could earn more money.

"In Rio I earn more," he insisted. "There I bless children and get a lot of money."

I knew that when the gypsy was talking to somebody he could go on for hours and hours, until the person offered money. There is no advantage in being friendly with a gypsy.

I started out and he asked me to stay. I went out and went to the store. I bought rice, coffee, and soap. Then I went to the Bom Jardim Butcher Shop to buy meat. When I got there the clerk looked at me with an unhappy eye.

"Do you have lard?"

"No."

"Meat?"

"No."

A Japanese came in and asked:

"Do you have lard?"

She waited until I had gone out to tell him:

"Yes we have."

I returned to the favela furious. Then the money of a *favelado* is worthless? I thought: today I'm going to write and am going to complain about that no-good clerk at the Bom Jardim Butcher Shop.

Common!

January 7

Today I fixed rice and beans and fried eggs. What happiness. Reading this you are going to think Brazil doesn't have anything to eat. We have. It's just that the prices are so impossible that we can't buy it. We have dried fish in the shops that wait for years and years for purchasers. The flies make the fish filthy. Then the fish rots and the clerks throw it in the garbage, and throw acid on it so the poor won't pick it up and eat it. My children have never eaten dried fish. They beg me.

"Buy it Mother!"

But buy it—how? At 180 cruzeiros a kilo? I hope if God helps me, that before I die I'll be able to buy some dried fish for them.

January 8

I met a driver who had come to dump sawdust here in the favela. He asked me to get into the truck. The blond driver then asked me if here in the favela it was easy to get a woman. And if he could come to my shack. He told me that he was still in form. His helper said he was on a pension.

I said good-by to the driver and went back to the favela. I lit a fire, washed my hands, and started to prepare food for the children.

January 10

Senhor Manuel came over. It was 8 o'clock. He asked me if I still talked to the gypsy. I told him that I did. And that the gypsy had some land in Osasco and that if they tore down the favela and I didn't have any place to go, I could go to his property. That he admired my spirit and if he could, would like to live at my side.

Senhor Manuel became angry and said he wasn't coming back any more. That I could stay with the gypsy.

What I admire in the gypsy is his calmness and understanding. Things that Senhor Manuel doesn't possess. Senhor Manuel told me he wouldn't show up any more. We'll see.

January 11

I am not happy with my spiritual state. I don't like my restless mind. I keep thinking about the gypsy, but I'm going to dominate these feelings. I know that when he sees me he gets happy. Me too. I have the feeling that I am one shoe and just now have found the other.

I've heard many things said about gypsies. But he doesn't have any of the bad qualities that they blab about. It seems that this gypsy wants a place in my heart.

In the beginning I distrusted his friendship. But now if it increases for me, it will be a pleasure. If it diminishes, I'll suffer. If I could only fasten myself to him!

He has two boys. One of them is always with me. If I go to wash clothes, he comes along, and sits at my side. The boys of the favela get jealous when they see me pampering the boy. Pleasing the boy, I get closer to the father.

The name of the gypsy is Raimundo. He was born in the capital of Bahia. He looks like Castro Alves.[4] His eyebrows meet.

January 13

I made supper and gave it to the children. Rosalina came over. She came looking for a few beans. I gave them.

Senhor Raimundo arrived. He came for his boys. He watched the children eating. I offered him some supper but he didn't want it. He picked out a sardine and asked me if I had any pepper. I don't put pepper in the food because of the children.

I thought: if I was alone I would give him a hug. What feelings I have seeing him at my side. I thought: if someday I was exiled and this man came along to accompany me, it would make the punishment easier.

I asked Rosalina to eat the sardines. I gave her the beans. Raimundo told me that he was going away to his house, and that if one day the favela was destroyed, for me to look for him there. He gave the same invitation to Rosalina. I didn't appreciate it. It wasn't egoism. It was jealousy. He left and I kept thinking. He never parks. He has gypsy blood. I thought: if someday this man was mine I would chain him to my side. I want to introduce him to another world.

January 14

I walked through the streets. I went to Dona Julita. I went to the Blue Cross to get money for the cans. I got home before the rain. Senhor Raimundo sent his son to call me. I changed myself and went to him. He told me he was going to Volta Redonda to work in the steel mill. I know I'm going to miss him. I hurried away saying that I needed to write and it was something that couldn't wait.

January 15

I got out of bed at 4 o'clock and went to carry water. I turned on the radio to hear the tango program.

Senhor Manuel said he was never going to come back. He walked through the water to get to my shack. He caught a cold.

Today I'm happy. I earned some money. I got 300! Today I'm going to buy meat. Nowadays when a poor man eats meat he keeps smiling stupidly.

January 16

I went to the post office to take out the notebooks that returned from the United States. I came back to the favela as sad as if they had cut off one of my arms. *The Readers' Digest* returned my novels. The worst slap for those who write is the return of their works.

To dispel the sadness that was making me blue, I went to talk with the gypsy. I picked up the notebooks and the ink bottle and went there. I told him that I had received the originals back in the mail and now wanted to burn the notebooks.

He started to tell me of his adventures. He said he was going to Volta Redonda and would stay in the house of a fourteen-year-old girl who was with him. If the girl went out to play he was right after her, watching her carefully. I didn't like the way he was looking at the girl. I thought: what does he want with this youngster?

My sons came into the shack. He was lying on the floor. I asked him if he used a knife.

"No. I prefer a revolver, like this one."

He showed me a .32 revolver. I am not very friendly with revolvers. He gave the gun to João to hold and said:

"You are a man. And a man must learn to handle these things."

João told him he had better not say anything to anyone, that he didn't want the people in the favela to know he had a revolver.

"I showed it to your mother because she likes me. And when a woman likes a man she never denounces him. I bought this revolver when I was a soldier."

"You were a soldier?"

"In Bahia. But I left the corps because I was earning very little."

He showed me a photo taken in uniform. When I got up to go he said:

"It's early!"

He ordered coffee to be made. The girl said there wasn't any sugar. I sent João to get some sugar and butter. He sent his son to buy six cruzeiros worth of bread. He said:

"I never eat without meat. I never eat bread without butter. Here in this shack I eat. This shack made me put on weight."

His boy returned with the bread. José Carlos came in and started to fight with the boy. He told them not to fight because they were all brothers.

"I'm not his brother. Oh, no!"

"You are brothers because of Adam and Eve!"

He grabbed José Carlos by the arms, forcing him to lie down beside him on the floor. José Carlos got loose and ran into the street.

I put my eyes to the notebook and started to write. When I raised my head his eyes were on the girl's face. I didn't like the strange look he had.

My mind began to unmask the sordidness of this gypsy. He used his beauty. He knows that women can be fooled with pretty faces. He attracts girls telling them he will marry them, then satisfies his desires and sends them away. Now I understand his eyeing that girl. This is a warning to me. I would never let Vera in the same house with him.

I looked at the gypsy's face. A beautiful face. But I got nauseated. It was the face of an angel with the soul of the devil. I went back to my shack.

Notes

1. Shantytown, slum—ED.

2. A "Baiano" is a person from Bahia, a state on the Atlantic coast of Brazil—ED.

3. São Silvestre race: a traditional footrace through the downtown streets of São Paulo every New Year's Eve.

4. Castro Alves: Brazilian nineteenth-century abolitionist poet.

Language and Shame

Meena Alexander

There is something molten in me. I do not know how else to begin, all over again as if in each attempt something needs to be recast, rekindled, some bond, some compact between flesh, clothing, words. There is something incendiary in me and it has to do with being female, here, now, in America. And those words, those markers, of gender, of time, of site, all have an extraordinary valency. When they brush up against each other, each of those markers—"female," "here," "now," "America"—I find that there is something quite unstable in the atmosphere they set up. I do not have a steady, taken for granted compact with my body. Nor indeed with my language. Yet it is only as my body enters into, coasts through, lives in language that I can make sense.

I need to go backwards, to begin: think of language and shame.

As a child I used to hide out to write. This was in Khartoum, where I spent many months of each year—my life divided between that desert land and the tropical green of Kerala, where my mother returned with her children for the summer months. In Khartoum, I hid behind the house under a neem tree or by a cool wall. Sometimes I forced myself into the only room where I could close the door, the toilet. I gradually learnt that the toilet was safer, no one would thrust the door open on me. There I could mind my own business and compose. I also learnt to write in snatches. If someone knocked at the door, I stopped abruptly, hid my papers under my skirts, tucked my pen into the elastic band of my knickers, and got up anxiously. Gradually, this enforced privacy—for I absorbed and perhaps, in part, even identified with my mother's disapproval over my poetic efforts—added an aura of something illicit, shameful, to my early sense of my scribblings. Schoolwork was seen in a totally different light. It was good to excel there, interpreting works that were part of a great literary past. The other writing, in one's own present, was to be tucked away, hidden. No wonder then that my entry into the realm of letters was fraught.

The facts of multilingualism added complexity to this split sense of writing in English. Hindi washed over me in my earliest years. I chattered aloud in it to the children around. It was my first spoken language, though Malayalam, my mother tongue, has always been there by its side, indeed alongside any other language I have used. What is my mother tongue now, if not a buried stream? At times, in America, I feel my mother tongue approaches the condition of dream. Its curving syllables blossom for me in so many scripts: gawky, dazzling letters spray painted in fluorescent shades onto the metal sides of subway cars or the dark walls of inner tunnels, shifting, metamorphic. Sometimes in chalk I read letters a man draws out laboriously on the sidewalks of Manhattan, spelling out the obvious, as necessity so often compels: I AM HOMELESS, I NEED FOOD, SHELTER. A smattering of dimes and quarters lie near his bent knees. Those letters I read in the only script I know make for a ferocious, almost consumptive edge to knowledge in me.

I have never learnt to read or write in Malayalam and turned into a truly postcolonial creature, who had to live in English, though a special sort of English, I must say, for the version of the language I am comfortable with bends and sways to the shores of other territories, other tongues.

Yet the price of fluency in many places may well be loss of the sheer intimacy that one has with "one's own" culture, a speech that holds its own sway, untouched by any other. But perhaps there is a dangerous simplicity here. And, indeed, how might such an idealized state be maintained at the tail end of the century? And it is a dangerous idea that animates such simplicity, small and bloody wars have been fought for such ideals.

Of course, there are difficulties in the way of one who does not know how to read or write her mother tongue. For instance, I would love to read the prose of Lalithambika Antherjanam, the poetry of Nalapat Balamaniamma and Awappa Paniker rather than have them read to me. I would love to read Mahakavi K. V. Seemon's epic *Vedaviharam* rather than have it recited to me.

Or is there something in me that needs to draw on that old reliance, the voice of another reading, the sheer giveness of speech. After all, if it were just an issue of mother wit, I am sure I would be able to read and write Malayalam by now. So is there perhaps a deliberate dependency, revealing something of my childhood longings and fears, a community held in dream, a treasured orality? For the rhythms of the language first came to me not just in lullabies or in the chatter of women in the kitchen or by the wellside, but in the measured cadences of oratory and poetry, and nightly recitations from the Bible and the epics.

As a Blackwoman

Maud Sulter

As a blackwoman
the bearing of my child
is a political act.

I have
been mounted in rape
   bred from like cattle
   mined for my fecundity

I have
been denied abortion
   denied contraception
   denied my freedom to choose

I have
been subjected to abortion
   injected with contraception
   sterilized without my consent

I have
borne witness to the murders
of my children
by the Klan, the Front, the State

I have
borne sons hung for rape
for looking at a white girl

I have
borne daughters shot
for being liberationists

As a blackwoman
I have taken the power to choose
to bear a black child

—a political act?

As a blackwoman
every act is a personal act
every act is a political act

As a blackwoman
the personal is political
holds no empty rhetoric

The Colonel

Carolyn Forché

What you have heard is true. I was in his house. His wife carried a tray of coffee and sugar. His daughter filed her nails, his son went out for the night. There were daily papers, pet dogs, a pistol on the cushion beside him. The moon swung bare on its black cord over the house. On the television was a cop show. It was in English. Broken bottles were embedded in the walls around the house to scoop the kneecaps from a man's legs or cut his hands to lace. On the windows there were gratings like those in liquor stores. We had dinner, rack of lamb, good wine, a gold bell was on the table for calling the maid. The maid brought green mangoes, salt, a type of bread. I was asked how I enjoyed the country. There was a brief commercial in Spanish. His wife took everything away. There was some talk then of how difficult it had become to govern. The parrot said hello on the terrace. The colonel told it to shut up, and pushed himself from the table. My friend said to me with his eyes: say nothing. The colonel returned with a sack used to bring groceries home. He spilled many human ears on the table. They were like dried peach halves. There is no other way to say this. He took one of them in his hands, shook it in our faces, dropped it into a water glass. It came alive there. I am tired of fooling around he said. As for the rights of anyone, tell your people they can go fuck themselves. He swept the ears to the floor with his arm and held the last of his wine in the air. Something for your poetry, no? he said. Some of the ears on the floor caught this scrap of his voice. Some of the ears on the floor were pressed to the ground.

Six Days: Some Rememberings

Grace Paley

I was in jail. I had been sentenced to six days in the Women's House of Detention, a fourteen-story prison right in the middle of Greenwich Village, my own neighborhood. This happened during the American War in Vietnam. I have forgotten which important year of the famous '60s. The civil disobedience for which I was paying a small penalty probably consisted of sitting down to impede or slow some military parade.

I was surprised at the sentence. Others had been given two days or dismissed. I think the judge was particularly angry with me. After all, I was not a kid. He thought I was old enough to know better, a forty-five-year-old woman, a mother and teacher. I ought to be too busy to waste time on causes I couldn't possibly understand.

I was herded with about twenty other women, about 90 percent black and Puerto Rican, into the bull pen, an odd name for a women's holding facility. There, through someone else's lawyer, I received a note from home, telling me that since I'd chosen to spend the first week of July in jail, my son would probably not go to summer camp because I had neglected to raise the money I'd promised. I read this note and burst into tears, real running down the cheek tears. It was true: Thinking about other people's grown boys I had betrayed my little son. The summer, starting that day, July 1, stood up before me day after day, steaming the city streets, the after-work crowded city pool.

I guess I attracted some attention. You—you white girl you—you never been arrested before? A black woman about a head taller than I put her arm on my shoulder.—It ain't so bad. What's your time sugar? I gotta do three years. You huh?

Six days.

Six days? What the fuck for?

I explained, sniffling, embarrassed.

You got six days for sitting down in front of a horse? Cop on the horse?

Horse step on you? Jesus in hell, cops gettin' crazier and stupider and meaner. Maybe we get you out.

No, no, I said. I wasn't crying because of that. I didn't want her to think I was scared. I wasn't. She paid no attention. Shoving a couple of women aside.— Don't stand in front of me, bitch. Move over. What you looking at? She took hold of the bars of our cage, commenced to hang on them, shook them mightily, screaming—Hear me now, you mother fuckers, you grotty pigs, get this housewife out of here! She returned to comfort me.—Six days in this lowdown hole for sitting in front of a horse!

Before we were distributed among our cells, we were dressed in a kind of nurse's aide scrub uniform, blue or green, a little too large or a little too small. We had had to submit to a physical in which all our hiding places were investigated for drugs. These examinations were not too difficult, mostly because a young woman named Andrea Dworkin had fought them, refused a grosser, more painful examination some months earlier. She had been arrested, protesting the war in front of the U.S. mission to the UN. I had been there too, but I don't think I was arrested that day. She was mocked for that determined struggle at the Women's House, as she has been for other braveries, but according to the women I questioned, certain humiliating—perhaps sadistic—customs had ended, for that period at least.

My cellmate was a beautiful young woman, twenty-three years old, a prostitute who'd never been arrested before. She was nervous, but she had been given the name of an important long-termer. She explained it in a businesslike way that she *was* beautiful, and would need protection. She'd be OK once she found that woman. In the two days we spent together, she tried *not* to talk to the other women on our cell block. She said they were mostly street whores and addicts. She would never be on the street. Her man wouldn't allow it anyway.

I slept well for some reason, probably the hard mattress. I don't seem to mind where I am. Also I must tell you, I could look out the window at the end of our corridor and see my children or their friends, on their way to music lessons or Greenwich House pottery. Looking slantwise I could see right into Sutter's Bakery, then on the corner of 10th Street. These were my neighbors at coffee and cake.

Sometimes the cell block was open, but not our twelve cells. Other times the reverse. Visitors came by: they were prisoners, detainees not yet sentenced. They seemed to have a strolling freedom, though several, unsentenced, unable to make bail, had been there for months. One woman peering into the cells stopped when she saw me. Grace! Hi! I knew her from the neighborhood, maybe the park, couldn't really remember her name.

What are you in for? I asked.

Oh nothing—well a stupid drug bust. I don't even use—oh well forget it. I've been here six weeks. They keep putting the trial off. Are you OK?

Then I complained. I had planned not to complain about anything while living among people who'd be here in these clanging cells a long time; it didn't seem right. But I said, I don't have anything to read and they took away my pen and I don't have paper.

Oh you'll get all that eventually—she said. Keep asking.

Well they have all my hair pins. I'm a mess.

No no she said—you're OK. You look nice.

(A couple of years later, the war continuing, I was arrested in Washington. My hair was still quite long. I wore it in a kind of bun on top of my head. My hair pins gone, my hair straggled wildly every which way. Muriel Rukeyser, arrested that day along with about thirty other women, made the same generous sisterly remark. No no Grace; love you with your hair down, you really ought to always wear it this way.)

The very next morning, my friend brought me *The Collected Stories of William Carlos Williams*. These OK?

God! OK—Yes!

My trial is coming up tomorrow, she said. I think I'm getting off with time already done. Over done. See you around?

That afternoon, my cellmate came for her things—I'm moving to the fourth floor. Working in the kitchen. Couldn't be better.—We were sitting outside our cells, she wanted me to know something. She'd already told me, but said it again.—I still can't believe it. This creep, this guy, this cop, he waits he just waits till he's fucked and fine, pulls his pants up, pays me, and arrests me. It's not legal. It's not. My man's so mad, he like to kill *me*, but he's not that kind of—he's not a criminal type, *my* man. She never said the word pimp. Maybe no one did. Maybe that was our word.

I had made friends with some of the women in the cells across the aisle. How can I say "made friends." I just sat and spoke when spoken to, I was at school. I answered questions—simple ones. Why I would do such a fool thing on purpose? How old were my children? My man any good? Then, you live around the corner? That was a good idea, Evelyn said, to have a prison in your own neighborhood, so you could keep in touch, yelling out the window. As in fact we were able to do right here and now, calling and being called from Sixth Avenue, by mothers, children, boyfriends.

About the children: One woman took me aside. Her daughter was brilliant, she was in Hunter High School, had taken a test. No she hardly ever saw her, but she wasn't a whore—it was the drugs. Her daughter was ashamed, the grandmother, the father's mother made the child ashamed. When she got out in six months it would be different. This made Evelyn and Rita, right across from my cell, laugh. Different, I swear. Different. Laughing. But she *could* make it, I said. Then they really laughed. Their first laugh was a bare giggle compared to these convulsive roars. Change her ways? That dumb bitch? Ha!!

Another woman, Helen, the only other white woman on the cell block, wanted to talk to me. She wanted me to know that she was not only white, but Jewish. She came from Brighton Beach. Her father, he should rest in peace, thank God, was dead. Her arms were covered with puncture marks almost like sleeve patterns. But she needed to talk to me, because I was Jewish (I'd been asked by Rita and Evelyn—was I Irish? No, Jewish. Oh, they answered). She walked me to the barred window at the end of the corridor, the window that looked down on W. 10th Street. She said—How come you so friends with those black whores? You don't hardly talk to me. I said I liked them, but I like her too. She said, if you knew them for true, you wouldn't like them. They nothing but street whores. You know, once I was friends with them. We done a lot of things together, I knew them fifteen years Evy and Rita maybe twenty, I been in the streets with them, side by side, Amsterdam, Lenox, West Harlem; in bad weather we covered each other. Then one day along come Malcolm X and they don't know me no more, they ain't talking to me. You too white, I ain't all that white. Twenty years. They ain't talking.

My friend Myrt called one day, that is called from the street, called—Grace, Grace.—I heard and ran to the window. A policeman, the regular beat cop was addressing her. She looked up, then walked away before I could yell my answer. Later on she told me that he'd said—I don't think Grace would appreciate you calling her name out like that.

What a mistake! For years, going to the park with my children, or simply walking down Sixth Avenue on a summer night past the Women's House, we would often have to thread our way through whole families calling up—bellowing, screaming to the third, seventh, tenth floor, to figures, shadows behind bars and screened windows—How you feeling? Here's Glena. She got big. Mami mami you like my dress? We gettin you out baby. New lawyer come by.

And the replies, among which I was privileged to live for a few days—shouted down.—You lookin beautiful. What he say? Fuck you James. I got a chance? Bye bye. Come next week.

Then the guards, the heavy clanking of cell doors. Keys. Night.

I still had no pen or paper despite the great history of prison literature. I was suffering a kind of frustration, a sickness in the way claustrophobia is a sickness—this paper-and-penlessness was a terrible pain in the area of my heart, a nausea. I was surprised.

In the evening, at lights out (a little like the army or on good days a strict, unpleasant camp), women called softly from their cells. Rita hey Rita sing that song—Come on sister sing. A few more importunings and then Rita in the cell diagonal to mine would begin with a ballad. A song about two women and a man. It was familiar to everyone but me. The two women were prison sweethearts. The man was her outside lover. One woman, the singer, was being paroled. The ballad told her sorrow about having been parted from him when she was sentenced, now she would leave her loved woman after three years. There were about twenty stanzas of joy and grief.

Well, I was so angry not to have pen and paper to get some of it down that I lost it all—all but the sorrowful plot. Of course she had this long song in her head and in the next few nights she sang and chanted others, sometimes with a small chorus.

Which is how I finally understood that I didn't lack pen and paper but my own memorizing mind. It had been given away with a hundred poems, called rote learning, old-fashioned, backward, an enemy of creative thinking, a great human gift, disowned.

Now there's a garden where the Women's House of Detention once stood. A green place, safely fenced in, with protected daffodils and tulips; roses bloom in it too, sometimes into November.

The big women's warehouse and its barred blind windows have been removed from Greenwich Village's affluent throat. I was sorry when it happened; the bricks came roaring down, great trucks carried them away.

I have always agreed with Rita and Evelyn that if there are prisons, they ought to be in the neighborhood, near a subway—not way out in distant suburbs, where families have to take cars, buses, ferries, trains, and the population that considers itself innocent forgets, denies, chooses to never know that there is a whole huge country of the bad and the unlucky and the self-hurters, a country with a population greater than that of many nations in our world.

The Ritual of *Satī*

Gītā Chattopādhyāy

The dog has crossed the knee-deep dark stream of water,
that trickle oozing out of your eyes is your Baitaranī River.
Your *jāmrul*-tree body covered with poisonous ants,
a hard fist holds you down in case you want to come back.
You're going to burn here, now mount the funeral pyre.
You're going to burn here, now mount the memory pyre.
You're going to burn here—bloody lips, navel the color of copper.
Lift the face-cloth, take a last look at your husband's face.

Notes:

On September 4, 1987, in the village of Deorala in Rajasthan, an eighteen-year-old Rajput woman, Roop Kanwar, burned herself alive on the funeral pyre of her husband, setting off storms of controversy, and a flurry of legislation, in the country. Alleged eyewitnesses first claimed that the girl committed *satī* voluntarily, this being a long-revered custom for Rajput widows.

Later, however, after the central and state governments voiced tardy disapproval, and sent police to close off the area to thousands of fervent pilgrims and curiosity seekers, the story emerged that the young woman had been dragged to the pyre, screaming for mercy, by her in-laws who were anxious for the glory—and revenue—that accrue to Rajasthani villages where a *satī* has occurred. Although the custom was outlawed in 1829, it remains very much alive in cultural memory; but fortunately, despite the intense publicity this incident received, there have been no substantiated "copy-cat" cases.

Jāmrul wood is often used for funeral pyre fuel.

In Hindu mythology, the Baitaranī is the river which the spirits of the dead must cross to reach the afterworld, much like the Styx or the Jordan in Western mythology.

six

Resistance and Refusal

City of Fire

Joy Harjo

Here is a city built of passion
where live many houses
with never falling night
in many rooms.
Through this entrance cold
is no longer a thief,
and in this place your heart
will never be a murderer.
Come, sweet,
I am a house with many rooms.
There is no end.
Each room is a street to the next world.
Where live other cities beneath
incendiary skies. And you have made
a fire in every room.
Come.
Lie with me before the flame.
I will dream you a wolf
and suckle you newborn.
I will dream you a hawk
and circle this city in your
racing heart.
I will dream you the wind,
taste salt air on my lips until
I take you apart raw.
Come here.

We will make a river,
flood this city built of passion
with fire,
with a revolutionary fire.

That Other World That Was the World

Nadine Gordimer

More than three hundred years of the colonization of modern times (as distinct from the colonization of antiquity) have come to an end. This is the positive achievement of our twentieth century, in which so much has been negative, so much suffering and destruction has taken place. Colonization is passing into history, except for comparatively small pockets of the earth's surface where new conquest has taken a precarious hold and the conquered, far from being subdued into acquiescence, make life for the conquerors difficult and dangerous.

Surely the grand finale of the age of colonization took place in the three years, 1991 to 1994, when South Africa emerged amazingly, a great spectacle of human liberation, from double colonization.

For unlike other countries where the British, the French, the Portuguese and other European powers ruled the indigenous people and when these colonizers were defeated or withdrew, left the countries in indigenous hands, South Africa in the early twentieth century passed from colonization from without—Dutch, French, finally British—to perpetuated colonization within, in the form of white minority power over the black majority. All the features of colonization were retained: taxes and the appropriation of land by whites, so that blacks would have to come to town and provide cheap labour in order to survive; favoured status for the minority in civil rights, education, freedom of movement. Freed from British imperialism, South Africa was far from free; it was a police state based on the claim that the white skin of colonials was superior to black skin.

I think there is a definite distinction to be made, everywhere, between what were the first settlers, the so-called pioneers who fought their way into a country, killing Indians or blacks, and the people of later generations who were born into a society that had long established its ruling accommodation with the indigenous people: a society removed from all danger that had made itself comfortable with injustice, in this case the theory that there are genetically inferior races with lower needs than others.

I emerged into this milieu with my birth in South Africa in the Twenties. I shall never write an autobiography—I am much too jealous of my privacy, for that—but I begin to think that my experience as a product of this social phenomenon has relevance beyond the personal; it may be a modest part of alternative history if pieced together with the experience of other writers. And it has a conclusion I did not anticipate would be reached in my lifetime, even when I became aware of my situation.

We lived in a small gold-mining town thirty miles from Johannesburg, lost in the veld nearly 6,000 feet above sea level. The features of the landscape, its shapes and volumes, were made of waste. We were surrounded by yellow geometrical dumps of gold tailings and black hills of coal slag. I thought it ugly when I was a child brought up on English picture books of lush meadows and woods—but now I find the vast grassland beautiful and the memory of it an intimation to me, if I had known it then, that the horizons of existence are wide and that the eye and the mind could be carried on and on, from there.

My mother came from England when she was six years old. My father came from Latvia at thirteen. She had a solid, petty middle-class, piano-playing background, a father lured to emigration by the adventure of diamond prospecting rather than need. My father was sent away by his father to escape pogroms and poverty.

Perhaps because of their youth when they left, and because of this economic and social disparity, my parents kept no connections with the countries they emigrated from. They could not talk of a common "home" across the water, as many other whites in the town did. My father was ashamed of his lack of formal education and my mother did not disguise the fact that she felt she had demeaned herself by marrying him. There was a certain dour tact in not talking about where they had sprung from.

Though both Jewish, they did not take part in Jewish communal life in the town, or join the Zionist associations of the time; they did not belong to a synagogue—my mother was an agnostic and my father, who had had an orthodox childhood, could not withstand her gibes about the hypocrisy of organized religion.

In one of Albert Camus's novels, the child Jacques, born and living in Algeria, asks his mother: "Maman, qu'est que c'est la patrie?" And she replies, "Je ne sais pas. Non." And the child says, "C'est la France."

If I had been asked the question as a child, I probably would have said, "It's

England." South Africa's British dominion status had ended the year after I was born, but South Africa was a "sovereign independent state" whose allegiance still was to the British Crown. At school we celebrated the Twenty-fifth Jubilee of "our" King, George V. The so-called mother country: that was the focus of inculcated loyalty, of allegiance, identification for English-speaking South Africans.

And yet it was so remote, that England, that Northern Hemisphere we learnt about in geography class. In the Twenties and Thirties it was four weeks away across the seas. We were at the bottom of the map; we did not count, had little sense of ourselves beyond the performance of daily life.

Italo Calvino was not a colonial but he knew the sense an imaginative child, living in a small town even in an integrated, Italian society, may have of living in an ante-room of life. He describes how, as a boy, passing the cinema where dubbed voices on the sound track of American films came through the projectionist's window, he could "sense the call of that other world that was the world."

This conveys perfectly, at a graver and more enduring—a damaging—level what was my sense of my own existence.

From a very early age I had the sense that that other world—the world of books I took from the library, the world of the cinema—was that other world that was the world. We lived outside it.

It called. Perhaps some day, if one were very lucky, very good, worked very hard, one might get to see it; and as I grew older that world took form, Dickens's and Virginia Woolf's London, Balzac's and Proust's Paris. As for America, I passed from Huck Finn to Faulkner and Eudora Welty; but America was not on the itinerary of the retired mine captains and shift bosses and their wives, my mother's friends, who saved all their lives to afford one trip "home" to England on retirement.

That other world that was the world.

For me, this was not merely a charming childish romanticism; I would not simply grow out of it, grow into my own world effortlessly, as Calvino would.

I had no lineal connection with the past around me, the dynasties of black people.

I had the most tenuous of connections with the present in which I was growing up.

My parents never talked politics; the only partisanship they displayed was during the war, when they wanted "la patrie," the British, to defeat the Germans. I was not even dimly aware of the preparation for the struggle for political power that was beginning between Afrikaners, who more than twenty years before my birth had lost the Boer War to the British, and English-speaking South African whites who were the victors.

I saw the bare-foot children of poor-white Afrikaners, victims of defeat and drought, selling newspapers, just as I saw black people, victims of a much greater defeat, the theft of their land and the loss of all rights over the conduct of their lives, sent back to their ghetto after the day's work serving the town.

Reading a biography of Marguerite Duras recently, I see in her colonial childhood in Indochina my own in South Africa. Her family "had the right not to be kept waiting at administration counters, and were served everywhere before the local Vietnamese. They benefited by the privileges reserved for the French colonials. Marguerite does not complain about this difference in treatment. The distinction between the races is a natural reality for her."

As it was for me.

What was my place? Could it know me?

On the one hand there was that other world that was the world, where Ginger Rogers and Fred Astaire danced in a cloudscape (I had ambitions to be a dancer, myself, as an entry to that world) and Maurice Chevalier sang about Paris. There were the moors where Heathcliff's Cathy wandered, and the London park where Mrs. Dalloway took her walks.

On the other hand, just outside the gate of our suburban house with its red-polished stoep and two bow-windows, there was the great continuous to-and-fro of life, the voice of it languages I didn't understand but that were part of my earliest aural awakening; the spectacle of it defined by my adult mentors as something nothing to do with me.

This totally surrounding, engulfing experience was removed from me not by land and sea but by law, custom and prejudice.

And fear. I was told by my mother to avoid passing, on my way to school, the mine compound where black miners lived; she did not explain why, but the reason seeped to me through adult innuendo: there was the idea that every black man was waiting to rape some toothy little white schoolgirl.

Many years later, my friend and fellow writer Es'kia Mphahlele told me he was instructed by his mother to turn his bicycle down another street if he saw he was going to pass white boys. He did not know why until, in the same way as I learned my fear of black men, he gathered that he must believe every white was only waiting for the opportunity to attack him.

There was certainly more substance behind the fear instilled in him than the fear instilled in me, since blacks were physically maltreated by some whites; but the extreme unlikelihood that he or I was in any danger in the manner anticipated was part of the paranoia of separation that prevailed, matched each to the colour of his or her skin.

Archbishop Desmond Tutu—he and I have discovered—as a child lived for some time in the black ghetto across the veld from the town where I, too, was growing up; there was as much chance of our meeting then as there was of a moon landing.

Did we pass one another, sometimes, on Saturday mornings when the white town and the black ghetto all stocked up for the weekend at the same shops? Did I pass him by when I went into the local library to change books, a library he was barred from because he was black?

Perhaps there were explanations for all this, but they were not evident at home, at school, or among the contemporaries who were chosen for me, to whom I was confined by law, so to speak. And if there were to be some explanations in that other world that was the world, over the seas, it was not open to me; you could not expect it to be bothered with us.

Albert Camus's unfinished, posthumously published novel, from which I quoted earlier, has what appears to be a puzzling title, *Le Premier Homme*; but this is not some Neanderthal romance. Jacques is a colonial boy born and growing up in Algiers. He's white, not Arab; therefore, as we have seen in his answer to his mother, he must be French. But he has never seen France. For fictional Jacques and for the child I was, the premise is: Colonial: that's the story of who I am.

The one who belongs nowhere.

The one who has no national mould.

As Jacques grows up he comes to the realization that he must *make himself*. The precept is: if he is not to be the dangling participle of imperialism, if he is not to be the outsider defined by Arabs—a being non-Arab—what is he? A negative. In this sense, he starts from zero. He is the constructor of his own consciousness. He is The First Man.

Let us not worry about the gender: I was to come to the same necessity; to *make myself*, in the metaphor of The First Man, without coherent references, up on his own two legs, no model on how to proceed.

Of course the realization of the necessity did not come quickly; one must not exaggerate, or rather one cannot exaggerate sufficiently the tendency of human beings to keep sipping the daily syrup of life in a cosy enclave.

Our place as whites outside that world that was the world, overseas, was suitably humble—what effrontery to think that we could write a poem or compose a song that would be "good enough," over there—but ours was a place secure and comfortable, so long as one kept to the simple rules, not walking by too close to the compound where the black miners lived. The ordinary components of childhood were mine, at least until the age of eleven when circumstances that have no relevance here put a curious end to it.

But with every adolescence there comes to everyone the inner tug of war—the need to break away, and the need to bond.

I had more passionate emotion for the first than courage to carry it out, but that would have resolved itself anyway, with time and confidence.

What was dismaying was the lack of discovery of what one might turn *to*, bond *with*.

Young white people in the town gathered in sports clubs and religious groups; they met the same people at tennis on Sunday as they had danced with on Saturday night. It was a prelude to going to one another's weddings, attending bridge afternoons and charity cake-sales (the white women) and meeting to exchange chaff in the club bar after golf (the white men). As Camus says, a life "with no other project but the immediate."

A life ordered, defined, circumscribed by the possession of a white skin. I did not know anything else, yet I knew I could not commit myself there; I felt it as a vague but menacing risk, bondage, not bonding. My reaction was to retreat, turn even further away from the reality of our life than the club life of colonials, which at least was an enclave within the life that swarmed around it.

That world that was the world, overseas, now lived my life as proxy for me; it was no longer the cloudscape of Fred Astaire and Ginger Rogers, but the world of literature. I ate and slept at home, but I had my essential being in books. Rilke roused and answered the emptiness in me where religious faith was missing. Chekhov and Dostoevsky opened for me the awesome mysteries of human behaviour. Proust taught me that sexual love, for which every adolescent yearns, is a painful and cruel affair as well as the temptation of bliss. Yeats made me understand there was such a thing as a passion for justice, quite as strong as sexual passion.

These and other writers were my mentors, out of whom I tried to make an artificial construct of myself. When young people are said to "live in books" rather than in themselves, this is regarded as an escape; it is more likely a search.

For me, of course, the search was not a success in terms of the unconscious purpose I had. I could not make myself out of the components of that other world, though I could and did appropriate it for my delight and enlightenment. What it could do for me, and did, was turn me to face a possibility; a possibility for myself. In my desire to write, in the writing that I was already doing out of my pathetically limited knowledge of the people and the country where I lived, was the means to find what my truth was, what was there to bond with, how I could manage to become my own First Man, woman-man, human being.

I had, in fact, been engaged with this possibility for some time, without understanding what I was doing.

An early story of mine harked back to a childhood impression I had thought forgotten.

On that same way to school when I avoided crossing the path of the black miners in the open veld, I would pass the row of "Concession" stores—trading concessions on mine property—which served the miners and had the intended effect of keeping them out of the town. I had taken my time, as children will dawdle, seeing through the shop doors every day how the miners were treated by the white shopkeepers, spoken to abusively, not allowed to linger in choice of purchases as we whites did. At the time, to me this was just another example of the way adult life was ordered; something accepted, not disturbing. But the images had fermented below the surface impressions of childhood as I developed the writer's questioning concentration.

What I was coming to understand, in writing that story, was one of the essential features of colonialism: the usefulness to the regime of the poor immigrant's opportunity, at last, to feel superior to someone, and thereby support the regime's policy of keeping the indigenous population decreed inferior.

My story's title was "The Defeated," and it did not refer only to the black miners. They were despised, and bullied across the counter by white immigrants who themselves had a precarious economic and social footing: ill-educated, scarcely able to speak the two languages of the white community, carrying in their minds and bodies the humiliations and deprivation of pogroms and quotas they had fled in Eastern Europe.

In keeping with my ignorance at the time, the story makes too much of an equation between the defeated—the shopkeeper who relieves his feelings of inferiority within the white community by maltreating blacks, the black miners who are so stripped of every context of human dignity that they must submit to abuse even from someone at the lowest level in the white community.

For the shopkeeper and the black miner were, in fact, *not* in the same social pit.

I could have written a sequel set ten or twenty years on and the shopkeeper would have had a business in town and a son at a university, he would have been a naturalized full citizen with the vote—while the black miner still would have been drilling the rock-face or back in his rural home living on the meagre savings of a lifetime spent underground, and still without citizenship rights or the vote in the country of his birth and ancestry.

But if out of a muddled desire to juggle justice where there was none—a kind of reconciliatory conclusion I might have thought was the correct literary approach—I equated the measure of defeat in the lives of the two men, black and white, I did at least reveal in the story that important phenomenon whereby the balance of oppression is maintained not just by laws, but in every situation of social intercourse. I was learning that oppression thrives on all manner of prejudicial behavior, is fostered by all kinds of insecurity.

With small beginnings such as this I started, tentatively, held back by the strictly controlled environment of the white enclave, to live in the country to which, until then, I had no claim but the fact of birth.

In my stories I was continuing to turn over, this way and that, events in the conduct of my narrow life that had seemed to have a single meaning. The only communal activity in which I'd taken part was amateur theatricals; the first uneasy stirrings of liberalism in the town came to be expressed in the mode the churches and individual consciences were accustomed to—charity. No one thought to petition the town council to open the library to blacks, but it was decided to take a play to the only public hall in the black ghetto.

The play was *The Importance of Being Earnest*, and I had the role of Gwendolen. I was twenty and had never been into a black township before; I believe none of us in the cast had. I believe that no one in the audience had ever seen a play before; how could they? The Town Hall, which doubled as a theatre, was closed to blacks. The audience started off close-kneed and hands folded but was soon laughing and exclaiming. We thought we had had a great success, and drank to it back-stage with our usual tipple, some gaudy liqueur.

When the scenes of that evening kept returning to me in aspects turned this way and that, and I began to write a piece of fiction, make a story out of them, what emerged was a satire—on us.

On the absurdity of taking what we imagined was bountiful cultural uplift, an Oscar Wilde play, to the ghetto the town had created. I came to the full appreciation that the audience, those people with drama, tragedy and comedy in their own lives about which we knew *nothing*, were laughing at us.

Not at the play, but us. They did not understand the play with its elaborate, facetious and ironic use of the language they half-knew, English; but they understood us, all right. And we in our pretensions, our idea of what we were "giving" them, were exquisitely funny. Oscar Wilde perhaps would have been amused to think that his play became doubly a satire, functioning as such far from Lady Bracknell's drawing-room.

I think I have been fortunate in that I was born into the decadence of the colonial period.

It has been ravelling out during my lifetime. This is so, even though the mid-century saw the hardening of South African racism in huge forced removals of the black population in order to satisfy white separatism and economic greed, the outlawing of all opposition to these policies as subversion, and for millions the suffering of imprisonment and exile. These were the ghastly paroxysms of a monstrous regime thrashing about in death throes.

The reaction of the white community to strikes and mass demonstrations was to raise the drawbridges over which blacks might commingle with whites. Sexual relations between black and white became a criminal offence, no mixed membership of political parties was allowed, even ambulances were segregated so that an accident victim might lie by the roadside until the vehicle mandated to the appropriate skin colour could be summoned.

A larger and larger army and police force were deployed to keep blacks out of white lives, and all the devices of bugging, opening mail, infiltrating, trapping, spying were gratefully tolerated by the white community within itself for what it believed was its own safety. For, of course, there were dissidents among whites who actively supported blacks against discrimination, and who, going about undetected in their white skin, could be hunted out only in this way.

Diary

Anne Frank

Monday, July 26, 1943

Dear Kitty,

Yesterday was a very tumultuous day, and we're still all wound up. Actually, you may wonder if there's ever a day that passes without some kind of excitement.

The first warning siren went off in the morning while we were at breakfast, but we paid no attention, because it only meant that the planes were crossing the coast. I had a terrible headache, so I lay down for an hour after breakfast and then went to the office at around two. At two-thirty Margot had finished her office work and was just gathering her things together when the sirens began wailing again. So she and I trooped back upstairs. None too soon, it seems, for less than five minutes later the guns were booming so loudly that we went and stood in the hall. The house shook and the bombs kept falling. I was clutching my "escape bag," more because I wanted to have something to hold on to than because I wanted to run away. I know we can't leave here, but if we had to, being seen on the streets would be just as dangerous as getting caught in an air raid. After half an hour the drone of engines faded and the house began to hum with activity again. Peter emerged from his lookout post in the front attic, Dussel remained in the front office, Mrs. van D. felt safest in the private office, Mr. van Daan had been watching from the loft, and those of us on the landing spread out to watch the columns of smoke rising from the harbor. Before long the smell of fire was everywhere, and outside it looked as if the city were enveloped in a thick fog.

A big fire like that is not a pleasant sight, but fortunately for us it was all over, and we went back to our various chores. Just as we were starting dinner: another air-raid alarm. The food was good, but I lost my appetite the moment I heard the siren. Nothing happened, however, and forty-five minutes later the all clear was sounded. After the dishes had been washed: another air-raid warning, gunfire and swarms of planes. "Oh, gosh, twice in one day," we thought, "that's twice too many." Little good that did us, because once again the bombs rained down, this time on the other side of the city. According to British reports, Schiphol Airport was bombed. The planes dived and climbed, the air was abuzz with the drone of engines. It was very scary, and the whole time I kept thinking, "Here it comes, this is it."

I can assure you that when I went to bed at nine, my legs were still shaking. At the stroke of midnight I woke up again: more planes! Dussel was undressing, but I took no notice and leapt up, wide awake, at the sound of the first shot. I stayed in Father's bed until one, in my own bed until one-thirty, and was back in Father's bed at two. But the planes kept on coming. At last they stopped firing and I was able to go back "home" again. I finally fell asleep at half past two.

Seven o'clock. I awoke with a start and sat up in bed. Mr. van Daan was with Father. My first thought was: burglars. "Everything," I heard Mr. van Daan say, and I thought everything had been stolen. But no, this time it was wonderful news, the best we've had in months, maybe even since the war began. Mussolini has resigned and the King of Italy has taken over the government.

We jumped for joy. After the awful events of yesterday, finally something good happens and brings us . . . hope! Hope for an end to the war, hope for peace.

[. . .]

Yours, Anne

Wednesday, May 3, 1944

Dearest Kitty,

[. . .]

As you can no doubt imagine, we often say in despair, "What's the point of the war? Why, oh, why can't people live together peacefully? Why all this destruction?

The question is understandable, but up to now no one has come up with a satisfactory answer. Why is England manufacturing bigger and better airplanes and bombs and at the same time churning out new houses for reconstruction? Why are millions spent on the war each day, while not a penny is available for medical science, artists or the poor? Why do people have to starve when mountains of food are rotting away in other parts of the world? Oh, why are people so crazy?

I don't believe the war is simply the work of politicians and capitalists. Oh no, the common man is every bit as guilty; otherwise, people and nations would have rebelled long ago! There's a destructive urge in people, the urge to rage, murder and kill. And until all of humanity, without exception, undergoes a metamorphosis, wars will continue to be waged, and everything that has been carefully built up, cultivated and grown will be cut down and destroyed, only to start all over again!

I've often been down in the dumps, but never desperate. I look upon our life in hiding as an interesting adventure, full of danger and romance, and every privation as an amusing addition to my diary. I've made up my mind to lead a different life from other girls, and not to become an ordinary housewife later on. What I'm experiencing here is a good beginning to an interesting life, and that's the reason—the only reason—why I have to laugh at the humorous side of the most dangerous moments.

[...]

Yours, Anne M. Frank

Friday, July 21, 1944

Dearest Kitty,

I'm finally getting optimistic. Now, at last, things are going well! They really are! Great news! An assassination attempt has been made on Hitler's life, and for once not by Jewish Communists or English capitalists, but by a German general who's not only a count, but young as well. The Führer owes his life to "Divine Providence": he escaped, unfortunately, with only a few minor burns and scratches. A number of the officers and generals who were nearby were killed or wounded. The head of the conspiracy has been shot.

This is the best proof we've had so far that many officers and generals are fed up with the war and would like to see Hitler sink into a bottomless pit, so they can establish a military dictatorship, make peace with the Allies, rearm themselves and, after a few decades, start a new war. Perhaps Providence is deliberately biding its time getting rid of Hitler, since it's much easier, and cheaper, for the Allies to let the impeccable Germans kill each other off. It's less work for the Russians and the British, and it allows them to start rebuilding their own cities all that much sooner. But we haven't reached that point yet, and I'd hate to anticipate the glorious event. Still, you've probably noticed that I'm telling the truth, the whole truth and nothing but the truth. For once, I'm not rattling on about high ideals.

Furthermore, Hitler has been so kind as to announce to his loyal, devoted people that as of today all military personnel are under orders of the Gestapo, and that any soldier who knows that one of his superiors was involved in this cowardly attempt on the Führer's life may shoot him on sight!

A fine kettle of fish that will be. Little Johnny's feet are sore after a long march and his commanding officer bawls him out. Johnny grabs his rifle, shouts, "You, you tried to kill the Führer. Take that!" One shot, and the snooty officer who dared to reprimand him passes into eternal life (or is it eternal death?). Eventually, every time an officer sees a soldier or gives an order, he'll be practically wetting his pants, because the soldiers have more say-so than he does.

[. . .]

Yours, Anne M. Frank

Tuesday, August 1, 1944

Dearest Kitty,

[. . .]

As I've told you many times, I'm split in two. One side contains my exuberant cheerfulness, my flippancy, my joy in life and, above all, my ability to appreciate the lighter side of things. By that I mean not finding anything wrong with flirtations, a kiss, an embrace, an off-color joke. This side of me is usually lying in wait to ambush the other one, which is much purer, deeper and finer. No one knows Anne's better side, and that's why most people can't stand me. Oh, I can be an amusing clown for an afternoon, but after that everyone's had enough of me to last a month. Actually, I'm what a romantic movie is to a profound thinker—a mere diversion, a comic interlude, something that is soon forgotten: not bad, but not particularly good either. I hate having to tell you this, but why shouldn't I admit it when I know it's true? My lighter, more superficial side will always steal a march on the deeper side and therefore always win. You can't imagine how often I've tried to push away this Anne, which is only half of what is known as Anne—to beat her down, hide her. But it doesn't work, and I know why.

I'm afraid that people who know me as I usually am will discover I have another side, a better and finer side. I'm afraid they'll mock me, think I'm ridiculous and sentimental and not take me seriously. I'm used to not being taken seriously, but only the "lighthearted" Anne is used to it and can put up with it; the "deeper" Anne is too weak. If I force the good Anne into the spotlight for even fifteen minutes, she shuts up like a clam the moment she's called upon to speak, and lets Anne number one do the talking. Before I realize it, she's disappeared.

So the nice Anne is never seen in company. She's never made a single appearance, though she almost always takes the stage when I'm alone. I know exactly how I'd like to be, how I am . . . on the inside. But unfortunately I'm only like that with myself. And perhaps that's why—no, I'm sure that's the reason why—I think of myself as happy on the inside and other people think I'm happy on the outside. I'm guided by the pure Anne within, but on the outside I'm nothing but a frolicsome little goat tugging at its tether.

As I've told you, what I say is not what I feel, which is why I have a reputation for being boy-crazy as well as a flirt, a smart aleck and a reader of romances. The happy-go-lucky Anne laughs, gives a flippant reply, shrugs her shoulders and pretends she doesn't give a darn. The quiet Anne reacts in just the opposite way. If I'm being completely honest, I'll have to admit that it does matter to me, that I'm trying very hard to change myself, but that I'm always up against a more powerful enemy.

A voice within me is sobbing, "You see, that's what's become of you. You're surrounded by negative opinions, dismayed looks and mocking faces, people who dislike you, and all because you don't listen to the advice of your own better half." Believe me, I'd like to listen, but it doesn't work, because if I'm quiet and serious, everyone thinks I'm putting on a new act and I have to save myself with a joke, and then I'm not even talking about my own family, who assume I must be sick, stuff me with aspirins and sedatives, feel my neck and forehead to see if I have a temperature, ask about my bowel movements and berate me for being in a bad mood, until I just can't keep it up anymore, because when everybody starts hovering over me, I get cross, then sad, and finally end up turning my heart inside out, the bad part on the outside and the good part on the inside, and keep trying to find a way to become what I'd like to be and what I could be if . . . if only there were no other people in the world.

Yours, Anne M. Frank

ANNE'S DIARY ENDS HERE.

Arriving at the Plaza

Matilde Mellibovsky

One Thursday, during our walks in the circle, I feel the urge to find out what exactly the Plaza had been like in earlier days. So I delve into a fat book of Argentinian history: "The Plaza was always bustling, movement never ceased. Around 1810 neighborhood people would come: children, black women and vendors. They would add to the shouting and the din."[1] Looking at the illustrations from that time, my own childhood memories of them come alive: countrymen on horseback, poultry vendors, black women selling pastries or sweets, above all the water sellers' carts.

Washerwomen on their way back from the river carrying enormous bundles on their heads. Lots of dogs. And strolling ladies wearing dresses with very wide skirts. By 1844 we can already see the "pyramid"[2] in the Plaza, a new market, the Government House, the Cabildo's outline, and coaches drawn by four or six horses. . . .

Actually, I always thought of it as a foolish place and to me it still seems so; but not when I find myself there together with the Mothers.

But after so many marches I came to imagine it a small liberated zone separated from the rest of the country. Then I began to discover that it has beautiful trees, and I started to look for some beauty in its two or three standing monuments. On Thursdays when we are there, I love to see the children running, climbing onto the "pyramid." . . . At that moment I feel as if I were in a very intimate place. We have stepped on each street-tile surrounding the "pyramid" so many times. . . . Invariably, I ask myself how many miles have we Mothers walked around this monument. . . .

When we are all together, the Plaza is *my* place, it is *our* Plaza, and *all the disappeared are there and everybody is there.*

Moreover, as we Mothers have sometimes commented, it was in this Plaza that the Assembly of 1813 resolved that all instruments of torture had to be burnt: "The use of instruments of torture to get information about crimes is forbidden," and they decreed that "all instruments of torture should be burnt *by the executioner's hands* on May 25 at the Plaza Victoria."[3]

Over a hundred years later, we stand in horror in this place thinking about our savagely tortured children and their fate.

It is true that we Mothers did not choose the Plaza de Mayo because it is itself a political center or because it is very close to Argentina's great political center, still . . . how very odd, something like destiny came about, because it is precisely in the Plaza de Mayo that very important events in the life of the country have occurred.

This place, center of celebrations and of rejoicing during colonial times, was also the place where tragic sentences of justice were executed . . . before everybody's eyes. . . . It is not mere happenstance either that Garay, the founder of Buenos Aires, had the "Tree of Justice," or "el Rollo," erected nearby. And it is here that we Mothers come every Thursday to demand that justice be done.

The Plaza is a throbbing heart. . . . It appears to be a spot predestined to be a center of world interest, a window to the world, for half an hour one day a week. . . .

Yesterday I went to the Plaza and I was watching my companions—and everybody else—observing what takes place there, and I insist that at these very moments the Plaza is a throbbing heart, perhaps with a touch of tachycardia. . . . People approach full of curiosity, some from California, others from Australia. One of these foreigners, who could not express himself very well, said something like: "What is it that keeps you in a state of such high emotion besides the suffering, of course? What makes you keep moving?" And I spent the night asking myself that question until I found the answer: the fact that they have eliminated the generation that comes after me, that they have isolated me from the future, that they have separated me completely from my sense of continuity . . . and that I want to recover it, through Memory.

Without Memory, continuity in life does not exist.

Memory is the well-hidden roots which nourish the flowers with their sap and the fruits that we can see. Without the roots neither the flowers nor the fruits are possible.

I would say that Memory is the root that culminates in the seed which makes the circle of life cycle.

"You have to feel the fire of the desert under the soles of your feet," Rabbi Marshall Meyer used to tell us Mothers.

Memory gives life.

And the Plaza, with all its multitudes, is the perennial Memory of all that has happened since its origin. . . .

Everybody leaves their testimony . . . but the children? Where are they? I miss something . . . those children who made me thrill more than I ever had before, who jumped so happily that it looked as if they caused the clouds to run faster. . . . To see them so united by their songs and catch-words filled me with illusion and brought me closer than ever to a fairer, more human world. . . . Never in my entire life have I spent such happy hours . . . of real fellowship.

That is why when I walk around the Plaza I feel the Plaza asking me: *What has happened? I miss those children.*

Notes

1. Ricardo de la Fuente Machain's *La Plaza Trágica*, Municipalidad de la Ciudad de Buenos Aires, 1973. [MM]

2. This "pyramid" is actually an obelisk.

3. Diego Abad de Santillán's *Historia Argentina*, Editora Argentina, Buenos Aires, 1965. [Plaza de Mayo was then called Plaza Victoria.]

The Trikeri Journal

Victoria Theodorou

Far, very far, I hear life
high, very high hang the lights
the lights they stole from us
lights from the city they stole from us
and the memory of the last sunset when the hills
    were still our hills
far, very far you exist, you must exist
                    —"Marina," *State of Siege*

Trikeri is a tiny, virtually deserted island at the foot of Mount Pelion, immediately to the north of Pagasitikon Bay in the north of Greece. Cut off from the rest of the country by the surrounding mountain ranges of Rumeli to the west, the Evia mountains to the south, and Pelion to the east, it was considered an excellent site for the establishment of a concentration camp for political prisoners.

One can walk around Trikeri in a matter of three hours—a pleasant stroll in the summer, along paths shaded by evergreens and olive trees. But in the winter the little island is constantly beaten by icy winds, rain, and snow.

A monastery was built in 1841 on the highest point of the island. The church, dedicated to the Assumption of the Holy Virgin, stands in the middle of the courtyard. Its lovely reredos was restored by an exiled artist, who was later executed nearby. The ground floor and upper cells, built around the courtyard, are connected by a roofed, wooden porch, which in summer was used as a living space by the women exiled there. The ground floor cells, always dark and moldy, with half-rotten floorboards and no doors or windowpanes, were used for storage, bathhouses, and stables.

The sea surrounds Trikeri like a moat, and the mountains form a naturally impassable wall. Because of this isolation and inaccessibility, it was used during the Balkan wars as a camp for prisoners of war, without additional fortification. When in 1947 it was chosen as an ideal site for a camp for women political prisoners, it was deemed necessary to fortify it further, with even harsher security than that offered by nature. Guards, armed with machine guns, barbed-wire fences were installed in double and triple rows around all the areas used by the women, and naval vessels were positioned along the entire shoreline. Not a soul could approach Trikeri except policemen, the sailors who brought in supplies, and public speakers, whose job was to instruct the prisoners on how to "repent" and return to the "bosom of Greece." In spite of all the security measures, the women were forbidden to go outside the barbed-wire cages even to look for mushrooms and wild vegetables in the fields and olive groves nearby, or to go to the shore to swim and bathe their sore bodies. The eyes of the guards were constantly on them. Lights and fires were strictly forbidden for fear the women might flash signals to guerrillas in the mainland.

Early in the summer of 1945, almost immediately after the end of the war, the persecution of the left-wing resistance movement started. The government began to arrest men and women who had played an active part in the resistance against the Germans. If they had escaped to the mountains or to the Balkan countries, their families were arrested and confined on the island of Trikeri. In 1949, when the men were relocated at the Makronisos camp, Trikeri became exclusively a women's camp.

The first women exiled there were relatives—mothers, grandmothers, wives and children—of members of EAMELAS, and the Democratic Army. Most of these women came from villages in the north of Greece. Many of them had small children and had brought nothing more than the clothes on their backs. The government called these arrests "a preventative measure." Their numbers were always fluctuating because almost daily many would sign the Declaration of Repentance and leave, and new ones would arrive. From 1947 to 1949, these were the only women on Trikeri, and they were confined within the area of the monastery. But by September 1949, new arrivals (guerrillas and political activists) from the concentration camps of Chios, Macedonia, Rumeli, and Thessaly increased their number to 4,700.

Outside the monastery, only a few yards from the main gate, there was a small cemetery for those who died at Trikeri—a small, square plot, always with some freshly dug graves, which with the first rains would become green with clover and bright with wild flowers. The first men exiled there planted an oleander and marked the place with a large cross carved from olive wood.

The tents were a few steps away from the cemetery. On sunny days the children would play hide and seek there, hiding in the thick foliage of the blooming oleander behind the cross. The knowledge that yellow fever or T.B. or even a simple cold could put any of them under the salty earth had given them such familiarity with death that this cemetery, a place that under ordinary circumstances they would have shunned, held no special fear for them. It was simply a spot where they were allowed to run and shout away from the guards and the sad faces of their mothers.

On April 4, 1949, three cargo ships, carrying 1,200 women and children, left the concentration camp of Chios for Trikeri. The ships were painted black on the outside, and their interior was black with soot.

At nightfall a ferocious storm developed. The captain wanted to return to port, but the officers pressed him to continue the journey. The ship battled huge waves across the Aegean and almost lost the struggle. We lived through the first night of terror packed inside suffocatingly narrow sooty cabins, fearing that after having survived two wars we would perish at sea. All night long we were tossed about, knocking against each other like drunks. Many had lost consciousness and lay on the floor in puddles of blood, vomit, and excrement from the overflowing toilets. Others lamented and pulled their hair, hugging their frightened children to their breasts. Only Kate Memeli and Tila were on their feet, trying to take care of us and comfort the children.

By the next evening, as we approached the shores of Pelion, the storm calmed down somewhat, and we were able to discern Trikeri on the horizon, green with olive groves and pine forests. Among the olive groves stretching to the shore were scattered small grey houses. Half a dozen fishing boats were moored at the small pier.

Our official destination was the campsite on the north shore of the island, but the officers in charge ordered the captain to dock two miles away, giving us the additional burden of carrying our bundles, the children, and the stretchers with the sick up a steep and thorny path, which that day we named Golgotha.

The camp, originally occupied by men, was located on the top of the hill beyond the olive groves and was enclosed by rows of barbed wire. We stopped for a short break under the shade of the olive trees and ate our few ounces of "dry nourishment"—half a piece of salty whitefish—and drank a mouthful of brackish, lukewarm water. Our future home, a barbed-wire enclosure, was entirely exposed to the elements, without a single tree in sight.

The tents we found within this cage were tilted over, many had neither poles nor ropes. They were low and narrow, with room enough for only one person to squat or lie down. Inside some of them there were makeshift fireplaces and small stoves made from tin cans.

We gazed in terror at the desolation on the top of the bare hill, stark witness to man's struggle with the sea and sky. We began to realize how much more difficult survival would be in this desert, without even the comforting thought of being near the sympathetic and compassionate people of Chios. Our one hope was that they would keep us here only through the fall, that they would not let women, who lacked men's strength and expertise, face the winter isolated in a place as terrible as this.

For weeks we slept on the ground without fires or blankets, exposed to the night damp and surrounded by pounding waves and the cries of owls. Finally we were divided into three groups and placed within separate barbed-wire cages. In spite of everything, spring had filled our bodies with strength and our hearts with joy, and we began to repair and set up the small tents, thankful to be out of the dark, stinking cells of our prisons. To avoid having to crawl in and out of the tents, some of us (using only our hands and fingernails for tools) built a five-foot wall, and over it we tied the canvas. We wondered why the men who had lived there before us had not thought of doing that. The first summer storms gave us the answer by bringing our hard work down in heaps of bricks and mud. But we were young, the sun was warm and bright, and we would not give up trying. We built over and over, countless times, until we found the way. In the end our huts stood impregnable against the fury of the storm.

The Dance in Jinotega

Grace Paley

In Jinotega women greeted us
with thousands of flowers   roses
it was hard to tell   the petals
on our faces and arms falling

Then embraces and the Spanish language
which is a little like a descent of
petals pink   and orange

Suddenly out of the hallway   our
gathering place   AMNLAE the
Associacion de Mujeres women
came running   seat yourselves dear
guests from the north we   announce
a play   a dance   a play the women
their faces mountain   river Indian
European   Spanish   dark haired
women

dance   in grey green
fatigues   they dance the Contra who
circles the village waiting
for the young teacher   the health worker
(these are the strategies)   the farmer
in the high village walks out into the
morning toward the front which is a
circle of terror

                    they dance
the work of women and men   they dance

the plowing of the field   they kneel
to the harrowing with the machetes   they
dance the sowing of seed (which is always
a dance) and the ripening of corn   the
flowers of grain   they dance the harvest
they raise their machetes for
the harvest   the machetes are high
                              but no!

out of the hallway in green and grey
come those who dance the stealth
of the Contra   cruelly they
dance the ambush   the slaughter of
the farmer   they are the death dancers
who found the school teacher   they caught
the boy who dancing   brought seeds in
his hat   all the way from Matagalpa they
dance the death of the mother the
father   the rape of the daughter   they
dance the child murdered the seeds
spilled and trampled   they dance
sorrow   sorrow

          they dance the
search for the Contra   and the defeat
they dance a comic dance   they make a
joke of the puppetry of the Contra of
Uncle Sam who is the handler of puppets
they dance rage and revenge they place
the dead child (the real sleeping baby)
on two chairs   which is the bier for
the little actor they dance prayer
bereavement   sorrow   they mourn

Is there applause for such theater?

Silence then   come let us dance
together   now you know   the usual
dance of couples Spanish or North
American   let us dance in two and
threes   let us make little circles let us
dance as though at a festival or in peace
time together and alone   whirling   stamping
our feet   bowing to one another

Encounter

Grace Akello

Teach me to laugh once more
let me laugh with Africa my mother
I want to dance to her drum-beats
I am tired of her cries
Scream with laughter
roar with laughter
Oh, how I hate this groaning

Africa groans
under the load of her kwashiorkored children
she weeps
what woman would laugh
over her children's graves

I want to laugh once again
let me laugh with you
yes, even you my brother who blames me for breeding . . .
I laugh with you
even you who sell me guns
preserving world peace
while my blood, Africa's blood stains Earth
let laughter be my gift to you
my generous heart overflows with laughter
money and vanity harden yours
clogged in your veins, the blood no longer warms your heart
I will teach you yet

I am not bush, lion, savagery
mine are the sinews which built your cities
my sons fighting your wars

gave you victory, prestige
wherein lies the savagery in Africa . . .
Your sons in Africa looted our family chests
raping the very bowels of our earth
our gold lines the streets of your cities . . .
where are pavements in Africa

Laugh with me
Do not laugh at me
my smile forgives all
but greed fetters your heart
the nightmare of our encounter is not over
your overgrown offspring
swear by the western god of money and free enterprise
that they are doing their best for Africa
indeed, Africa the dumping ground
Africa the vast experimental ground
the army bases in the developing parts
enhanced military aid in the loyal parts
family planning programmes in the advanced parts

My son built your cities
What did your son do for me . . .

E. F. Schumacher Memorial Lecture

Petra Kelly

"We can best help you prevent war, not by repeating your words and repeating
your methods, but by finding new words and creating new methods."

Virginia Woolf

On 3 November 1983, I read in the German newspapers with great shock
about the warnings of the British Defence Minister Michael Heseltine, in which
he made clear that the Military Police would shoot at peaceful demonstrators
near the American Base of Greenham Common. His warnings led to very
strong reactions on the side of the opposition and the peace movement. For it
is now clear, very clear, that the laws in the Western democracies protect the
bombs and not the people. The warning that the State is ready to kill those
engaged in non-violent resistance against nuclear weapons, shows how criminal this atomic age has become.

Great Britain, I am told, has more nuclear bases and consequently targets
per head of population—and per square mile—than any country of the world.
And I am coming from a country, the Federal Republic of Germany, that is
armed to the teeth with atomic and conventional weapons. I come here on this
weekend to hold the E. F. Schumacher Memorial Lecture and would like to
dedicate this lecture to the Greenham Common women. I dedicate a poem to
them by Joan Cavanagh:

I am a dangerous woman
Carrying neither bombs nor babies,
Flowers nor molotov cocktails.
I confound all your reason, theory, realism
Because I will neither lie in your ditches
Nor dig your ditches for you
Nor join your armed struggle
For bigger and better ditches.
I will not walk with you nor walk for you,

I won't live with you
And I won't die for you
But neither will I try to deny you
The right to live and die.
I will not share one square foot of this earth with you
While you are hell-bent on destruction,
But neither will I deny that we are of the same earth,
Born of the same Mother.
I will not permit
You to bind my life to yours
But I will tell you that our lives
Are bound together
And I will demand
That you live as though you understand
This one salient fact.

I am a dangerous woman
Because I will tell you, Sir,
Whether you are concerned or not
Masculinity has made of this world a living hell,
A furnace burning away at hope, love, faith and justice.
A furnace of My Lais, Hiroshimas, Dachaus.
A furnace which burns the babies
You tell us we must make.
Masculinity made femininity,
Made the eyes of our women go dark and cold
Sent our sons—yes Sir, our sons—
To war
Made our children go hungry
Made our mothers whores
Made our bombs, our bullets, our "food for peace,"
Our definitive solutions and first-strike policies.
Masculinity broke women and men on its knee,
Took away our futures,
Made our hopes, fears, thoughts, and good instincts
"Irrelevant to the larger struggle,"

And made human survival beyond the year 2000
An open question.

I am a dangerous woman
Because I will say all this
Lying neither to you nor with you
Neither trusting nor despising you.
I am dangerous because
I won't give up or shut up
Or put up with your version of reality.
You have conspired to sell my life quite cheaply
And I am especially dangerous
Because I will never forgive nor forget
Or ever conspire
To sell your life in return.

Women all over the world are taking the lead in defending the forces of life—whether by demanding a nuclear-free constitution in the Pacific islands of Belau, campaigning against the chemical industry after Seveso, or developing a new awareness of the rights of animals, plants and children.

We must show that we have the power to change the world and contribute towards the development of an ecological/feminist theory, capable of challenging the threat to life before it is too late. Just a few days ago the American House of Representatives agreed to go ahead with the construction of the first 21 of 100 planned MX inter-continental missiles. I have just returned from a trip to the men at the Kremlin in Moscow and to those powerful men in East Germany. And this year I have been to Washington several times to meet those in power there too. And during each trip, whether it was to Moscow or Washington or East Berlin, I tried at the same time to speak with the people at the grass-roots level, those struggling against the military-industrial complex whether it be capitalist or state socialist. And while I sat listening to those men, those many incompetent men in power, I realized that they are all a mirror image of each other. They each threaten the other side and try to explain that they forced to threaten the other side; that they are forced to plan more evil things to prevent other evil things. And that is the heart of the theory of atomic deterrence.

We must find a way to demilitarize society itself if we are to succeed. And so we must deny votes to the proponents of rearmament. We must organize alternative production in the arms industry and move towards the production of socially-useful goods, and we must organize political strikes and war tax boycotts. We want to change the structures and conditions of our society non-violently and move towards a system of social and alternative defence. We declare ourselves responsible for the security policies within our own immediate surroundings.

At a time where one fourth of all the world's nations are currently involved in wars and where 45 of the world's 164 nations are involved in 40 conventional and guerrilla conflicts—in a world where over 4 million soldiers are today directly engaged in combat and where about 500,000 foreign combat troops are involved in 8 conflicts and at a time when the United States, Great Britain, Germany, France and the Soviet Union are major arms suppliers to about 40 of those nations at war—I would like to leave you with these words:

O sisters come you sing for all you're worth
Arms are made for linking
Sisters, we're asking for the Earth.

Gandhi has stated that non-violence is the greatest force man has ever been endowed with. And love has more force and power than a besieging army. The power of love, as Martin Luther King said, is "passive physically, but active spiritually . . . the non-violent resister is passive in the sense that he is not physically aggressive toward his opponent, but his mind and his emotions are constantly active, constantly seeking to persuade the opposition."

These spiritual weapons do what guns and arms only pretend to do—they defend us. These spiritual weapons can bring about, I believe, the kind of social force and the great social change we need in this destructive age.

The Hour of Truth

Isabel Allende

Alba was curled up in the darkness. They had ripped the tape from her eyes and replaced it with a tight bandage. She was afraid. As she recalled her Uncle Nicolás's training, and his warning about the danger of being afraid of fear, she concentrated on trying to control the shaking of her body and shutting her ears to the terrifying sounds that reached her from outside. She tried to visualize her happiest moments with Miguel, groping for a means to outwit time and find the strength for what she knew lay ahead. She told herself that she had to endure a few hours without her nerves betraying her, until her grandfather was able to set in motion the heavy machinery of his power and influence to get her out of there. She searched her memory for a trip to the coast with Miguel, in autumn, long before the hurricane of events had turned the world upside down, when things were still called by familiar names and words had a single meaning; when people, freedom, and *compañero* were just that—people, freedom, and *compañero*—and had not yet become passwords. She tried to relive that moment—the damp red earth and the intense scent of the pine and eucalyptus forests in which a carpet of dry leaves lay steeping after the long hot summer and where the coppery sunlight filtered down through the treetops. She tried to recall the cold, the silence, and that precious feeling of owning the world, of being twenty years old and having her whole life ahead of her, of making love slowly and calmly, drunk with the scent of the forest and their love, without a past, without suspecting the future, with just the incredible richness of that present moment in which they stared at each other, smelled each other, kissed each other, and explored each other's bodies, wrapped in the whisper of the wind among the trees and the sound of the nearby waves breaking against the rocks at the foot of the cliff, exploding in a crash of pungent surf, and the two of them embracing underneath a single poncho like Siamese twins, laughing and swearing that this would last forever, that they were the only ones in the whole world who had discovered love.

Alba heard the screams, the long moans, and the radio playing full blast.

The woods, Miguel, and love were lost in the deep well of her terror and she resigned herself to facing her fate without subterfuge.

She calculated that a whole night and the better part of the following day had passed when the door was finally opened and two men took her from her cell. With insults and threats they led her in to Colonel García, whom she could recognize blindfolded by his habitual cruelty, even before he opened his mouth. She felt his hands take her face, his thick fingers touch her ears and neck.

"Now you're going to tell me where your lover is," he told her. "That will save us both a lot of unpleasantness."

Alba breathed a sigh of relief. That meant they had not arrested Miguel!

"I want to go to the bathroom," Alba said in the strongest voice she could summon up.

"I see you're not planning to cooperate, Alba. That's too bad." García sighed. "The boys will have to do their job. I can't stand in their way."

There was a brief silence and she made a superhuman effort to remember the pine forest and Miguel's love, but her ideas got tangled up and she no longer knew if she was dreaming or where this stench of sweat, excrement, blood, and urine was coming from, or the radio announcer describing some Finnish goals that had nothing to do with her in the middle of other, nearer, more clearly audible shouts. A brutal slap knocked her to the floor. Violent hands lifted her to her feet. Ferocious fingers fastened themselves to her breasts, crushing her nipples. She was completely overcome by fear. Strange voices pressed in on her. She heard Miguel's name but did not know what they were asking her, and kept repeating a monumental *no* while they beat her, manhandled her, pulled off her blouse, and she could no longer think, could only say *no, no,* and *no* and calculate how much longer she could resist before her strength gave out, not knowing this was only the beginning, until she felt herself begin to faint and the men left her alone, lying on the floor, for what seemed to her a very short time.

She soon heard García's voice again and guessed it was his hands that were helping her to her feet, leading her toward a chair, straightening her clothes, and buttoning her blouse.

"My God!" he said. "Look what they've done to you! I warned you, Alba. Try to relax now, I'm going to give you a cup of coffee."

Alba began to cry. The warm liquid brought her back to life, but she could not taste it because when she swallowed it was mixed with blood. García held the cup, guiding it carefully toward her lips like a nurse.

"Do you want a cigarette?"

"I want to go to the bathroom," she said, pronouncing each syllable with difficulty with her swollen lips.

"Of course, Alba. They'll take you to the bathroom and then you can get some rest. I'm your friend. I understand your situation perfectly. You're in love, and that's why you want to protect him. I know you don't have anything to do with the guerrillas. But the boys don't believe me when I tell them. They won't be satisfied until you tell them where Miguel is. Actually they've already got him surrounded. They know exactly where he is. They'll catch him, but they want to be sure that you have nothing to do with the guerrillas. You understand? If you protect him and refuse to talk, they'll continue to suspect you. Tell them what they want to know and then I'll personally escort you home. You'll tell them, right?"

"I want to go to the bathroom," Alba repeated.

"I see you're just as stubborn as your grandfather. All right. You can go to the bathroom. I'm going to give you a chance to think things over," García said.

They took her to a toilet and she was forced to ignore the man who stood beside her, holding on to her arm. After that they returned her to her cell. In the tiny, solitary cube where she was being held, she tried to clarify her thoughts, but she was tortured by the pain of her beating, her thirst, the bandage pressing on her temples, the drone of the radio, the terror of approaching footsteps and her relief when they moved away, the shouts and the orders. She curled up like a fetus on the floor and surrendered to her pain. She remained in that position for hours, perhaps days. A man came twice to take her to the bathroom. He led her to a fetid lavatory where she was unable to wash because there was no water. He allowed her a minute, placing her on the toilet seat next to another person as silent and sluggish as herself. She could not tell if it was a woman or a man. At first she wept, wishing her Uncle Nicolás had given her a special course in how to withstand humiliation, which she found worse than pain, but she finally resigned herself to her own filth and stopped thinking about her unbearable need to wash. They gave her boiled corn, a small piece of chicken, and a bit of ice cream, which she identified by their taste, smell, and temperature, and which she wolfed down with her hands, astonished to be given such luxurious food, unexpected in a place like that. Afterward she learned that the food for the prisoners in that torture center was supplied by the new headquarters of the government, which was in an improvised building, since the old Presidential Palace was a pile of rubble.

She tried to count the days since she was first arrested, but her loneliness, the darkness, and her fear distorted her sense of time and space. She thought she saw caves filled with monsters. She imagined that she had been drugged and that was why her limbs were so weak and sluggish and why her ideas had grown so jumbled. She decided not to eat or drink anything, but hunger and thirst were stronger than her determination. She wondered why her grandfather still had not come to rescue her. In her rare moments of lucidity she understood that this was not a nightmare and that she was not there by mistake. She decided to forget everything she knew, even Miguel's name.

The third time they took her in to Esteban García, Alba was more prepared, because through the walls of her cell she could hear what was going on in the next room, where they were interrogating other prisoners, and she had no illusions. She did not even try to evoke the woods where she had shared the joy of love.

"Well, Alba, I've given you time to think things over. Now the two of us are going to talk and you're going to tell me where Miguel is and we're going to get this over with quickly," García said.

"I want to go to the bathroom," Alba answered.

"I see you're making fun of me, Alba," he said. "I'm sorry, but we don't have any time to waste."

Alba made no response.

"Take off your clothes!" García ordered in another voice.

She did not obey. They stripped her violently, pulling off her slacks despite her kicking. The memory of her adolescence and García's kiss in the garden gave her the strength of hatred. She struggled against him, until they got tired of beating her and gave her a short break, which she used to invoke the understanding spirits of her grandmother, so that they would help her die. But no one answered her call for help. Two hands lifted her up, and four laid her on a cold, hard metal cot with springs that hurt her back, and bound her wrists and ankles with leather thongs.

"For the last time, Alba. Where is Miguel?" García asked.

She shook her head in silence. They had tied her head down with another thong.

"When you're ready to talk, raise a finger," he said.

Alba heard another voice.

"I'll work the machine," it said.

Then she felt the atrocious pain that coursed through her body, filling it completely, and that she would never forget as long as she lived. She sank into darkness.

"Bastards! I told you to be careful with her!" she heard Esteban García say from far away. She felt them opening her eyelids, but all she saw was a misty brightness. Then she felt a prick in her arm and sank back into unconsciousness.

A century later Alba awoke wet and naked. She did not know if she was bathed with sweat, or water, or urine. She could not move, recalled nothing, and had no idea where she was or what had caused the intense pain that had reduced her to a heap of raw meat. She felt the thirst of the Sahara and called out for water.

"Wait, *compañera*," someone said beside her. "Wait until morning. If you drink water, you'll get convulsions, and you could die."

She opened her eyes. They were no longer bandaged. A vaguely familiar face was leaning over her, and hands were wrapping her in a blanket.

"Do you remember me? I'm Ana Díaz. We went to the university together. Don't you recognize me?"

Alba shook her head, closed her eyes, and surrendered to the sweet illusion of death. But she awakened a few hours later, and when she moved she realized that she ached to the last fiber of her body.

"You'll feel better soon," said a woman who was stroking her face and pushing away the locks of damp hair that hid her eyes. "Don't move, and try to relax. I'll be here next to you. You need to rest."

"What happened?" Alba whispered.

"They really roughed you up, *compañera*," the other woman said sadly.

"Who are you?" Alba asked.

"Ana Díaz. I've been here for a week. They also got my *compañero*, Andrés, but he's still alive. I see him once a day, when they take them to the bathroom."

"Ana Díaz?" Alba murmured.

"That's right. We weren't so close back then, but it's never too late to start.

The truth is, you're the last person I expected to meet here, Countess," the woman said gently. "Don't talk now. Try to sleep. That way the time will go faster for you. Your memory will gradually come back. Don't worry. It's because of the electricity."

But Alba was unable to sleep, for the door of her cell opened and a man walked in.

"Put the bandage back on her!" he ordered Ana Díaz.

"Please . . . Can't you see how weak she is? Let her rest a little while. . . ."

"Do as I say!"

Ana bent over the cot and put the bandage over her eyes. Then she removed the blanket and tried to dress her, but the guard pulled her away, lifted the prisoner by her arms, and sat her up. Another man came in to help him, and between them they carried her out because she could not walk. Alba was sure that she was dying, if she was not already dead. She could tell they were walking down a hallway in which the sound of their footsteps echoed. She felt a hand on her face, lifting her head.

"You can give her water. Wash her and give her another shot. See if she can swallow some coffee and bring her back to me," García said.

"Do you want us to dress her?"

"No."

Alba was in García's hands a long time. After a few days, he realized she had recognized him, but he did not abandon his precaution of keeping her blindfolded, even when they were alone. Every day new prisoners arrived and others were led away. Alba heard the vehicles, the shouts, and the gate being closed. She tried to keep track of the number of prisoners, but it was almost impossible. Ana Díaz thought there were close to two hundred. García was very busy, but he never let a day go by without seeing Alba, alternating unbridled violence with the pretense that he was her good friend. At times he appeared to be genuinely moved, personally spooning soup into her mouth, but the day he plunged her head into a bucket full of excrement until she fainted from disgust, Alba understood that he was not trying to learn Miguel's true whereabouts but to avenge himself for injuries that had been inflicted on him from birth, and that nothing she could confess would have any effect on her fate as the private prisoner of Colonel García. This allowed her to venture slowly out of the private circle of her terror. Her fear began to ebb and she was able to feel compassion for the others, for those they hung by their arms, for the newcomers, for the man whose shackled legs were run over by a truck. They brought all the prisoners into the courtyard at dawn and forced them to watch, because this was also a personal matter between the colonel and his prisoner. It was the first time Alba had opened her eyes outside the darkness of her cell, and the gentle splendor of the morning and the frost shining on the stones, where puddles of rain had collected overnight, seemed unbearably radiant to her. They dragged the man, who offered no resistance, out into the courtyard. He could not stand, and they left him lying on the ground. The guards had covered their faces with handkerchiefs so no one would ever be able to identify them in the improbable event that circumstances changed. Alba closed her eyes when she heard the truck's engine, but she could not close her ears to the sound of his howl, which stayed in her memory forever.

Ana Díaz helped her to resist while they were together. She was an indomitable woman. She had withstood every form of cruelty. They had raped her in the presence of her lover and tortured them together, but she had not lost her capacity to smile or her hope. She did not give in even when they transferred her to a secret clinic of the political police because one of the beatings had caused her to lose the child she was carrying and she had begun to hemorrhage.

"It doesn't matter," she told Alba when she returned to her cell. "Someday I'll have another one."

That night Alba heard her cry for the first time, covering her face with her blanket to suffocate her grief. She went to her and put her arms around her, rocking her and wiping her tears. She told her all the tender things she could think of, but that night there was no comfort for Ana Díaz, so Alba simply rocked her in her arms, lulling her to sleep like a tiny baby and wishing she could take on her shoulders the terrible pain of Ana's soul. Dawn found them huddled together like two small animals. During the day, they anxiously awaited the moment when the long line of men went by on their way to the latrine. They were blindfolded, and to guide themselves each had his hand on the shoulder of the man ahead of him, watched over by armed guards. Among the prisoners was Andrés. From the tiny barred window of their cell the women could see them, so close that if they had been able to reach out they could have touched them. Each time they passed, Ana and Alba sang with the strength of their despair, and female voices rose from the other cells. Then the prisoners would stand up tall, straighten their backs, and turn their heads in the direction of the women's cells, and Andrés would smile. His shirt was torn and covered with dried blood.

One of the guards was moved by the women's hymns. One night he brought them three carnations in a can of water to put in their window.

Another time he came to tell Ana Díaz that he needed a volunteer to wash one of the prisoners' clothes and clean out his cell. He led her to where Andrés was and left them alone together for a few minutes. When Ana Díaz returned, she was transfigured. Alba did not dare speak to her, so as not to break the spell of her happiness.

One day Colonel García was surprised to find himself caressing Alba like a lover and talking to her of his childhood in the country, when he would see her walking hand in hand with her grandfather, dressed in her starched pinafores and with the green halo of her hair, while he, barefoot in the mud, swore that one day he would make her pay for her arrogance and avenge himself for his cursed bastard fate. Rigid and absent, naked and trembling with disgust and cold, Alba neither heard nor felt him, but that crack in his eagerness to torture her sounded an alarm in the colonel's mind. He ordered Alba to be thrown in the doghouse, and furiously prepared to forget that she existed.

The doghouse was a small, sealed cell like a dark, frozen, airless tomb. There were six of them altogether, constructed in an empty water tank especially for punishment. They were used for relatively short stretches of time, because no one could withstand them very long, at most a few days, before beginning to ramble—to lose the sense of things, the meaning of words, and the anxiety of passing time—or simply, beginning to die. At first, huddled in her sepulcher, unable either to stand up or sit down despite her small size, Alba managed to stave off madness. Now that she was alone, she realized how much she needed Ana Díaz. She thought she heard an imperceptible tapping in the distance, as if someone were sending her coded messages from another cell, but she soon stopped paying attention to it because she realized that all attempts at communication were completely hopeless. She gave up, deciding to end this torture once and for all. She stopped eating, and only when her feebleness became too much for her did she take a sip of water. She tried not to breathe or move, and began eagerly to await her death. She stayed like this for a long time. When she had nearly achieved her goal, her Grandmother Clara, whom she had invoked so many times to help her die, appeared with the novel idea that the point was not to die, since death came anyway, but to survive, which would be a miracle. With her white linen dress, her winter gloves, her sweet toothless smile, and the mischievous gleam in her hazel eyes, she looked exactly as she had when Alba was a child. Clara also brought the saving idea of writing in her mind, without paper or pencil, to keep her thoughts occupied and to escape from the doghouse and live. She suggested that she write a testimony that might one day call attention to the terrible secret she was living through, so that the world would know about this horror that was taking place parallel to the peaceful existence of those who did not want to know, who could afford the illusion of a normal life, and of those who could deny that they were on a raft adrift in a sea of sorrow, ignoring, despite all evidence, that only blocks away from their happy world there were others, these others who live or die on the dark side. "You have a lot to do, so stop feeling sorry for yourself, drink some water, and start writing," Clara told her granddaughter before disappearing the same way she had come.

Alba tried to obey her grandmother, but as soon as she began to take notes with her mind, the doghouse filled with all the characters of her story, who rushed in, shoved each other out of the way to wrap her in their anecdotes, their vices, and their virtues, trampled on her intention to compose a documentary, and threw her testimony to the floor, pressing, insisting, and egging her on. She took down their words at breakneck pace, despairing because while she was filling a page, the one before it was erased. This activity kept her fully occupied. At first, she constantly lost her train of thought and forgot new facts as fast as she remembered them. The slightest distraction or additional fear or pain caused her story to snarl like a ball of yarn. But she invented a code for recalling things in order, and then she was able to bury herself so deeply in her story that she stopped eating, scratching herself, smelling herself, and complaining, and overcame all her varied agonies.

Word went out that she was dying. The guards opened the hatch of the doghouse and lifted her effortlessly, because she was very light. They took her back to Colonel García, whose hatred had returned during these days, but she did not recognize him. She was beyond his power.

On the outside, the Hotel Christopher Columbus looked as ordinary as an elementary school, just as I remembered. I had lost count of the years that had passed since I had last been there, and I tried to tell myself that the same Mustafá as before would come out to greet me, that blue Negro dressed like an Oriental apparition, with his double row of leaden teeth and the politeness of a vizier, the only authentic Negro in the country since all the others were painted, as Tránsito Soto had assured me. But that was not what happened. A porter led me to a tiny cubicle, showed me to a seat, and told me to wait. After a while, instead of the spectacular Mustafá, a lady appeared who had the unhappy, tidy air of a provincial aunt, dressed in a blue uniform with a starched white collar. She gave a start when she saw how old and helpless I was. She was holding a red rose.

"The gentleman is alone?"

"Of course I'm alone!" I shouted.

The woman handed me the rose and asked me which room I preferred.

"It makes no difference," I replied, surprised.

"We can offer you the Stable, the Temple, and the Thousand and One Nights. Which one do you want?"

"The Thousand and One Nights," I said, for no particular reason.

She led me down a long hallway that was lined with green lights and bright-red arrows. Leaning on my cane, dragging my feet along, I followed her with great difficulty. We arrived in a small courtyard with a miniature mosque that had been fitted with absurd arched windows made of painted glass.

"This is it. If you want something to drink, order it by phone," she said, pointing.

"I want to speak with Tránsito Soto. That's why I've come," I said.

"I'm sorry, but Madam doesn't see private individuals, only suppliers."

"I have to speak with her! Tell her that Senator Trueba is here. She knows who I am."

"I already told you, she won't see anyone," the woman replied, crossing her arms.

I picked up my cane and told her that if Tránsito Soto did not appear in person within ten minutes, I would break all the windows and everything else inside that Pandora's box. The woman in the uniform jumped back in fright. I opened the door of the mosque and found myself inside a cheap Alhambra. A short tiled staircase covered with false Persian carpets led to a hexagonal room with a cupola on the roof, where someone who had never been in an Arab harem had arrayed everything thought to have existed in one: damask cushions, glass incense burners, bells, and every conceivable trinket from a bazaar. Through the columns, which were infinitely multiplied by the clever placement of the mirrors, I saw a blue mosaic bathtub that was as big as the room and a pool large enough to bathe a cow in—or, more to the point, for two playful lovers to cavort in. It bore no resemblance to the Christopher Columbus I remembered. I lowered myself painfully onto the round bed, suddenly feeling very tired. My bones ached. I looked up, and the mirror on the ceiling returned my image: an old, shriveled body, the sad face of a biblical patriarch furrowed with bitter wrinkles, and what was left of a mane of white hair. "How time has passed!" I sighed.

Tránsito Soto entered without knocking.

"I'm glad to see you, *patrón*," she said, as she always greeted me.

She had become a slender, middle-aged woman with her hair in a bun, wearing a black woolen dress with two strands of simple pearls around her neck, majestic and serene; she looked more like a concert pianist than the owner of a brothel. It was hard for me to connect her to the woman I had known, who had a tattooed snake around her navel. I stood up to greet her, and found I was unable to be as informal as I'd been before.

"You're looking well, Tránsito," I said, figuring she must be past sixty-five.

"Life has been good to me, *patrón*. Do you remember that when we met I told you one day I'd be rich?" She smiled.

"Well, I'm glad you have achieved that."

We sat down side by side on the round bed. Tránsito poured us each a glass of cognac and told me that the cooperative of whores and homosexuals had done stupendously well for ten years, but that times had changed and they had had to give it a new twist, because thanks to the modern ways—free love, the pill, and other innovations—no one needed prostitutes, except sailors and old men. "Good girls sleep with men for free, so you can just imagine the competition," she said. She explained that the cooperative had begun to go downhill and that the partners had had to look for higher-paying jobs and that even Mustafá had gone back to his country. Then she had realized that what was really needed was a hotel for rendezvous, a pleasant place where secret couples could make love and where a man would not be embarrassed to bring a girl for the first time. No women: those were furnished by the customer. She had decorated it herself, following the whims of her imagination and taking her customers' taste into account. Thus, thanks to her commercial vision, which had led her to create a different atmosphere in every available corner, the Hotel Christopher Columbus had become the paradise of lost souls and furtive lovers. Tránsito Soto had made French sitting rooms with quilted furniture, mangers with fresh hay and papier-mâché horses that observed the lovers with their immutable glass eyes, prehistoric caves with real stalactites, and telephones covered with the skins of pumas.

"Since you're not here to make love, *patrón*, let's go talk in my office," Tránsito Soto said. "That way we can leave this room to customers."

On the way she told me that after the coup the political police had raided the hotel, a couple of times, but that each time they dragged the couples out of bed and lined them up at gunpoint in the main drawing room, they had found a general or two, so the police had quickly stopped annoying her. She had an excellent relationship with the new government, just as she had had with the preceding ones. She told me that the Christopher Columbus was a thriving business and that every year she renovated part of the decor, replacing the stranded hulls of Polynesian shipwrecks with severe monastic cloisters, and baroque garden swings with torture racks, depending on the latest fashion. Thanks to the gimmickry of the mirrors and lights, which could multiply space, transform the climate, create the illusion of infinity, and suspend time, she could bring all this into a residence of relatively normal size.

We arrived at her office, which was decorated like the cockpit of an airplane and from which she ran her incredible organization with the efficiency of a banker. She told me how many sheets had to be washed, how much toilet paper bought, how much liquor was consumed, how many quail eggs prepared daily—they're aphrodisiacs—how many employees she needed, and how much she paid for water, electricity, and the phone in order to keep that outsized aircraft carrier of forbidden love afloat.

"And now, *patrón*, tell me what I can do for you," Tránsito Soto finally said, settling into the reclining seat of an airplane pilot while she toyed with the pearls around her neck. "I suppose you've come because you want me to repay the favor that I've owed you for half a century, right?"

Then, having waited for her to ask me that, I opened the floodgates of my soul and told her everything; I didn't hold back anything and didn't stop for a second from beginning to end. I told her that Alba is my only granddaughter, that I'm practically all alone in the world, and that my body and my soul have shrunken away, just as Férula predicted with her curse; that all that awaits me now is to die like a dog, and that my green-haired granddaughter is all I have left, the only person I really care about; that unfortunately she turned out to be an idealist, a family disease, one of those people cut out to get involved in problems and make those closest to her suffer, that she took it into her head to help fugitives get asylum in the foreign embassies, something she did without thinking, I'm sure, without realizing that the country is at war, whether war against international Communism or its own people it's hard to tell, but war one way or the other, and these things are punishable by law, but Alba always has her head in the clouds and doesn't realize she's in danger, she doesn't do it to be mean, really, just the opposite, she does it because her heart knows no limits, just like her grandmother, who still runs around ministering to the poor behind my back in the abandoned wing of the house, my clairvoyant Clara, and anyone who tells Alba people are after him gets her to risk her life for him, even if he's a total stranger, I've already told her, I warned her time and again they could lay a trap for her and one day it would turn out that the supposed Marxist was an agent of the secret police, but she never listened to me, she's never listened to me in her life, she's more stubborn than I am, but even so, it's not a crime to help some poor devil get asylum every once in a while, it's not so serious that they should arrest her without taking into account that she's my granddaughter, the granddaughter of a senator of the Republic, a distinguished member of the Conservative Party, they can't do that to someone from my own family, in my own house, because then what the hell is left for everybody else, if people like us can be arrested then nobody is safe, that more than twenty years in Congress aren't worth a damn and all the acquaintances I have, I know everybody in this country, at least everyone important, even General Hurtado, who's my personal friend but in this case hasn't lifted a finger to help me, not even the cardinal's been able to help me locate my granddaughter, it's not possible she could just disappear as if by magic, that they could take her away in the night and that I should never hear a word of her again, I've spent a whole month looking for her and I'm going crazy, these are the things that make the junta look so bad abroad and give the United Nations reason to screw around with human rights, at first I didn't want to hear about the dead, the tortured, and the disappeared, but now I can't keep thinking they're just Communist lies, because even the gringos, who were the first to help the military and sent their own pilots to bombard the Presidential Palace, are scandalized by all the killing, it's not that I'm against repression, I understand that in the beginning you have to be firm if you want a return to order, but things have gotten out of hand, they're going overboard now and no one can go along with the story about internal security and how you have to eliminate your ideological enemies, they're finishing off everyone, no one can go along with that, not even me, and I was the first to throw corn at the military cadets and to suggest the coup, before the others took it into their heads, and I was the first to applaud them, I was present for the Te Deum in the cathedral, and precisely because I was I can't accept that this sort of thing should happen in my country, that people disappear, that my granddaughter is dragged from my house by force and I'm powerless to stop them, things like this never happened here and that's why I've come to see you, Tránsito, because fifty years ago when you were just a skinny little thing in the Red Lantern I never thought that one day I'd be coming to you on my knees to beg you to do me this favor, to help me find my granddaughter, I dare to ask you such a thing because I know you're on good terms with the new government, I've heard about you, Tránsito, I'm sure no one knows the top brass of the armed forces better than you do, I know you organize their parties for them and that you have access to places I could never penetrate and that's why I'm asking you to do something for my granddaughter before it's too late, I've gone weeks without sleeping, I've been to every office, every ministry, seen all my old friends, and no one's been able to do anything, they don't want to see me anymore, they make me wait outside for hours, please, Tránsito, ask me for anything you want, I'm still a wealthy man even though under the Communists things got a little tough for me, you probably heard, you must have seen it in the papers and on television, a real scandal, those ignorant peasants ate my breeding bulls and hitched my racing horses to the plow and in less than a year Tres Marías was in ruins, but now I've filled the place with tractors and I'm picking up the pieces, just as I did before, when I was young, I'm doing the same thing now that I'm an old man, but I'm not done for, while those poor souls who had the title to my property—my property—are dying of hunger like a bunch of miserable wretches, poor things, it wasn't their fault they were taken in by that damned agrarian reform, when it comes right down to it I've forgiven them and I'd like them to return to Tres Marías, I've even placed notices in the papers summoning them back, someday they'll return and I'll have no choice but to shake their hands, they're like children, but anyway that's not what I came to talk to you about, Tránsito, I don't want to waste your time, what counts is that I'm

The Reciters

Agate Nesaule

Once upon a time in Latvia all women knew how to recite. As girls we memorized lullabies, folk songs, poems, and hymns. Safe in our own beds, warm under goose-down quilts and embroidered linen sheets, we whispered lines to ourselves as we drifted off to sleep. On Christmas Eve, standing in front of trees ablaze with real candles, we swayed back and forth importantly to emphasize the rhythm of verses we had learned. If we recited correctly and loudly enough, we would be given creamy sweets wrapped in tasseled gold paper instead of bundles of switches reserved for bad children. During the brief white nights of summer, when along with visiting cousins we were allowed to sleep in fragrant hay in barns, we shouted verses we believed were uproariously funny, until gentle adult voices silenced us. On marketing days, in front of city shops or village stores, we turned our backs on boys who grinningly teased us. Holding hands, looking pleased with ourselves, reciting in unison, we skipped away.

Es meitiņa kā rozīte
Kā sarkana zemenīte,
Pienu ēdu, pienu dzēru,
Pienā muli nomazgāju.

I am a little girl like a little rose,
Like a red strawberry.
I eat milk, I drink milk,
And I bathe myself in milk.

Our feet, clad in fine white stockings and red shoes with thin straps, moved rhythmically together. Our chants might turn imperceptibly into song. We knew many melodies too, of course, but above all we knew the words.

Women sang everywhere, in kitchens kneading rye bread or slicing apples, in dairies skimming cream or churning butter, in fields, raking hay or gathering grain. Alone in parlors lit by kerosene lamps or newly installed electric lights, on dark verandas scented by lilacs, on lonely paths leading through forests, women sang to themselves. Young women walked from one country church to another to look at the new ministers said to be handsome and single, and then, having paid little attention to their sermons, they walked home again, arms linked, laughing and singing. Young men, dressed in dark suits and white shirts, called out to them as they passed in polished wagons pulled by lovingly groomed horses. On St. John's Eve in midsummer, from hill to hill ablaze with bonfires, women and men sang, first in competition, then in harmony. Old women sang together in churches, alone while tending gardens and working at looms.

But always in addition to singing, women recited. On postcards with photos of birches or roses, which women sent for birthdays and namedays, they wrote lines they had memorized. They inscribed poems in books given as school prizes, in leather bound albums presented to newlyweds, on notes accompanying flowers for sick friends. Women gave public speeches less often than men, but like them they quoted the words of Latvian poets on ceremonial and political occasions.

Lines recited spontaneously were even more meaningful. So a woman might quote from a play by major Latvian writer Aspazija to a friend passionately in love; she might murmur a lyric about suffering and loss by the same poet as she comforted her friend later. Women included stanzas from poems in hastily written letters to lovers and husbands away, to mothers welcoming new life, to old people marking the passing of years.

That is how it was, once upon a time.

As the independence of Latvia was increasingly threatened by Nazis and Soviets both, lines from poems accompanied flowers laid anxiously at the foot of the Monument to Freedom in the center of Riga. Later, as women prayed to be saved from exile and war, they recited.

The reciting stopped abruptly in 1940, the Year of Terror under Russian occupation, when thousands of Latvians were imprisoned or deported to Siberia. Nazi armies overran Latvia the following year, and Soviet armies took forcible possession again in 1945. For almost half a century, Latvian language was discouraged and Latvian literature neglected. Girls and women who remained in their own country were forced to speak Russian. Those in exile learned other languages. Only fifty-two percent of the inhabitants of Latvia are now Latvians.

I was six when my family fled Latvia on one of the last ships sailing for Germany. In a camp circled with barbed wire, threatened by Nazi guards barely restraining leashed dogs, we whispered fearfully to each other. Flags with swastikas flew overhead, and nightly bombings continued. The following spring we were forced to watch as occupying Russian soldiers beat a retarded boy, executed a man, raped women without children. Dazed and afraid, we remained silent for a long time.

But as hunger turned into starvation we had to speak. My mother taught me to recite in Russian. She washed my face, pinned an incongruously cheerful wreath of blue bachelor's buttons and red clover above my blonde braids, and sent me away from the German village. Holding an empty bowl in my hands, I stood behind a barbed wire fence watching soldiers drinking, shouting, and stumbling. I waited for the briefest pause and then began "*Petushok . . . petushok. . . .*"

I did not know the meaning of the Russian children's rhymes I had learned by rote. I had to make the soldiers notice me so I used all my will power to speak loudly and distinctly. My legs and arms trembled but my voice did not fail. Usually the soldiers ignored the hungry children behind the fence, they turned away from their comrades and towards us only to vomit or urinate. Or they tried to drive us off with furious gestures.

But sometimes a soldier would hear me and motion to the others to listen. Surprised at me mouthing Russian words, the soldiers laughed delightedly, as they might at a goose singing or a dog dancing. They flung a chunk of heavy dark rye bread or a piece of raw liver into my bowl.

Walking back to the village, I felt the envy and anger of the other children scorching my back. I tried not to think, I recited instead. Over and over again, I whispered the meaningless sounds. I had to remember them for whatever came next. I set the bowl on the ground in front of my mother, turned away from her, ran to a tree, pressed against it, prayed to grow into it, failed.

Later, in Displaced Persons camps in Germany, I recited in Latvian for the last time. Without books or supplies, Latvians started make-shift schools in every camp. Actresses, ministers, writers, historians, all lovers of words recalled lines they knew and taught them to us. Every week we had to recite "with appropriate feeling" a poem in front of the whole class. I learned lines about the white birches, fragrant grasses, and misty blue hills of Latvia. We declaimed defiant speeches of ancient heroes who died defending Latvia against foreign invaders. We chanted hundreds of *dainas*, folksongs about brave girls and proud women, and about the healing powers of nature and work. Teachers repeatedly quoted a poem which included the line, "The riches of the heart cannot be destroyed." They said it meant that we should study hard, because only our knowledge could never be taken from us. We might lose our family members, our country, and our possessions, but the riches of the heart would remain ours.

Reciting in Latvian ended for me when I left the camps in Germany for the United States. I learned English, won scholarships, completed degrees at universities, taught British poems to American students. I married an American and moved to a small town in the Midwest, away from my mother, away from communities of exiled Latvians. Slowly, through disuse, I forgot most of the Latvian poems I knew.

But life, while harsh, is also miraculous. In 1991 Latvia declared independence from the Soviet Union and was recognized as a sovereign nation. Although the shores of the Baltic sea are polluted, people now walk more freely on its white sands and pine-bordered paths. They may even find amber there, though they are cautious about picking it up. Some of the lovely translucent yellow pieces are not crystallized pine resin at all, but explosives carelessly disposed of by Soviet military troops, many of whom are still stationed there.

I returned to Latvia last summer, after an exile of forty-seven years. I eagerly looked forward to meeting relatives, but of my father's family of six brothers and sisters, only one of my cousins survived. After several painful encounters, I was forced to recognize that our relationship could never be reestablished. Our lives had been too different, our experiences too separate and painful.

Nor could the house where I had lived until I was six give me the connection that I longed for. The large, comfortable country parsonage was now a run down collective farm, so changed that I passed it three times without recognizing it. Gone were the wide verandas and the silvery thatched roof, gone the apple-trees, lilacs, and mock orange, gone the flower beds filled with sweet william, iris, and lilies. Even the pond, where storks used to wade, was dry.

Standing alone in the desolate rutted yard, I prayed not to give in to bitterness. If only I could stay open to experience, something else might happen. I had to believe that it would. I did not know yet that a stranger, an old woman reciting, would give me what I needed, and more.

Most people in Latvia have excruciatingly painful stories. They seize a visitor from the outside world by the hand, insist upon attention, prevent departure. They speak about the grim Soviet occupation, of Latvians being subjected to political repression and economic hardship, of being treated as second class citizens in their own country, of being denied access to education and advancement. Latvians were imprisoned and deported, many died in Siberia, some committed suicide upon returning, others remained physically and psychologically damaged. In spite of the new independence, daily life in Latvia is still unbelievably harsh.

Listening to these recitations, I was rocked by conflicting emotions: sympathy for the people, anger at the devastation of the land, desire to help, guilt that I could never do enough. I wavered between high energy and absolute exhaustion. Desiring connection, I nevertheless found myself longing to be alone.

At an outdoor concert of Latvian folksongs, I allowed my mind to wander from a speaker who said that only in song did the spirit of Latvia still live undamaged. In January 1991, when Soviet Black Berets had killed five unarmed men, among them two prominent young film makers, Latvians had not turned to violence, but to singing. Indoors and out, in churches and concert halls, on street corners in Riga and Liepaja, Latvians sang in defiance of Soviet authorities. Journalists had been right in dubbing the independence movement in Latvia the Singing Revolution.

Too depleted to follow the rest of the speech, I watched the choirs arriving instead. Dressed in colorful costumes from various districts of Latvia, young men and old were lining up to sing. Women carried bunches of flowers, girls with wreaths of flowers in their hair walked by with arms linked. The fragrance of pines intensified as massed rain clouds parted for the late afternoon sun. Finally the singing began.

At first I strained to hear every word of songs I had known once. I tried to remember them, I had to repossess them. But gradually I realized there were too many songs completely unfamiliar to me, which had been composed during the long separation from Latvia. Try as I might, I inevitably failed to make out the words. Feeling separate from all the people and the common emotions the songs evoked, I closed my eyes.

When I looked again, my focus had shifted. The choirs had receded into the background, but individual people were now much more distinct. On the steps in front of a women's choir was a seven-year-old girl. She was sitting very still, looking past the audience to the line of birches across an open meadow. Her blue eyes had that clear, almost other worldly gaze that one sometimes sees in children at moments when they feel absolutely secure. She made no movement to brush away a strand of blonde hair escaping from her braids beneath a small wreath of red clover. Her hands rested lightly in her lap, over a long string of tiny, very dark amber beads. She wore an embroidered white linen blouse and a full red wool skirt, also embroidered. Her long legs and sturdy feet, clad in white thin stockings and highly polished shoes, were planted firmly on the ground.

A woman bent down to whisper to her, another woman brushed away the escaping tendril of her hair, and the little girl stood up. She was ready to sing. Complete in herself, she was also an essential part of the choir. Totally self-possessed, she was cherished and supported by the circle of women around her.

I felt an envy so surprising and so sharp I could hardly breathe. Holding onto myself, rocking silently back and forth, I concentrated on regulating my breathing until the pain began to subside. Shame followed quickly. How could I, a middle-aged economically secure, politically privileged, well dressed and well fed university professor from America envy this little girl in Latvia? Hadn't I been paying attention as people told me repeatedly of extreme poverty, humiliation, hopelessness? Didn't I know the endless contriving and bribing and patching every mother had to do to send her child out fully clothed in the morning?

I forced myself to imagine the effort this mother had expended finding the string of amber beads, standing in line for a piece of unbleached linen to sew her daughter's blouse, collecting plants to make dye, saving and bartering for the polished black shoes. I could not know every detail, but I was touched nevertheless by the immense devotion and determination that must have gone into raising and clothing this little girl, who now looked as natural as a small berry.

Yet still I envied her. She was exactly where she belonged, in her own country, with people she had known all her life, singing in her own language. She knew all the words, and she could sing together with others. With courage and almost bravado the women were singing now:

Bēda mana liela bēda
Es par bēdu nebēdāju
Liku bēdu zem akmena
Pāri gāju dziedādama

I had a great sorrow,
But I didn't dwell on it
I put it under a stone
I stepped over it singing

Perhaps if one were so connected to other people and to the land, one could indeed put sorrow under a stone. But I was sentimentalizing the experience of the girls and women singing. I must remember the harsh lives of all Latvians, I must stop feeling sorry for myself as well.

I tried to imagine the little girl making her way home to a shabby apartment or a run-down collective farm. But I could only see her walking on familiar roads past pine woods and banks of wild strawberries. She was holding her mother's hand and perhaps her aunt's. Tired but satisfied with the events of the day, they were talking softly together. The two women listened attentively as the girl recited a poem she had memorized for school, then lapsed into silence. But soon one of them began to hum, the others joined in. They seemed vulnerable now in the dusk, and I felt a tender protectiveness towards them. I wished fervently for their good fortune, and I regretted my envy once more. But something hard and rough, like a stone shard, remained in my heart.

Just outside the city of Riga lies Brīvdabas Muzējs, a large outdoor museum of farm buildings, churches, and mills dating back to the sixteenth century. Established during the brief period of independence between the two World Wars, the museum has been kept open by Soviet authorities, though it seems sparsely attended, at least on weekdays. Walking on the wooded paths from one cluster of buildings to another, one can almost forget one is in a museum. The effect is of roaming about in the countryside, going from farm to flourishing farm, stopping by the side of a lake, climbing a hill to a Lutheran church.

I was surrounded by blossoming trees, swaying flowers, and ripe berries, several of which I remembered vividly from my childhood but had never seen growing outside of Latvia. Here and there a museum worker dressed as a farm wife encouraged me and the few other visitors to taste the currants, to smell the camomile, to pluck a blue bell-flower to press in a book for remembrance.

I accepted everything so generously offered, but my spirits did not lift. For the past two weeks I had heard people speak constantly about the war and its grim aftermath, and I had listened, sympathized, offered help. But not one person had asked me what had happened to my family or me during the war, no one was interested in hearing about the struggle of beginning life in a foreign country, no one believed me when I said not everyone in the United States lived in luxury. Having fought against my own envy, I recognized it in others as they spoke of all Americans as millionaires, without any experience of hunger or fear, totally incapable of imagining hardship. I felt completely depleted, the stone grated my heart.

I closed behind me the wooden gate of an orchard by an eighteenth-century farmhouse, walked up a flower bordered path, and entered a dim barn. At first I could see only a shadowy wagon, a few rakes and other implements, some empty bins. Letting my shoulders sag, I leaned against a wall. I wished I could stay in the restful darkness forever.

"Come," a woman's voice called out, "come with me. You look like someone who needs to hear me reciting."

A sturdy, small person, no more than five feet tall, grasped my hand and guided me firmly out into the sunlight, then into the dappled shade under a white birch. She was much older than I had first judged her by her decisive movements. Hundreds of lines marked her round weathered face, dozens of long white hairs grew on her chin, her pale blue eyes were merry and knowing. For a brief moment I was confused, the person before me seemed to be a woman and a man both, and yet neither. But then I saw the gray braids secured at the nape of her neck, the long skirt with its finely embroidered border, the worn gray shawl pinned with a small amber pin. Judged by such externals, she was clearly a woman. But being certain of her gender seemed less important than usual. I felt as if I, though fully awake, had suddenly fallen into a dream.

"Listen," she said, "this is the poem for you."

She let go my hand, stepped onto a slight elevation, closed her eyes, and started reciting. All my doubts about her being a woman vanished: her voice was melodious and strong, in a word, womanly. She had chosen "Sauciens Tāle," "Call into the Distance," a long poem of eight elaborate stanzas. I suddenly remembered that I too had memorized it once, when I was ten, in a Displaced Persons camp in Germany. But that had been more than forty years ago, so that now I could only feel the absolute rightness of each line as she spoke it, without being able to produce the next one myself.

"Sauciens Tāle" was written by Fricis Bârda for the Latvians who were driven into exile in 1905. Directly addressing a wanderer who has lost his country and everything else, the poet speaks of the pain of separation and the anguish of exile. He urges the wanderer not to forget Latvia and promises a final homecoming. On that distant joyous day of new freedom, trumpets will sound, flags and blossoms will lie in snowdrifts on rooftops, but the wanderer will bring with him the pain of his long years of exile. He will question what he can accomplish in the ashes and ruins of his country, he will be uncertain whether he has the strength to do anything at all. But return he must. He can at least offer to Latvia his heart which has suffered so much.

The professor inside me began by noting the formal characteristics of the poem, classifying it as too nationalistic, filing away words and metaphors I was glad to relearn. But by the second or third stanza none of that mattered.

The old woman had *recognized* me, and she was speaking directly to me about my depletion and alienation. She understood that even though I was now living a comfortable life in the United States, it had been painful for me to separate from family members, to leave home, to experience exile and war. She knew too that returning at the beginning of new independence was more complex than simply joyous.

I felt tears rising to my eyes, then flowing down my face. By the time she was finished reciting, I was crying freely. The hard stone in my heart seemed to be dissolving and flowing away, taking with it the pain of exile as well. I was known and totally accepted. She had welcomed me home. I felt connected to every tree and cloud and blade of grass.

She took my hand and waited in silence until I had more or less finished crying.

"Thank you for that," I said when I could finally speak.

"That was good," she patted my hand. "Crying is healing like some herbs that grow here."

She stepped away from me again, dropped her arms to her sides, lifted her face towards the sky, and recited three brief poems about the beautiful trees, hills, and roadsides of Latvia. These too were poems I had once known well.

The feeling of being in a dream, the sense that the odd and unusual was un-surprising and even fitting, persisted. As if to make certain that I really was awake, I drew myself up straight and rubbed my eyes, but the strangeness did not dissipate.

"This has meant the world to me," I said.

"I know," she nodded.

We stood looking at each other not quite willing to part yet. And then sud-denly I thought of it, a question I could ask, almost a test I could give her. It would bring this significant exchange to a close, and it would certainly return me to the everyday, rational world.

"Tell me," I said, "do you happen to know a poem which contains the line 'the riches of the heart cannot be destroyed'?" For the last three years I had been searching for the poem that teachers quoted to us in Displaced Persons camps. I wanted to include it in a book I was writing, but I was no longer sure I had it right. I had not found the line in a collection by Kārlis Skalbe, which I had gone to great trouble to locate. I was not certain now of the author or the title or whether I was quoting the line accurately.

I had asked every Latvian I knew in the United States about it: my father, old teachers, and women and men more or less my contemporaries, who had also spent part of their childhood in camps. Everyone said it sounded familiar, a few volunteered their approval or disapproval of the sentiment expressed, but no one could identify it precisely.

"What were those words again?" the old woman asked.

"The riches of the heart cannot be destroyed."

"Oh, yes," she murmured, "oh yes, that's the last line in a poem 'For Friends' by Kārlis Skalbe. But it's a little different. 'The riches of the heart do not rust,' is how it goes."

And of course, I knew it was so as soon as she said it. The riches of the heart were safe. Not only could they not be destroyed by displacement and war as I had been taught, but they could also not perish through disuse.

Es nezinu, kas vakar bija,
Es nezinu, kas rītu būs,
Tik ausīs sālc kā melodija:
Sirds bagātība nesarūs.

I do not know what was yesterday,
I do not know what will be,
I only hear as a melody,
The riches of the heart don't rust.

The past and the present were uncertain, but the riches of the heart were real. She had completed the poem and my return to Latvia for me.

Like so much in Latvia, the old woman seemed enchanted. Yet for me and for other exiles, returning to the countries of our childhood, looking for clues how to face our coming old age, the angle of vision determines magic. For the present, I hope to see clearly without sentimentality.

In the years of independence between the two World Wars, Latvia was indeed full of women reciting in safety and comfort. But nostalgia and envy had blotted out my memory of other reciters.

When she was seven years old, the future poet Aspazija recited to an examining Lutheran minister. Patting her on the head, he sighed regretfully, "It's too bad that you aren't a boy," he said. "Great things could come of you, but you're only a girl." My mother, who taught school girls from orphanages to recite, had been told essentially the same thing when she was sent to a teachers' institute instead of the University.

Once, when I was five or six, a thin, almost emaciated old woman dressed in gray came to the back door of the comfortable country parsonage. Her lips blue with cold, she stood out in the muddy yard, on a low round stump, reciting the Twenty-third Psalm. From the unhurried, matter of fact way the housekeeper gave her a bowl of porridge and a *centims*, I could tell that it was not unusual for old women to come begging to supplement their rations at the poorhouse in the next village.

The old woman ate very quickly, handed back the empty bowl to our robust housekeeper, and kissed her hand in gratitude. Then she lifted her face towards the sky, and sang "Nearer my God to Thee," in a sweet, quavering voice. The housekeeper sighed in exasperation and ladled another serving of porridge, a half a bowl this time. "No more reciting now," she said as she handed the food to the old woman, who looked ashamed.

Once upon a time in Latvia, all women and girls knew how to recite. Reciting united us, hurt and divided us, reciting could heal us. Once upon a time in Latvia, there were so many kinds of reciters.

Justice

Maro Markarian

There is something in this world
called Justice.
Compensation, Restitution
are its other names.
But it is never called Punctual.
On the contrary it always comes
too late. Like a missed love,
timed wrong, worse when it arrives
than if it had never come.
Causing more pain.
There is something in this world
named Justice that arrives late
to find a new name on its door:
Injustice.

The Writer's Commitment

Claribel Alegría

Political commitment, in my view, is seldom a calculated intellectual strategy. It seems more like a contagious disease—athlete's foot, let's say, or typhoid—and if you happen to live in a plague area, the chances are excellent that you will come down with it. Commitment is a visceral reaction to the corner of the world we live in and what it has done to us and to the people we know. Albert Camus penned a phrase in "The Myth of Sisyphus" that impressed me profoundly. "If a man believes something to be true yet does not live in accordance with that truth," he said, "that man is a hypocrite."

Each of us writers, I have found, is obsessed with the personal equation and, however successfully he or she camouflages it, is surreptitiously pushing a world view.

"What am I doing here? Where am I going?"

These are the eternal existential—and profoundly political—questions, and the creative writer dedicates his life to communicating the answers he has stumbled across while negotiating the booby traps and barbed wire barricades of this twentieth-century obstacle course.

Let me be unashamedly personal, then. I spent the greater part of my life writing poetry, without the slightest notion that I had an obligation to commit myself literarily or politically to what was happening in my country—El Salvador—or my region—Central America.

There were political antecedents that marked me, of course. Thirty thousand peasants were slaughtered in El Salvador when I was seven years old. I remember with hard-edged clarity when groups of them, their crossed thumbs tied behind their backs, were herded into the National Guard fortress just across the street from my house, and I remember the *coup de grace* shots startling me awake at night. Two years later, I remember just as clearly my father, a Nicaraguan exile, telling me how Anastasio Somoza, with the benediction of the Yankee minister, had assassinated Sandino the night before.

I left El Salvador to attend a U.S. University; I married, had children, and wrote poetry, convinced that Central American dictators—Martínez, Ubico,

Carías, Somoza—were as inevitable and irremediable as the earthquakes and electrical storms that scourge my homeland.

The Cuban revolution demonstrated that social and political change was possible in Latin America, but surely the Yankees with their helicopter gunships and Green Berets would never permit such a thing to happen again. Nevertheless Fidel and Che sensitized me to the currents of militant unrest just below the surface of the American *mare nostrum* in the Caribbean. We watched the eddies and whirlpools from Paris and later from Mallorca while I nourished my growing burden of middle-class guilt. What was I doing sitting on the sidelines while my people silently suffered the implacable repression of the Somoza dynasty in Nicaragua and the rotating colonel-presidents in El Salvador? Some of my poems took on an edge of protest, and my husband and I wrote a novel about my childhood nightmare: the 1932 peasant massacre.

I caught the political sickness from the Sandinista revolution. Shortly after Somoza's overthrow in 1979, my husband and I went to Nicaragua for six months to research a book about the historical epic of Sandino and his successors of the FSLN. We were in Paris, on our way home to Mallorca, when we heard of the assassination of Archbishop Oscar Arnulfo Romero, the only Salvadoran figure of international prestige who had served as the voice of the millions of voiceless in my country. In response to that brutal and tragic event, all but two or three of El Salvador's artists and intellectuals made the quiet decision, without so much as consulting each other, to do what we could to try to fill the enormous vacuum left by his death.

Since then, I have found myself writing more and more poems and prose texts that reflect the misery, the injustice, and the repression that reign in my country. I am fully aware of the pitfalls of attempting to defend a transient political cause in what presumes to be a literary work, and I have tried to resolve that dilemma in a roughshod way by dividing my writing into two compartments: the "literary-poetic," if you will, and what I have come to think of as my "crisis journalism."

Political concerns do have a way of creeping into my poetry, however—simply because the Central American political situation is my major obsession, and I have always written poetry under obsession's spur. When I think back, though, I can truly say that my "commitment" to literature has always been, and remains, a simple attempt to make my next poem less imperfect than the last.

But there is something further: in Central America today, crude reality inundates and submerges the ivory tower of "art for art's sake." What avantgarde novelist would dare write a work of imagination in which the Salvadoran people, in supposedly free elections could only choose between Robert D'Aubuisson, the intellectual author of Monseigneur Romero's assassination and the recognized mentor of the infamous "Squadrons of Death," and José Napoleón Duarte, who, as the nation's highest authority for the greater part of the last four years, has systematically failed to bring the known perpetrators and executors of that sacrilegious deed to justice?

What Hollywood writer four short years ago could have envisioned a script in which all the horrors of Vietnam are being reenacted on the Central American isthmus?

America! America!
God shed his grace on thee
And crowned thy good with brotherhood
From sea to shining sea!

Can this be the America that sends Huey helicopter gunships, A-37 Dragonflies, and "Puff, the magic dragon" to rain napalm and high explosives on the women, children, and old people in El Salvador's liberated zones, to convert the village of Tenancingo among others into a second Guernica? Is this the nation that christens Somoza's former assassins of the National Guard as "freedom fighters" and "the moral equivalent of the Founding Fathers" and sends them across the Nicaraguan border night after night to spread their message of democracy by slaughtering peasants, raping their women, and mowing down defenseless children while blowing up the cooperatives and health clinics and schools the Nicaraguans have so painfully constructed over the past six years?

How has America become entrapped in this morass of blood and death?

An American President, John F. Kennedy, made a prophetic statement twenty-five years ago. His words were: "Those who make peaceful evolution impossible, make violent revolution inevitable."

Anastasio Somoza, Jr., made peaceful evolution impossible in Nicaragua, so the Nicaraguan people had no choice but to overthrow him. Again today, as it has so often in the past, the U.S. government has allied itself with the forces in El Salvador who make peaceful evolution impossible: the forces that have put an abrupt end to the limping agrarian reform program, have encouraged a recrudescence of the Squadrons of Death—and have forced a suspension of peace negotiations with the FMLN-FDR.

The burning question for all of us today is: how will America find its way out of this bloody swamp?

Central American reality is incandescent, and if there be no place there for "pure art" and "pure literature" today, then I say so much the worse for pure art and pure literature. I do not know a single Central American writer who is so careful of his literary image that he sidesteps political commitment at this crucial moment in our history, and were I to meet one, I would refuse to shake his hand.

It matters little whether our efforts are admitted into the sacrosanct precincts of literature. Call them newspapering, call them pamphleteering, call them a shrill cry of defiance. My people, sixty percent of whom earn less than eleven dollars per month, know that only through their efforts today will it be possible for their children and grandchildren to eventually have equal opportunity to learn the alphabet and thus gain access to the great literature of the world: a basic human right that has been denied most of their elders.

world view

Hattie Gossett

theres more poor than nonpoor
theres more colored than noncolored
theres more women than men

>   all over the world the poor woman of color is the mainstay of
>   the little daddy centered family which is the bottom-line of big
>   daddys industrial civilization

>   when she gets off her knees and stands up straight the whole thing
>   can/will collapse

>   have you noticed that even now she is flexing her shoulder muscles
>   and strengthening her thigh and leg muscles?

>   and her spine is learning to stretch out long her brain and heart
>   are pumping new energy already you can see the load cracking at
>   the center as she pushes it off her

she is holding up the whole world
what you gonna do?
you cant stop her
you gonna just stand there and watch her with your mouth open?
or are you gonna try to get down?
you cant stop her
she is holding up the whole world

notes on contributors

Mahnaz Afkhami is the executive director of Sisterhood Is Global Institute and a member of Human Rights Watch. She has done extensive work on women's rights in the Middle East and has examined gender issues in Islamic societies. She is the author of *Women in Exile*, a collection of essays about women and displacement.

Grace Akello is a Ugandan poet and author who attended Makerere University and worked in Kenya and Tanzania before settling in England in 1981. She is the author of *Iteso Thought Patterns in Tales*. The poems in her collection, *My Barren Song*, have a strong traditional setting.

Anna Akhmatova was born before the Russian Revolution, and her work was unofficially banned in the former Soviet Union from 1921 until 1940, and then again for a decade after World War II. Her best-known work, *Requiem*, arose out of the experience of her son's imprisonment. Only in the late 1950s did she begin to once again gain recognition. Her work has a wide following in the West today, and she is revered for her courage and tenacity in her struggles for human rights in the former Soviet Union. She died in 1966.

Claribel Alegría was born in 1924. She is one of the central voices in the human rights movement in Nicaragua during the Sandinista revolution. Alegría has published almost twenty collections of poetry and anthologies, as well as testimonial works about Central American women written in collaboration with her husband. These include *They Want to Take Me Alive* and *Breaking the Silence*.

Meena Alexander, born in 1936, is a South Asian poet and novelist who teaches at Hunter College. Her work focuses on the issues of displacement, alienation, and the lives of postcolonial immigrants in the United States. She is the author of several collections of poetry and prose. Her memoir *Faultlines* portrays the effect of migration on adolescents and the prejudices they face.

Isabel Allende was born in Lima, Peru, in 1942. Due to her father's work as a diplomat, she traveled throughout Latin America and the Middle East with her family as a child. The family finally settled in Chile when she was an adolescent. She was later exiled and became known as a daring columnist for the women's magazine *Paula*. Her first novel, *The House of the Spirits*, is a haunting saga about contemporary Chilean politics and the overthrow of President Salvador Allende, her great-uncle. Many of her works explore the conditions of women and the human rights struggles in Latin America.

Nuha Al Radi is the daughter of an Iraqi diplomat. She moved back to Baghdad as an adult, where she is presumed to be living; her whereabouts are unknown. "Baghdad Diary," written during the Gulf War, is her first published work.

Salwa Bakr, who currently works and resides in Cairo, has traveled around the Middle East and has worked as a journalist. Due to her political activities, she was arrested and held in prison. This experience inspired her to write her first novel. She has published a collection of short stories, a novel, and many journalistic works.

Maria Banus was born in 1911 in Romania and became famous at the age of fourteen with her first publication. Since then she has published many volumes of poetry and translations.

Sheila Cassidy is a British physician and internationally renowned writer and political activist. She went to Chile at the time of the Salvador Allende government (1971 to 1973) and was arrested during the reign of terror of the Pinochet dictatorship, which had overthrown the Allende regime the following year. In 1977 she published *Audacity to Believe*, a courageous testimony of her arrest and imprisonment in Chile. Dr. Cassidy now works at Plymouth General Hospital in London. She is the author of several other highly acclaimed books, *Sharing the Darkness*, *Light from the Darkness*, and *The Loveliest Journey*.

Rosario Castellanos was born in Mexico City in 1925 and was raised in the Mexican state of Chiapas. Many of her writings are descriptions of life there. Castellanos's work reveals a profound sensitivity to human rights, social justice, and the role of women in society. She wrote plays, novels, stories, and poetry. She served as Mexico's ambassador to Israel, where she died in 1974.

Gītā Chattopādhyāy was born in Calcutta and writes in Bengali. She is the author of two books of poetry. Recently her work has begun to be translated into English by Caroline Wright. Chattopādhyāy is a professor of literature at the University of Calcutta.

Judith Ortíz Cofer is a poet, writer, and playwright who came to mainland United States at the age of four from Hormigueros, Puerto Rico. She has written several books of poetry, including *Letters from a Caribbean Island*, *Peregrina*, and *The Latin Deli. Latin*

Women Pray was performed as a three-act play in 1984 at Georgia State University in Atlanta. Cofer has also contributed to several magazines.

Carolina María de Jesus lived in the slums of São Paulo and received only a second-grade education. She supported her three children and lived in uttermost poverty. In 1960 she published a diary of her life in the slums that became an immediate best-seller, allowing her to change her life for a short time before she returned to poverty. Carolina María de Jesus's diary is a moving account of destitution and urban life.

Charlotte Delbo, playwright and human rights activist, was born in 1913 in Vigneux-sur-Seine, France, and died in Paris in 1985. She participated actively in the French Resistance during World War II and was sent to Auschwitz in 1942. After her liberation by the Red Cross in 1944, Delbo wrote *Auschwitz and After*, a trilogy about life in the concentration camp. She also wrote *Convoy to Auschwitz*, an oral history collection of women's voices in the French Resistance.

Diana Der-Hovanessian is a New England–born poet of Armenian ancestry whose work has appeared in such journals as *American Scholar*, *Partisan*, *APR*, and in sixteen volumes of her poetry and translations. She has received awards from NEA, PEN, Columbia Translation Center, and the Fulbright Commission.

Carol Dine has published two books, *Trying to Understand the Lunar Eclipse* and *Naming the Sky*. Her work appears in *Women's Review of Books*, *Prairie Schooner*, *Spoon River Poetry Review*, and *Blue Mesa Review*. She has been a resident at Ragdale, Virginia Center for Creative Arts. "Light and Bone/Luz y hueso" was presented in a multimedia performance at the Boston Conservatory.

Assia Djebar comes from the Maghreb, Algeria; she had written four novels before her thirtieth birthday. She has been a professor of history at the University of Algeria. *Fantasia: An Algerian Cavalcade* is her first book translated into English.

Slavenka Drakulic is a journalist and writer as well as a cultural commentator in Croatia. Her work can be found in the *New York Times*, *Time*, *The Nation*, *The New Republic*, and *New York Review of Books*. She wrote about life under a communist government in *How We Survived Communism and Even Laughed*, and about issues of ethnic conflict in *Balkan Express*. Because of the strong opinions expressed by Drakulic in these books, neither has been published in Croatia. Drakulic has received international awards and acclaim for her writing.

Ursula Duba was born in postwar Germany, in Cologne. Her first collection of poetry, *Tales from a Child of the Enemy*, explores her childhood in her native city.

Ferida Durakovic was born in 1957 in Olovo, Bosnia-Herzegovina, and now lives in Sarajevo. In 1980 she graduated from the faculty of philosophy at Sarajevo University. She has published five collections of poetry and two children's books, including *A Ball of Masks*, *The Eyes That Keep Watching Me*, *A Little Night Lamp*, *Look, Someone Has Moved from a Beautiful Neighbourhood Where Roses Die*, *Heart of Darkness*, *Another Fairy-*

tale About a Rose, and *Miki's Alphabet*. Her poetry has been translated into six languages and published in various literary magazines. She won many prizes in the former Yugoslavia for her poetry. She is also a winner of the Hellman-Hammet Grant for Free Expression.

Marguerite Duras was born in French Indochina (Vietnam) and moved to France at the age of seventeen. During World War II, she became part of a resistance group fighting the Nazi occupation. In 1943 she began a career as a screenwriter; most memorable is her screenplay for *Hiroshima Mon Amour*. Her best-known novel is *The Lover*.

Nawal El Saadawi is an Egyptian feminist, human rights activist, socialist, and novelist. Her political writings led to her dismissal from her post as general director of health and education in Cairo. She was later imprisoned by Anwar Sadat for alleged crimes against the state. Her collection of prison memoirs describes women's resistance to violence and the way in which they create a true community behind prison bars.

Carolyn Forché is a poet and human rights activist in both the United States and Central America. Her collection of poems, *The Country Between Us*, won the Lamont Poetry Prize in 1981. She is a translator and professor of creative writing at George Mason University.

Eleni Fourtouni was born in 1933 in Vassara, Greece, a small town in the mountains of Sparta. In 1952 she emigrated to the United States. She has been active in the Greek women's movement, and has written two volumes of poetry about the life of women during the Greek dictatorship, as well as unpublished memoirs of a woman during the Greek civil war.

Anne Frank was a Jewish girl who was born in Germany in 1929 and grew up in Amsterdam, where her family had sought refuge from the Nazis. Before being arrested and sent to Auschwitz in 1944, the family had been in hiding for two years. It was during this time that Anne kept a diary which received worldwide attention upon publication after the war as one of the most powerful and moving documents about the Holocaust. She died at Bergen-Belsen concentration camp in the spring of 1945.

Natalia Ginzburg is a novelist, short story writer, dramatist, and essayist. She has worked as a publisher for the Einaudi publishing company and is a member of the Italian parliament. She has received several prizes for her works and is one of the most popular writers in postwar Italy. Her works include *A Light for Fools*, *Family Sayings*, and *The Little Virtues*.

Nadine Gordimer is a South African novelist and short story writer who has also written nonfiction. Her dedication to the global community of writers earned her a vice presidency of PEN International. In 1991 she received the Nobel Prize in Literature. She holds honorary degrees from Harvard University and Yale University.

Hattie Gossett was born in New Jersey in 1942; she now lives in Harlem. Her work has appeared in many publications, including *Conditions*, *Essence*, *Jazz Spotlite News*, *Pleasure and Danger*, *Exploring Female Sexuality*, and *Southern Africa*, and she has published a poetry collection, *Sister No Blues*.

Saida Hagi-Dirie Herzi was born in Mogadishu, Somalia. She has a B.A. in English literature from King Abdulaziz University in Jedda, Saudi Arabia, where she currently teaches English, and a master's degree from American University in Cairo. "Against the Pleasure Principle" was her first published story, appearing in *Index on Censorship* in 1990.

Joy Harjo is a member of the Creek (Muscogie) Nation. She was born in Tulsa, Oklahoma, and grew up in New Mexico. Her poetry has been highly acclaimed and received many awards, including the Academy of American Poetry Award. Among her books are *What Moon Drove Me to Do This*, *The Last Song: Secrets from the Center of the World*, and *In Mad Love*. She is a professor of English at the University of Arizona at Tucson.

Taiko Hirabayashi was a novelist, biographer, social and literary critic, and political activist. A radical socialist, she was the chairperson of the Japan Communist Party and was arrested several times for her political beliefs. Some of her major works include *Underground*, *I Will Live*, *Desert Flowers*, and *One Life*. Hirabayashi died in 1972.

Eva Hoffman is a native of Krakow, Poland. She lived her early emigrant years in Canada and later moved to the United States, where she obtained a degree from Harvard University. Hoffman is the former editor of *The New York Times Book Review*. Her acclaimed *Lost in Translation* explores language, exile, and identity.

June Jordan is a poet and political activist who was born in New York City in 1936. She has published more than fifteen volumes of poetry and prose. She is currently professor of African American Studies at the University of California, Berkeley.

Ilona Karmel was born in Krakow, Poland, in 1925 and emigrated to the United States in 1948. She is the author of two novels written in English. She is best known for *An Estate of Memory*, a novel about life in the prison camps of Nazi Europe.

Petra Kelly was born in Germany in 1947. She studied international politics at American University in Washington, D.C., and at the University of Amsterdam. Inspired by her experience with the civil rights movement in United States during the 1960s, Kelly brought the philosophies of nonviolence and civil disobedience to her political activism in Germany. She helped establish the German Green "antiparty" in 1979 and held numerous legislative posts throughout the 1980s. In 1982, Kelly received the Alternative Nobel Prize in recognition of her leadership in international peace and human rights activism. She died in 1987 in East Germany under suspicious circumstances.

Barbara Kingsolver describes herself as a "political artist." A poet, essayist, journalist, and fiction writer, she addresses the issues of environmental degradation, political oppression, and the dislocation of Native Americans. Kingsolver grew up in rural

Nicholas County, in eastern Kentucky, and now resides in Tucson, Arizona. She received a citation of accomplishment from the United Nations Council of Women in 1989, as well as many other literary awards and fellowships. She is best known for her novels *The Bean Trees*, *Animal Dreams*, and *Pigs in Heaven*.

Gerda Weissman Klein was born in Poland in 1924. She has written five books; most of them deal with her experience in Nazi slave labor camps. Her memoirs were the basis for the HBO Best Documentary Academy Award–winning *One Survivor Remembers*. She lives in Arizona with her husband, who liberated her from a concentration camp in Germany on May 7, 1945.

Tatyana Mamonova was born in Leningrad, Russia. She was exiled from Russia in 1980 for writing poems and essays against the communist regime. An activist, she is the author of several Russian essays on sexism in the former Soviet Union and is the founder and director of an international magazine, *Women and Earth*, dedicated to ecology, gender, and human rights.

Maro Markarian, a lyrical poet, was born in 1915 in Georgia to Armenian parents, refugees from the Turkish genocide. In the last decade she has become a strong advocate of human rights, freedom for Karabagh, and child care.

Demetria Martínez is an award-winning poet and author. A Princeton University graduate, she began her career as a journalist in her native New Mexico. She has covered religious issues for *The Albuquerque Journal* and *The National Catholic Reporter*. Martínez gained widespread attention as the defendant (she was acquitted in 1988) in a sanctuary case, the first such case involving federal prosecution against a journalist.

Lê Thi Mây was born in Quang Tri province, Vietnam, in 1949. She served in the youth brigades of the army during the war in Vietnam after graduating from high school. In 1975, she entered Nguyen Du Writers' Training College. She is now editor-in-chief of the magazine *Cua Viet*. Her published works include seven collections of poems and three works in prose. She won the poetry award of the Vietnam Writers' Association in 1990 for *Tang Rieng Mot Ngu'oi (For One Person Only)*.

Matilde Mellibovsky, the mother of a disappeared son, lives in Buenos Aires, Argentina, and is one of the founding members of Mothers of the Plaza de Mayo. This is her first work to be published, and it reflects her experience as a grassroots activist.

Fatima Mernissi was born in Fez, Morocco, and spent her childhood in this city amid European and Maghreb cultures. Mernissi studied political science at Mohammed University, and has a Ph.D. from Brandeis University. She has written several books on Islamic feminism. Her best-known book translated into English is *Dreams of Trespass*. Mernissi lives in Rabat and teaches at Mohammed University.

Janice Mirikitani is a third-generation Japanese American, born in California. She was sent with her family to an internment camp in Rohwer, Arkansas, during World War

II. Much of her poetry deals with life in the camp, as well as the plight of incest victims. Among her works are *A Wake in the River* and *Shedding Silence*.

Angelina Muñiz-Huberman was born in Hyènes, France, in 1936, the daughter of Spanish exiles who settled in Mexico in 1938. Muñiz-Huberman is the author of more than twenty books of poetry, fiction, and essays. Among her works translated into English is *Enclosed Gardens*, in which she explores the roots of prejudice and anti-Semitism.

Taslima Nassrin was born in 1962. In 1989 she became an international dissident, speaking and advocating change for women within the Islamic Bangladesh society. She was banned from Bangladesh after publishing her best-selling novel, *Shame*. Since 1994 she has been in hiding due to death threats by Islamic fundamentalists. She is the author of eight collections of poetry and a novel.

Agate Nesaule was born in Latvia. While fleeing during World War II she was captured first by German and then by Russian troops. She graduated from Indiana University and has a Ph.D. from the University of Wisconsin. Her book *A Woman in Amber* is her first memoir. It was selected for Outstanding Achievement Recognition by the Wisconsin Library Association and won a 1996 American Book Award. Nesaule is a professor of English and women's studies in Whitewater, Wisconsin.

Alicia Nitecki was born in Warsaw to a Catholic family active in the anti-Nazi resistance movement. She and her family were dispersed to German camps as prisoners of war. Her first memoir is *A Recovered Land*.

May Opitz is coeditor of the 1992 book *Showing Our Colors: Afro-German Women Speak Out*. She is an activist living in Berlin.

Dzvinia Orlowsky is a Ukrainian poet presently residing in Marshfield, Massachusetts. She is the editor of Four Way Books.

Grace Paley is a longtime human rights activist, a pacifist especially during the Vietnam War, and a short story writer. Her many publications include *Later the Same Day*, *Enormous Chances at the Last Minute*, *The Little Disturbances of Man*, and *Leaning Forward*. Her most recent collection of poems and stories is *Long Walks and Intimate Talks*.

Ana Pizarro is a Chilean novelist and literary critic. She left Chile in 1974 and became a political exile, living in France and in several Latin American countries until her return to Chile in the late 1990s. Her first novel, *La luna, el viento, el año, el día*, depicts the political situation in Chile after democracy.

Dahlia Ravikovitch was born in Ramat Gan, Israel. She has published several volumes of poetry, books of children's verse, and a collection of short stories. Most of her poetry deals with the conflicts of women in war and with the legacy of a post-Holocaust society. Ravikovitch is the recipient of many Israeli prizes. She lives in Tel Aviv and writes reviews for *Maariv* newspaper.

Adrienne Rich is a feminist poet, teacher, and writer. She has received several awards and fellowships for her work. Some of her works include *Snapshots of a Daughter-in-Law: Poems 1954–1962*, *Of Woman Born*, *Secrets*, and *Silence*, and *Blood, Bread, and Poetry*. She is a professor of English and feminist studies at Stanford University.

Muriel Rukeyser was a poet and political activist. She was jailed together with Grace Paley for protesting against the Vietnam War. As a poet she was committed to showing the relationship between spirituality, politics, and art. Some of her works include *Theory of Flight*, *Beast in View*, *The Gates*, and *Out of Silence*.

Nelly Sachs was born in 1891 in Berlin, Germany. Her poetry, plays, and dramatic fragments about the Holocaust were a way of protesting against inhumanity and terror. In 1966 Sachs received the Nobel Prize for Literature.

Joyce Sikakane, an author of nonfiction, fiction, and poetry, was born in South Africa and brought up in the Orlando district of Soweto. She worked as a reporter for *The World*, a newspaper run by whites for the black community, and was the first black woman employed by the *Rand Daily Mail*. When Sikakane became engaged to a white Scottish doctor, she was arrested on charges of political subversion and was detained for seventeen months until she was finally acquitted after many trials. She left for Zambia in 1973 and eventually lived in Scotland. An active antiapartheid campaigner, she is a member of the African National Congress and is currently based in Zimbabwe. *A Window on Soweto* is her autobiography.

Leslie Marmon Silko has written poems, short stories, and novels about the experience of Native Americans. In 1977 she first received critical attention for her novel *Ceremony*. She is associated with the University of New Mexico and is an assistant professor of English at the University of Arizona. She has received several awards and prizes for her poetry.

Elsa Spartioti, a native of Naoussa, Greece, has lived in Athens since 1948. She is a graduate of Pierce College, and a former employee of the U.S. Embassy (Administrative Section) in Athens. She has also worked as a freelance book editor. Her prose piece "A Traditional Recipe" was included in the Women's Creative Writing Collective publication "Landscapes of Empowerment." Since 1974 Spartioti has been an active member of the Greek and International Women's Union.

Rose Styron has published three books of poetry: *From Summer to Summer*, *Thieves Afternoon*, and *By Vineyard Light*, and one of translations and biography: *Modern Russian Poetry*. She is a journalist and human rights activist who has contributed articles and essays to newspapers, magazines, and books on human rights and government policy.

Susan Rubin Suleiman is a professor of French and women's studies at Harvard University. Her books include *Subversive Intent: Gender, Politics and the Avant Garde* and *Risking Who One Is: My War in Four Episodes*, a memoir of her childhood in Budapest.

Maud Sulter was born in Glasgow, Scotland, in 1960 to a Scottish mother and a Ghanian father. Her poem "As a Blackwoman" won the Vera Bell Prize in the Afro-Caribbean Education Resource's 1984 Black Penmanship Awards in London. The following year her collection of the same title was published. Her subsequent publications include *Zabat: Poetics of a Family Tree* and a novel, *Necropolis*. She is also an artist and photographer whose work has appeared in exhibitions. She was awarded the MoMart Fellowship at the Tate Gallery in Liverpool in 1990–1991.

Aung San Suu Kyi is a women's rights and human rights activist and leader of Burma's National League for Democracy. She was detained in 1989 and remains under house arrest in Rangoon as a prisoner of conscience. She was a 1991 winner of the Nobel Peace Prize.

Anna Swir was born in Poland in 1909. Her poetry explores feminism, human rights, eroticism, and language. She was a member of the Polish resistance movement to the Nazi occupation and worked as a nurse in a makeshift hospital during the 1944 Warsaw uprising. She died in 1984.

Wislawa Szymborska is a Polish poet, critic, editor, and columnist. Not widely known outside her native Poland, Szymborska received international attention after she was given the Nobel Prize for Literature in 1996. She has written several volumes of poetry, including *That's Why We Are Alive* and *Sounds, Feelings, Thoughts: Seventy Poems*. She also contributes to several magazines and edits a literary magazine.

Victoria Theodorou participated in the resistance during World War II and was jailed in various concentration camps for a period of five years for her activity. She is a human rights activist, poet, essayist, and author of a series of oral histories recounting her experiences in the resistance movement.

Fadwa Tuqan was born in 1917 in Jordan. Her biography, *The Mountainous Journey: A Poet's Autobiography*, addresses issues of displacement and life under the occupation. She was raised in Nablus, where she presently lives.

Luisa Valenzuela was born in 1939 in Buenos Aires, Argentina, to a literary family. She worked as a journalist; her essays dealing with Argentine politics were published in Argentina's leading papers and later on in the United States, in *The Village Voice* and the *New York Review of Books*. During the Argentine "Dirty Wars," Valenzuela began writing novels that revealed the political oppression of Argentine society during the dictatorship. Her work also explores the relationship between women and language and the struggle for gender equality. She left Buenos Aires during the junta and became a writer in exile, living and teaching in New Jersey.

Yona Wallach was born in Israel in 1944 and died in 1985. Her poetry is characterized by extraordinary brilliance of language and imagery; most of her later work is in the form of monologues about her condition as a woman and about her illness.

Christa Wolf emerged in the 1970s as one of the voices of consciousness of her own Eastern European vision and commitment to the struggles for peace and justice. Her novels include *Accident* and *The Quest for Christa T.* She has worked as an editor, lecturer, journalist, and critic. Wolf presently lives in Berlin.

Xi Xi began to write and publish in the crucial years of negotiation between China and Britain, from 1982 to 1996. Her fiction eloquently explores issues of identity and the status of the refugees who arrived in Hong Kong in the early 1950s.

Mitsuye Yamada was born in Kyushu, Japan, and grew up in Seattle, Washington, where she lived until World War II, when she and her family were sent to an internment camp in Idaho. Her collection *Campnotes and Other Poems* recounts this experience.

Hisaye Yamamoto was born in 1921 in Redondo Beach, California. Her work explores the daily lives of Japanese American women in and out of American World War II internment camps. In 1986 she received the American Book Award for Lifetime Achievement from the Before Columbus Foundation. Her work has received international acclaim and has been widely published in anthologies. Among her most important collections is *Seventeen Syllables and Other Stories.*

copyrights and permissions

about the editor

Marjorie Agosín is an award-winning poet, short story writer and human rights activist. She has won numerous awards for her work in human rights, among them the Good Neighbor Award and the Jeanette Rankin Award for Human Rights. She has also been honored with the United Nations Leadership Award on Human Rights. Her writings have gained the Letras de Oro prize for poetry. She has written two memoirs about the life of her parents in Chile: *A Cross and A Star* and *Always from Somewhere Else*. Her most recent books of poetry are *Dear Anne Frank* and *In the Absence of Shadows*.

Marjorie Agosín is professor and chair of the Spanish department at Wellesley College. She lives in the town of Wellesley, Massachusetts, with her husband and two children.